P9-ARW-931

FERNS

of the

Vicinity of New York

Being descriptions of the fern-plants
growing naturally within a hundred
miles of Manhattan Island.
With Notes.

(Illustrated)

By

JOHN KUNKEL SMALL

DOVER PUBLICATIONS, INC., NEW YORK

Published in Canada by General Publishing Company, Ltd., 30 Lesmill Road, Don Mills, Toronto, Ontario.
Published in the United Kingdom by Constable and Company, Ltd., 10 Orange Street, London WC 2.

This Dover edition, first published in 1975, is an unabridged and unaltered republication of the work originally published by The Science Press, Lancaster, Pennsylvania, in 1935.

International Standard Book Number: 0-486-23118-6
Library of Congress Catalog Card Number: 74-12655

Manufactured in the United States of America
Dover Publications, Inc.
180 Varick Street
New York, N. Y. 10014

CONTENTS

METRIC SYSTEM

INCHES

PREFACE

Manhattan Island has outstanding botanical characteristics. So far as ferns are concerned, Nature, after the last Ice Age, set about to build up a new growth on the island. This or its descendants survived until the activities of the white man from Europe inaugurated changes on the surface of the land. Since modern history began on Manhattan the fern growth has gradually dwindled to almost nil. The same processes of destruction that reduced the fern growth on Manhattan have been and are operating nearly throughout the Local Flora Area, but in a less drastic degree.

In its geological formation Manhattan represents one of the two southern tips of the northeastern plant-province—the New England Coast Region; the other one ending in Bucks County, Pennsylvania. It was originally a wedge of ancient crystalline rock flanked on either side by portions of other plant-provinces, one the latest formation, the Coastal Plain, the other the oldest formation, the Piedmont.[1] These two plant-provinces coincide with definite groups of geological formations.

The amateur botanists of Manhattan and vicinity were the first on the Atlantic seaboard to organize themselves into an association—The Torrey Botanical Club[2]—for the study of plants from a botanical stand-

[1] Just after the Ice Ages Manhattan was for the most part a bare rocky island. As the Coastal Plain province was formed sand was deposited with the remains of the glacial drift over the lower parts of the eastern edge and the low positions south of the present 59th Street.

[2] The Torrey Botanical Club is the oldest botanical society in the United States, its present organization dating from December, 1867; its incorporation was effected in January, 1873. The *Bulletin of the Torrey Botanical Club*, the oldest botanical journal in America, was commenced in 1870; it is now in its 61st volume.

point, growing naturally within a certain region, in this case an area two hundred miles in diameter with Manhattan Island at the center was designated. This region has come to be known as the Local Flora Area.

Exploration for plants and the collecting of specimens within this area has been carried on officially and otherwise for over a half century. The specimens were preserved in various private herbaria. Mainly through the activities of the Local Flora committee, the Torrey Botanical Club gradually built up an herbarium of the local plants. The enthusiasm with which the work of the Local Flora committee was carried on varied according to the time, opportunity, and interests of the members and their associates. Eventually, the Club presented its local flora herbarium to the Board of Managers of The New York Botanical Garden.

One of the early activities of the Garden's botanical work, before the accession of the herbarium of the Torrey Botanical Club, was the beginning of a local flora herbarium. When the Club's herbarium was turned over to the Garden, the two collections were merged. During the past three decades miscellaneous collections of plants from the Local Flora Area and several large private herbaria have been incorporated with the original nucleus. Now, there is a large herbarium of local plants available for consultation or study to any one qualified for such work.

In the following taxonomic arrangement of our local ferns, pre-Linnaean publications are not directly considered. Carolus Linnaeus interpreted our fern-plants under twelve generic names, or in other words,

---

The Club also publishes a journal called *Torreya*, and a series entitled *Memoirs*. The membership, at first only about 30, all living in or near New York City, now numbers about 500, widely distributed geographically, although the meetings are still held in New York. The Club was responsible for the establishment of The New York Botanical Garden.—JOHN HENDLEY BARNHART.

under so many unorganized genera. (See page following.) After the Linnaean period many ferns and groups of ferns were removed from their earlier generic associations and classed in more natural or, at least, less complex groups. Curiously enough, after a lapse of nearly two centuries untidy genera are still maintained in the classifications of some fern students. This uneven division of the ferns, *i.e.*, into simple or natural groups and complex or unnatural groups under generic headings, is confusing to the amateur. So, in the following treatment an attempt has been made to interpret the fern-plants involved in more simple or natural generic concepts.

The names adopted for species and genera in this volume are those which, to the best of the author's knowledge, were first applied to each, accompanied or supported by an adequate description, and in the case of genera by specific references, from the time (1753) when binomial designation of species was definitely introduced into botanical nomenclature, unless preoccupied for another species or genus.

In the matter of terminology for the gross parts of a fern-plant Anglo-Saxon derivatives, as far as possible, are preferred by the writer. Thus for the underground stem, *rootstock* rather than *rhizome* is used; for the aërial parts *leaf, blade,* and *petiole* are preferred to the Latin *frond, lamina, stipe,* respectively. Of course, for the minute organs the almost universally accepted fern terminology is used in the following pages.

The preparation of this work was prompted by the lack of a book devoted to the ferns of the Local Flora Area. It is based mainly on collections of ferns preserved in the herbarium of The New York Botanical Garden, besides studies in the field, both within and without the Local Flora Area.[3]

[3] The word fern is used here in the broad sense covering the groups of fern-allies as well as the true ferns.

Records made by W. Herbert Dole on the growing of some of our native ferns are given on the following pages under the respective species. Mr. Dole's fern garden is centrally located in our area, and thus may be considered an index for the whole local flora region. James L. Edwards, in the course of cultivating our native ferns in northern New Jersey has found a great difference in the drought resistance of the different genera and species, especially where a continuous supply of ground moisture is lacking. For example, such ordinarily vigorous ferns as the osmundas, *Pteretis nodulosa, Anchistea virginica, Diplazium acrostichoides, Dryopteris Goldiana, D. Clintoniana,* and *D. cristata,* wither and die down after a prolonged dry spell, even as early as July. On the other hand, *Pteris latiuscula, Athyrium angustum, Thelypteris noveboracensis, Dryopteris marginalis, D. intermedia, D. spinulosa, Polystichum acrostichoides, Phegopteris hexagonoptera, Dennstaedtia punctilobula,* and *Onoclea sensibilis,* are less dependent on a continuous supply of moisture and thrive during dry spells.

This work is published to facilitate the study and determination of the ferns of the Local Flora Area, and also with the hope of inciting students to explore the fern growth of the wilder and more inaccessible mountainous parts of the area.

During the preparation for the press detailed information and constructive criticism was furnished by Edgar T. Wherry after the preliminary manuscript was finished. Both copy and proof were read by Edgar T. Wherry, John H. Barnhart, James L. Edwards, Edward J. Alexander, who also supervised the drawing of the details in most of the enlargements in the figures, and by Bertha Pickering, who also made the index. Proof was read, in part, by Ralph C. Benedict. The chapters: Taxonomic List with Citations, and Authors cited in the work, were furnished by John H. Barnhart and the Comparative lists of Genera and Species by James L. Edwards.

The figures on the following pages are, for the most part, from drawings made by Ruth George. Others were made by Margaret Sorensen and Eva Melady. A few have been adapted from the writer's "Ferns of Florida," originally made by Mary E. Eaton. A three-centimeter rule accompanies figures that have been reduced from natural size. The preparation of the manuscript and many of the drawings were made possible by the cooperation of the Board of Managers of The New York Botanical Garden through the former Director, E. D. Merrill.

JOHN KUNKEL SMALL

THE NEW YORK BOTANICAL GARDEN

OCTOBER 31, 1935

INTRODUCTION

The Local Flora Area is an arbitrary assemblage of parts of several major and minor plant-provinces. Curiously enough, this area represents the most complicated assemblage of plant-provinces, five in number, to be found in any similar-sized portion of the earth's surface. The flora is thus large for the size of the area, and its relations complicated. The very ancient history of the land has had a profound effect on the floristics. The outstanding influences in modifying the more ancient floristics involving the direct ancestors of our modern plants were the Ice Ages. During these periods more than half of the Local Flora Area was buried beneath prodigious ice sheets. The vegetation was wiped out and configuration of the surface of the land was more or less modified.

The greater part of the more southern portion of the Local Flora Area has had a continuous plant covering since very early times, whereas the portion north of the terminal moraine[4] was repopulated largely by immigrants after the ice receded to the north.

PLANT PROVINCES

The plant provinces involved in the Local Flora Area are five. The newest formation is the coastal region of our area—the Coastal Plain. The boundary of this province extends from the northern tip of Delaware diagonally across New Jersey, thence to Staten Island and Long Island Sound.

Northwestward the Coastal Plain abuts on two provinces of the very old formations: one, the Pied-

---

[4] The terminals of the glaciers formed a line across Long Island, Staten Island, northern New Jersey, northern Pennsylvania, south of the Great Lakes and westward.

mont, extending up from Georgia through eastern
Pennsylvania, and as a tongue, along the Hudson
River to Rockland County, New York; beyond this
point the Coastal Plain abuts on the New England
province. This extends southward as two tongues or
wedges, one ending near Reading in eastern Pennsylvania, the other wedge comprising most of Manhattan
Island, or New York City.

The remaining two provinces are northward exten-
sions from less ancient eroded uplifts from the south.
The one bordering the New England province is the
Appalachian Valley province, which begins in central
Alabama, extending northeastward just west of the
Blue Ridge province, which however ends in southern
Pennsylvania, a short distance southwest of Harris-
burg and outside our area. The most western part of
the Local Flora Area belongs to the northern extension of the Appalachian Plateaus province which, beginning in northwestern Alabama, extends in a northeasterly direction up to the Adirondack province in
northern New York, which also lies out of our area.

The interlocking of plant-provinces and the altitudinal range from below sea-level, where aquatics
grow, to mountain-tops, where alpines thrive, results
in a great variety of plants, ferns included. The
major groups of temperate fern-plants are well represented in the Local Flora Area—all of them by more
than one species.

FERNS AS KNOWN TO LINNAEUS

In 1753 Carolus Linnaeus[5] was acquainted with almost 50 per cent of the fern-plants now represented

[5] Carolus Linnaeus was born 13/14 May, 1707, at
Rashult, Smoland, Sweden. His interest in botany dated
from his youth. At twenty be began his university
studies at Lund, going to Upsala in the following year.
In 1732 he traveled in Lapland, under the auspices of
the Upsala academy, and during the next few years
visited various parts of Sweden, Denmark, Germany,
Holland, and England. In 1735 he received the degree

in the Local Flora range. They are as follows (this
list shows the Linnaean interpretation of our fern-
plants and their present-day generic interpretations) :

Polypodium virginianum L.
Adiantum pedatum L.
Pteris atropurpurea L. = Pellaea atropurpurea (L.) Link.
Blechnum virginicum L. = Anchistea virginica (L.) Presl.
Acrostichum areolatum L. = Lorinseria areolata (L.)
　　Presl.
Achrostichum platyneuros L. = Asplenium platyneuron
　　(L.) Oakes.
Asplenium rhizophylla L. = Camptosorus rhizophyllus (L.)
　　Link.
Polypodium noveboracense L. = Thelypteris noveboracen-
　　sis (L.) Nieuwl.
Acrostichum Thelypteris L. = Thelypteris Thelypteris (L.)
　　Nieuwl. T. palustris (Salisb.) Schott.
Polypodium marginale L. = Dryopteris marginalis (L.) A.
　　Gray
Polypodium cristatum L. = Dryopteris cristata (L.) A.
　　Gray
Polypodium Phegopteris L. = Phegopteris Phegopteris
　　(L.) Keyserl.
Polypodium Dryopteris L. = Phegopteris Dryopteris (L.)
　　Fée
Polypodium fragile L. = Cystopteris fragilis (L.) Bernh.
Polypodium bulbiferum L. = Cystopteris bulbifera (L.)
　　Bernh.
Acrostichum ilvense L. = Woodsia ilvensis (L.) R. Br.
Onoclea sensibilis L.
Osmunda regalis L.

---

of doctor of medicine in Holland, and made his home
in that country for several years. It was while there
that he published the details of his artificial ''sexual
system'' of plant classification, which soon made his
reputation world-wide, and was used exclusively by nearly
all botanists for almost a hundred years. In 1738 he
returned to Sweden, and became a practising physician
in Stockholm; from 1741 he was a professor in the university of Upsala, where he remained until his death,
10 January, 1778, publishing meanwhile numerous works,
botanical and zoological; the most famous is his ''Species
plantarum,'' 1753, which is now accepted as the starting point of modern botanical nomenclature.—JOHN
HENDLEY BARNHART.

Osmunda cinnamomea L.
Osmunda Claytoniana L.
Ophioglossum vulgatum L.
Osmunda virginiana L. = Botrychium virginianum (L.) Sw.
Marsilea quadrifolia L.
Equisetum arvense L.
Equisetum sylvaticum L.
Equisetum palustre L.
Equisetum fluviatile L.
Lycopodium Selago L.
Lycopodium inundatum L.
Lycopodium alopecuroides L.
Lycopodium carolinianum L.
Lycopodium obscurum L.
Lycopodium annotinum L.
Lycopodium clavatum L.
Lycopodium apodum L. = Selaginella apoda (L.) Fernald.
Lycopodium rupestre L. = Selaginella rupestris (L.) Spring.

As a result of the complicated geological structure, and consequent interlocking of the provinces, plus the history of the area concerned and the rather uniform climatic conditions, the ferns of the Local Area are as a rule generally distributed. However, the plant provinces show some individuality and isolation of genera and species. Tentatively the following cases of limitation to individual provinces may be recorded:

A.—For the Coastal Plain province: curly-grass (*Schizaea pusilla*), Fox-tail clubmoss (*Lycopodium alopecuroides*), Carolina-clubmoss (*Lycopodium carolinianum*).

B.—For the Piedmont province: lobed spleenwort (*Asplenium pinnatifidum*), (except perhaps in Warren County, New Jersey).

C.—For the New England Coast province: marsh-horsetail (*Equisetum palustre*), Tuckerman's quill-wort (*Isoetes Tuckermani*).

D.—For the Appalachian Valley province: smooth cliff-brake (*Pellaea glabella*), Bradley's-spleenwort

(*Asplenium Bradleyi*), fir-clubmoss (*Lycopodium Selago*).

E.—For the Appalachian Plateaus province: rock-clubmoss (*Lycopodium porophilum*).

OUTSTANDING REGIONS

The area under consideration, for the convenience of the study of plant distribution, may be divided into major and minor regions.

1. Major Regions

A. Glaciated Region. Here we find the oldest area, for the most part, geologically, and the newest floristically. The plant covering that had developed here before the Ice Ages was exterminated by the ice sheets that covered the region, varying from a few feet to thousands of feet in thickness. The ancestors of the present vegetation came in and developed after the recession of the last ice sheet. The maximum altitude in the glaciated area is 4,204 feet in the Catskills.

Ferns restricted to the glaciated area today are several; the following may be mentioned:

Cryptogramma Stelleri. (Slender cliff-brake)
Dryopteris campyloptera. (Spreading shield-fern)
Woodsia glabella. (Smooth cliff-fern)
Polystichum Braunii. (Holly-fern)
Equisetum palustre. (Marsh-horsetail)
Equisetum variegatum. (Variegated-horsetail)
Lycopodium Selago. (Fir-clubmoss)
Lycopodium annotinum. (Stiff-clubmoss)
Isoetes Eatoni. (Eaton's-quillwort)
Isoetes macrospora. (Lake-quillwort)
Isoetes Tuckermani. (Tuckerman's-quillwort)

B. Unglaciated Region. Here we find, at least in the case of the Coastal Plain, the newest area geologically and, for the most part, the oldest floristically. The original plant covering survived after the ice sheets had worked destruction north of the terminal moraine, and it is likely that various species that would have

remained northern types were forced down into the
southern lowlands and highlands. The maximum
altitude in the unglaciated region is approximately
2000 feet.

The ferns restricted to the unglaciated area are:

Asplenium pinnatifidum. (Lobed-spleenwort)
Schizaea pusilla. (Curly-grass)
Lycopodium alopecuroides. (Foxtail-clubmoss)
Lycopodium carolinianum. (Carolina-clubmoss)

2. Minor Regions

Within the boundaries of the major regions are
various minor regions.

A. Rivers and River Valleys. North of the moraine
the country is copiously cut by mostly short rivers
and creeks. Most prominent are those rising beyond
our range. The Connecticut River, with small tribu-
taries, rises in the White and Green Mountains, and
adjacent Canada. The Housatonic River rises in
Massachusetts east and north of the Taconic Mountains. The Hudson River with mostly small tribu-
taries, rises in the Adirondack Mountains. These
rivers and their confluents are wholly confined to the
glaciated part of our range. The Delaware River, on
the other hand, although it rises in the glaciated region in the western and southern part of the Catskill
Mountains, and has a long course north of the moraine, crosses the moraine and receives two large trib-
utaries, the Lehigh River and the Schuylkill River,
both of which, however, rise in the glaciated area.
The Lehigh crosses the moraine in Pennsylvania, and
the Schuylkill crosses the Blue Mountains in the same
State, their drainage through the Delaware River con-
tinuing on to Delaware Bay. Their influence, however, is for the most part in the unglaciated area.
The Susquehanna River affects only two counties
(Luzerne and Lackawanna) on the western edge of
our range.

The surface of the glaciated area, as a result of glaciation and attendant deposition of débris, shows many confined wet places, such as swamps, marshes, bogs, and lakes, suitable places for wood-ferns and swamp-ferns, and, on the other hand, boulders, rock-outcrops, cliffs, and crags to the liking of rock-ferns. South of the moraine, confined water and water-courses are conspicuously fewer. The moist and wet regions harbor what may be termed bog-ferns and swamp-ferns. These habitats are more or less dove-tailed, so that it is often difficult to assign a fern species definitely to one or the other. However, as the dominant habitat appears to be indicated in the region under consideration, we find:

1. Wood-ferns:

Polypodium virginianum. (Polypody)
Pteris latiuscula. (Bracken)
Adiantum pedatum. (Maidenhair)
Asplenium platyneuron. (Ebony-spleenwort)
Athyrium asplenioides. (Lowland lady-fern)
Athyrium angustum. (Upland lady-fern)
Diplazium acrostichoides. (Silvery-spleenwort)
Homalosorus pycnocarpus. (Glade-fern)
Thelypteris noveboracensis. (New York-fern)
Dryopteris marginalis. (Marginal shield-fern)
Dryopteris Goldiana. (Giant shield-fern)
Dryopteris intermedia. (American shield-fern)
Dryopteris spinulosa. (Toothed shield-fern)
Dryopteris campyloptera. (Spreading shield-fern)
Polystichum acrostichoides. (Christmas-fern)
Polystichum Braunii. (Holly-fern)
Phegopteris hexagonoptera. (Triangle-fern)
Phegopteris Phegopteris. (Beech-fern)
Phegopteris Dryopteris. (Oak-fern)
Dennstaedtia punctilobula. (Hay-scented fern)
Pteretis nodulosa. (Ostrich-fern)
Osmunda Claytoniana. (Interrupted-fern)
Ophioglossum vulgatum. (Adder's-tongue)
Botrychium lanceolatum. (Lance grape-fern)
Botrychium matricariaefolium. (Daisy-leaf grape-fern)
Botrychium simplex. (Little grape-fern)
Botrychium obliquum. (Grape-fern)
Botrychium dissectum. (Cut-leaved grape-fern)

Botrychium multifidum. (Leathery grape-fern)
Botrychium virginianum. (Rattlesnake grape-fern)
Equisetum arvense. (Field-horsetail)
Equisetum pratense. (Meadow horsetail)
Equisetum sylvaticum. (Wood-horsetail)
Equisetum variegatum. (Variegated horsetail)
Equisetum praealtum. (Scouring-rush)
Lycopodium lucidulum. (Staghorn-moss)
Lycopodium obscurum. (Ground-pine)
Lycopodium annotinum. (Stiff-clubmoss)
Lycopodium clavatum. (Running-pine)
Lycopodium flabelliforme. (Crowfoot-clubmoss)
Lycopodium tristachyum. (Ground-cedar)

2. Swamp-ferns:

Anchistea virginica. (Broad chain-fern)
Lorinseria areolata. (Narrow chain-fern)
Homalosorus pycnocarpus. (Glade-fern)
Thelypteris Thelypteris. (Marsh-fern)
Thelypteris simulata. (Bog-fern)
Dryopteris cristata. (Crested shield-fern)
Dryopteris Boottii. (Boott's-fern)
Dryopteris Clintoniana. (Clinton's-fern)
Dryopteris spinulosa. (Toothed shield-fern)
Phegopteris Phegopteris. (Beech-fern)
Onoclea sensibilis. (Sensitive-fern)
Pteretis nodulosa. (Ostrich-fern)
Schizaea pusilla. (Curly-grass)
Lygodium palmatum. (Climbing-fern)
Osmunda regalis. (Royal-fern)
Osmunda cinnamomea. (Cinnamon-fern)
Ophioglossum vulgatum. (Adder's-tongue)
Botrychium simplex. (Little grape-fern)
Equisetum palustre. (Marsh-horsetail)
Equisetum litorale. (Shore-horsetail)
Equisetum fluviatile. (Swamp-horsetail)
Lycopodium lucidulum. (Staghorn-moss)
Selaginella apoda. (Creeping-spikemoss)
Isoetes Engelmanni. (Engelmann's-quillwort)

3. Bog-ferns:

Anchistea virginica. (Broad chain-fern)
Thelypteris Thelypteris. (Marsh-fern)
Thelypteris simulata. (Bog-fern)
Dryopteris cristata. (Crested shield-fern)
Dryopteris Clintoniana. (Clinton's-fern)
Onoclea sensibilis. (Sensitive-fern)

Schizaea pusilla. (Curly-grass)
Lygodium palmatum. (Climbing-fern)
Osmunda regalis. (Royal-fern)
Osmunda cinnamomea. (Cinnamon-fern)
Ophioglossum vulgatum. (Adder's-tongue)
Lycopodium inundatum. (Bog-clubmoss)
Lycopodium adpressum. (Chapman's-clubmoss)
Lycopodium alopecuroides. (Foxtail-clubmoss)
Lycopodium carolinianum. (Carolina clubmoss)

Wood-ferns and swamp-ferns predominate in River
and River-Valley regions. They also occur in the two
following regions. Rock-ferns also occur here but
they form more prominent groups in the Ridges and
Highlands region. In this region most of the ferns
occur at the minimum altitudes. Specific altitudes
are given in the notes following the various species of
ferns.

Native floating aquatic ferns are lacking in the
Local Flora Area. Anchored aquatic or palustrine
ones are represented by the genus Isoetes, as follows:

Isoetes Braunii. (Braun's-quillwort)
Isoetes Eatoni. (Eaton's-quillwort)
Isoetes riparia. (River-bank-quillwort)
Isoetes macrospora. (Lake-quillwort)
Isoetes Tuckermani. (Tuckerman's-quillwort)
Isoetes Engelmanni. (Engelmann's-quillwort)

Three other aquatics, one anchored and two free-
floating, have found their way into the limits either
through cultivation or accident:

Marsilea quadrifolia. European
Azolla caroliniana. American
Salvinia auriculata. South American

B. Ridges and Highlands. North of the moraine
there are several ridges with northeast-southwest
trend. First, the Taconic Mountains on the New
York-Connecticut state line. The maximum altitude
within our area is 2,340 feet. Second, the ridge that
begins in Ulster County, New York, as the Shawan-

gunk Mountains, with a maximum altitude of 2,273 feet, continues as Kittatiny Mountain in New Jersey, with a maximum altitude of 1,800 feet, and, crossing the Delaware into Pennsylvania, becomes the Blue Mountain with an altitude of 2,000 feet.

In New Jersey, on the eastern edge of the Piedmont abutting on the New England Province along the Hudson River, are the Palisades, an outcrop of diabase in columnar form, with recurring ridges westward. The maximum altitude of the Palisades along the Hudson is about 500 feet, while an elevation slightly set off rises to 532 feet. In New York north of the Palisades in the vicinity of the Hudson River there are the Highlands of the Hudson. The Hudson River bisects this ridge at Cornwall. The ridge has a northeasterly trend, and attains a maximum altitude of 1,640 feet above sea-level. A minor elevation just west of the Hudson Highlands is Schunemunk Mountain; this shows a maximum altitude of 1,690 feet.

Glaciation on the one hand and general erosion on the other have prepared many habitats suitable for rock-loving ferns:

Rock ferns:
  On acid rocks, only or chiefly;

Cheilanthes lanosa. (Hairy lip-fern)
Asplenium pinnatifidum. (Lobed-spleenwort)
Asplenium montanum. (Mountain-spleenwort)
Asplenium Bradleyi. (Bradley's-spleenwort)
Woodsia ilvensis. (Rusty cliff-fern)
Dennstaedtia punctilobula. (Hay-scented fern)
Lycopodium Selago. (Fir-clubmoss)
Lycopodium porophilum. (Rock-clubmoss)
Selaginella rupestris. (Spike-moss)

  On calcareous rocks, only or chiefly;

Pellaea atropurpurea. (Cliff-brake)
Pellaea glabella. (Smooth cliff-brake)
Cryptogramma Stelleri. (Tender cliff-brake)
Asplenium cryptolepis. (Rue-fern)
Camptosorus rhizophyllus. (Walking-fern)

Cystopteris bulbifera. (Bulblet-fern)
Woodsia glabella. (Smooth cliff-fern)

Indifferent as to kind of rock;
Polypodium virginianum. (Polypody)
Asplenium ebenoides. (Scott's-spleenwort)
Asplenium Trichomanes. (Dwarf-spleenwort)
Asplenium platyneuron. (Ebony-spleenwort)
Phegopteris Phegopteris. (Beech-fern)
Cystopteris fragilis. (Brittle-fern)
Woodsia obtusa. (Cliff-fern)

The Ridges and Highlands region contains, in addition, many habitats for wood-ferns and swamp-ferns. This region also furnishes the medium high altitudes in the local flora region. Specific altitudes are given in the notes under the species on the following pages.

C. Dissected Plateaus. The Catskill Mountains represent one of the two most rugged areas in New York State, the other area being the Adirondacks, which, however, lies outside our range. The entire region is deeply dissected, even sharply so, with many areas of sheer cliff, especially around and near the summit of the peaks. Since the rocks of this area are not folded as are true mountains, but nearly horizontal with a slight northwesterly dip, there is no definite trend to the ridges: they are set at all sorts of angles to one another. The higher elevations in the Local Flora Area occur in this region, the climax being reached in Slide Mountain, 4,204 feet above sea-level, while there are numerous peaks above 3,500 feet.

Here the maximum of altitude and ruggedness is reached. Of course there are habitats for all groups of ferns in the Catskills. Many of the common ferns reach their maximum altitudinal distribution there. The following may be mentioned which reach nearly or quite to the 4,000-foot contour:

Asplenium montanum. (Mountain-spleenwort)
Asplenium cryptolepis. (Rue-fern)
Homalosorus pycnocarpus. (Glade-fern)

Diplazium acrostichoides. (Silvery-spleenwort)
Camptosorus rhizophyllus. (Walking-fern)
Dryopteris Goldiana. (Giant-fern)
Dryopteris spinulosa. (Toothed shield-fern)
Dryopteris campyloptera. (Spreading shield-fern)
Polystichum acrostichoides. (Christmas-fern)
Polystichum Braunii. (Holly-fern)
Phegopteris hexagonoptera. (Triangle-fern)
Phegopteris Phegopteris. (Beech-fern)
Phegopteris Dryopteris. (Oak-fern)
Cystopteris fragilis. (Brittle-fern)
Woodsia ilvensis. (Rusty cliff-fern)
Woodsia glabella. (Smooth cliff-fern)
Woodsia obtusa. (Cliff-fern)
Lycopodium lucidulum. (Staghorn clubmoss)
Lycopodium annotinum. (Stiff-clubmoss)

The Pocono Mountains in northeastern Pennsylvania represent a maturely dissected plateau about 2,100 feet in altitude, consisting of numerous rather flat ridges, with a sharp escarpment fronting on the Delaware River. The plateau grades southwestward into the more sharply and deeply dissected portion of the Alleghenies, where the gorge of the Lehigh River is a sharply outstanding physical feature. The ridges in this southwestern area are much more pronounced in their northeast-southwest trend and more highly folded in structure.

EXTRALIMITAL RELATIONSHIPS

The ferns of the local flora and their relatives are largely those whose genera show a north and south trend in their distribution. This fact comes out both in the species and in certain points in their structure. In the matter of an increase of species either north or south the following notes are of interest.

Ninety species of ferns are now recorded for the Local Flora Area. This is about 45 per cent of the 211 fern-plants in North America east of the Mississippi River. It is about 72 per cent of the 120 ferns of the northeastern United States and eastern Canada. It is nearly 50 per cent of the 182 ferns of the southeastern United States. Considered under family headings we find:

1. POLYPODIACEAE—Fern Family

The genera *Polypodium, Pteris, Adiantum, Cheilanthes, Asplenium, Thelypteris,* and *Dryopteris* are more generously or wholly represented by additional species in the south. The genera *Cystopteris* and *Woodsia,* on the other hand, are augmented northward. The genus *Dennstaedtia* has one relative, a tropical species, in southern Florida.

2. SCHIZAEACEAE—Curly-grass Family

The curly-grass, *Schizaea pusilla,* represented by the same species northward, has a generic counterpart of the extreme south in one species, the tropical *Actinostachys Germani.*

3. OPHIOGLOSSACEAE—Adder's-tongue Family

The local flora ferns have interesting relationships beyond our geographic area: A closely related *Ophioglossum, O. Engelmannii,* occurs to the southward and two additional species are in the Gulf States and contiguous territory. On the other hand, the genus *Botrychium* is more abundantly represented in the local flora area than elsewhere.

4. MARSILEACEAE and SALVINIACEAE— Pepperwort Family and Salvinia Family

The three species representing these families are introduced plants. *Marsilea quadrifolia* is European, although the genus is well represented in our southwest. *Azolla caroliniana* is native north, west, and south of our area, but not so within it. *Salvinia auriculata* is originally South American, and its only generic relative in the Eastern United States is an introduced species, *S. natans* of Europe.

5. EQUISETACEAE—Horsetail Family

The genus *Equisetum* has additional species northward.

6. LYCOPODIACEAE—Clubmoss Family

The genus *Lycopodium* is augmented by several species northward and by two additional species in the southeast.

7. SELAGINELLACEAE—Spikemoss Family

The genus *Selaginella,* besides having one additional species in the northeast, is abundantly augmented in the southeast by seven species.

8. ISOETACEAE—Quillwort Family

The quillworts show a northern relationship by an augmentation of fifty per cent more species. Two additional species occur in the southeast.

A study of the specimens and records of the ferns among the local flora has shown that a great deal of collecting remains to be done, mainly for gaining a proper knowledge of the geographic and altitudinal distribution. The ferns of the more populated and agricultural parts are pretty well known and in many places they have been exterminated. It is the uninhabited and virgin river and creek courses and swamps, ridges, plateaus, and mountains and other elevations with exposed rocks, cliffs, and escarpments that need concentrated collecting and study.

Up to the beginning of the present century this lack of detailed knowledge was pardonable, for access to the more remote parts by horse conveyance was at best a slow and tedious task. Since botanical work has been organized in various parts of the Local Flora Area, and with the advent of the automobile and better roads, time necessarily spent for attacking distant points may be largely eliminated and thus saved for foot work among the more inaccessible places. The failure of a complete fern survey is not pardonable in these days.

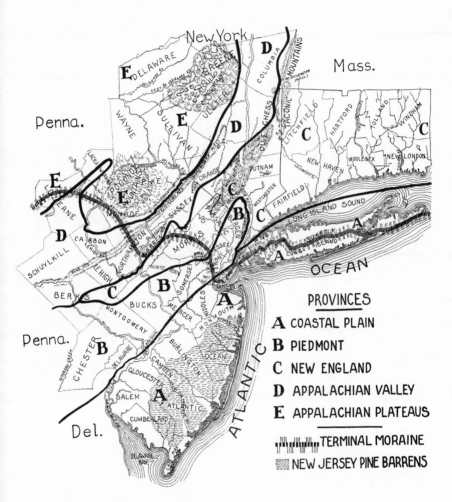

MAP OF THE LOCAL FLORA AREA.—All of the states of New Jersey and Connecticut, certain counties of eastern Pennsylvania and southeastern New York. The state boundaries are shown by light black lines and rivers and the county boundaries by dotted lines. The limits of the plant provinces are shown by heavy black lines. The southern limit of the glaciers, the terminal moraine, is shown by the line in hachure running through Long Island Sound and northern New Jersey into Pennsylvania. The New Jersey pine barrens are indicated by the area of dashes.

SUBKINGDOM PTERIDOPHYTA

FERNS AND FERN ALLIES

Plants containing woody and vascular tissues. They produce spores asexually, each of which, on germination, develops into a prothallium, a small thalloid body (gametophyte). The prothallia bear the reproductive organs; the female organ is known as an archegone, the male as an antherid. As a result of the fertilization of an egg in the archegone by a motile spermatozoid produced in the antherid, the asexual state of the plant (sporophyte) is developed; this phase is represented by and popularly known as a fern, a lycopod, or a quillwort. This phase sometimes propagates by buds or bulblets which are borne on the leaves. About 6,000 species of living ferns and fern-allies are known; perhaps an equal number of fossil species have been discovered. A large majority of the living forms grow only in tropical regions.

KEY TO THE ORDERS

Foliage leaves with broad or narrow, entire, toothed, pinnate, or variously dissected blades.—Fern-like plants.
  Spores of one kind, minute.
    Sporangia membranous, opening irregularly by an elastic ring: plants not succulent: vernation spirally coiled or rarely bent.   Order 1. FILICALES.
    Sporangia coriaceous, opening by a transverse slit: plants succulent: vernation erect or inclined.   Order 2. OPHIOGLOSSALES.
  Spores of two kinds, minute microspores and larger megaspores, borne in sporocarps.   Order 3. SALVINIALES.
Foliage leaves scale-like or subulate, sometimes united into

sheaths.—Moss-like plants or
rush-like plants.

Sporangia borne under peltate scales which are collected into an apical cone: stem hollow, rush-like.	Order 4. EQUISETALES.
Sporangia borne in the axils of scale-like or relatively small leaf-like or long-subulate bracts: stem solid.	
Leaves scale-like, flat, borne on erect or creeping stems and branches: terrestrial or epiphytic plants.	Order 5. LYCOPODIALES.
Leaves long-subulate, borne on a short corm-like caudex: aquatic plants.	Order 6. ISOETALES.

ORDER 1. FILICALES

Terrestrial or epiphytic, or in one family aquatic, plants, various in habit. Sporangia developed normally from single epidermal cells, variously disposed, mainly upon the under surface of the leaf, commonly in clusters (sori) upon the veins, or within special marginal indusia, or, less commonly, irregularly or in rows upon slender more or less non-foliose pinnae or segments. Spores of one sort. Indusia of various forms, or wanting. Prothallia flattish or filamentous, green, terrestrial or epiphytic.—Includes several families, three of which occur in our range.

KEY TO THE FAMILIES

Sporangia borne on the back or on the margins of a leaf-blade or a division thereof.	Family 1. POLYPODIACEAE.
Sporangia in panicles or spikes developed from modified leaves or parts of leaves.	
Sporangia ovoid or pyriform, with a complete apical ring.	Family 2. SCHIZAEACEAE.
Sporangia nearly globose, with a rudimentary ring.	Family 3. OSMUNDACEAE.

FAMILY 1. POLYPODIACEAE

FERN FAMILY

Terrestrial or epiphytic, swamp, marsh, wood or rock plants. Rootstocks elongate, creeping or horizontal, or short and erect. Leaves sometimes dimorphic, coiled or bent in vernation, erect to pendulous when expanded, sometimes tufted: petioles continuous with or jointed to the rootstock; blades simple, once pinnatifid or several times pinnatifid or pinnate, or decompound. Veins simple or forked, free, or united and forming areolae. Sporangia borne either promiscuously or in clusters (sori) on the lower side or on the margins of the leaf-blades, stalked, provided with an incomplete vertical ring of thickened cells, opening transversely, the sori either with or without a membranous covering (indusium). Prothallia green.—The largest of the families of ferns. It includes nearly one hundred and fifty genera and about five thousand species. It is represented in arctic, temperate, and tropical regions.

KEY TO THE GENERA

Spore-bearing leaves with the blades, divisions, or leaflets flat, or with the edges merely revolute.
  Indusium wanting.
    Petioles jointed to the rootstock. .... I. POLYPODIEAE.
    Petioles not jointed to the rootstock. Genus *Phegopteris* in ... VI. DRYOPTERIDEAE.
  Indusium present.
    Sori marginal or dorsal, but not borne in cup-like or pocket-like indusia which open towards the apex of the leaf.
      Sori marginal or essentially so : indusium formed, in part, by the more or less modified leaf-margins.
        Sporangia borne on a continuous vein-like receptacle connecting the apices of the veins. ...... II. PTERIDIEAE.
        Sporangia borne at or near the apices of unconnected veins. .... III. ADIANTEAE.
      Sori dorsal, not marginal : indusium not formed by part of the leaf-margin.
        Sori narrow, linear to elliptic : indusium more than thrice as long as broad.
          Sori parallel to the midrib of the leaf-segments. ..... IV. BLECHNEAE.
          Sori oblique to the midrib of the leaf-blade or the leaf-segment. ..... V. ASPLENIEAE.
        Sori broad, roundish or reniform : indusium

less than twice as long
as wide.
Indusium (if present)
superior, orbicular or
reniform.   VI. DRYOPTERIDEAE.
Indusium wholly or
partly inferior, hood-
like or stellate.   VII. WOODSIEAE.
Sori borne in cup-like or pocket-
like indusia which open towards the apex of the leaf-
segment.   VIII. DAVALLIEAE.
Spore-bearing leaves with the divi-
sions closely rolled together, thus
necklace-like or berry-like.   IX. ONOCLEAE.

I. POLYPODIEAE

Veins free: leaf-segments several or
usually numerous and narrow:
sori superficial: leaves not scaly.   1. POLYPODIUM.

II. PTERIDEAE

Indusium double, an inner membranous portion arising from the
receptacle: leaf-blades more than
twice-pinnate.   2. PTERIS.

III. ADIANTEAE

Leaves with only the teeth or lobes
of the divisions or leaflets re-
curved on the sori as indusia.   3. ADIANTUM.
Leaves with the margins of the seg-
ments wholly recurved over the
sori.
Leaves not dimorphic, or only
slightly so.
Leaflets with pubescent blades:
sporangia in interrupted submarginal bands: veinlets with
much thickened tips.   4. CHEILANTHES.
Leaflets glabrous except the mid-
rib: sporangia forming continuous submarginal bands:
veinlets not thickened at the
tip.   5. PELLAEA.
Leaves decidedly dimorphic.   6. CRYPTOGRAMMA.

IV. BLECHNEAE

Leaves uniform: veins free between
the sori and the margins.   7. ANCHISTEA.
Leaves dimorphic: veins copiously
anastomosing, thus forming fine
areolae.   8. LORINSERIA.

V. ASPLENIEAE

Veins free: sori all oblique.
Leaves evergreen; blades or leaflets thin- or thick-coriaceous;
petiole or rachis firm, slender
and wiry.   9. ASPLENIUM.
Leaves not evergreen; blades of
the leaflets herbaceous; pet-

ioles soft and relatively
stout, not wiry, often stramineous.
Blades of the leaflets pinnatifid
or pinnate : veins or veinlets running into the teeth
of the margins.
Leaf-segments c o a r s e l y
toothed : sori very short,
the indusia, at least some
of them vaulted, bent and
extending across the vein,
opening all around. 10. ATHYRIUM.
Leaf-segments e n t i r e or
bluntly-toothed : sori rather
long, at least some of the
indusia double, placed back
to back and opening in opposite directions. 11. DIPLAZIUM.
Blades of the leaflets shallowly
toothed : veins or veinlets
running into the sinuses of
the margins. 12. HOMALOSORUS.
Veins copiously anastomosing : sori
variously and unevenly disposed. 13. CAMPTOSORUS.

VI. DRYOPTERIDEAE

Indusium present.
Indusium reniform or suborbicular
and with a narrow sinus.
Veins simple or 1-forked, one
from the base of each leaf-
segment uniting in the sinus
or converging in the nearby
tissues : leaf-segments entire :
leaves not evergreen. 14. THELYPTERIS.
Veins forking, like the branches
running to the margins remote from the sinus, leaf-segments more or less toothed,
or lobed or pinnatifid : leaves
mostly evergreen. 15. DRYOPTERIS.
Indusium orbicular-peltate, without a sinus. 16. POLYSTICHUM.
Indusium wanting. 17. PHEGOPTERIS.

VII. WOODSIEAE

Indusium attached by one side of
the base, at one side of the sorus,
hood-like. 18. CYSTOPTERIS.
Indusium attached by the middle of
the base, wholly inferior, roundish or cleft into irregular lobes
or stellate. 19. WOODSIA.

VIII. DAVALLIEAE

Indusium convex, adnate laterally
to the concave opposed lobule,
the soral-pouch cup-like : leaf-segments cuneate to ovate. 20. DENNSTAEDTIA.

IX. ONOCLEAE

Blades of the foliage leaves pinnatifid: veins anastomosing: sporophyls 2-pinnatifid.	21. ONOCLEA.
Blades of the foliage leaves pinnate: veins free: sporophyls 1-pinnatifid.	22. PTERETIS.

1. POLYPODIUM L.

Low epiphytic or terrestrial wood-plants, with creeping or horizontal rootstocks. Leaves single or approximate, erect or spreading: petioles jointed to the rootstock: blades lobed or pinnatifid, the segments thin or coriaceous, entire or toothed. Veins free or only casually anastomosing. Sori orbicular, borne in one row or in several rows on the back of the leaf-blade on either side of the midrib. Indusium wanting.—POLYPODYS.—Almost two hundred species are known in this genus. They are widely distributed in temperate and tropical regions.—This genus, based on the common polypody, *Polypodium vulgare* L., of Europe, was named in 1753. The name is Greek, alluding to the numerous scars on the rootstock.—Great extremes in altitude are represented by the following species.

1. P. virginianum L. Rootstock creeping, densely covered with cinnamon-colored scales: leaves evergreen, mostly 1–4 dm. long, clustered or spaced on the rootstocks; petioles light-colored, glabrous; blades ovate-oblong or narrowly oblong in outline, slightly coriaceous, glabrous, deep-green above, paler beneath, deeply pinnatifid, the segments few or several, linear to linear-oblong, or rarely lanceolate, mostly undulate or obscurely toothed and obtuse, or sometimes prominently toothed and rarely acute or acuminate: veins rather obscure, once or twice forked: sori rather large, medial, red or red-brown. [*P. vulgare* Michx., not L.]—(GOLDEN-POLYPODY. ROCK-CAP FERN.)—Thin soil on rocks or rocky banks, often on trees, various provinces, throughout our range, except the pine-barrens and contiguous regions.—Occurs in several variations from the typical form in the shape, the toothing, and the deeper cutting of the leaf-segments.—Spores mature, July to October.

On account of its wide range and usually great abundance in the northeastern states and in the higher parts

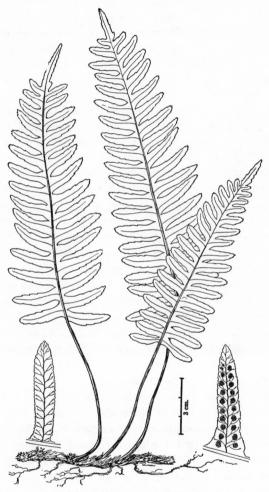

POLYPODIUM VIRGINIANUM

of the southeast, the common polypody is the first introduction the beginning botanist has to the smaller native ferns. Regions with rocks and cliffs are to the liking of this fern; consequently it is rare in the Coastal Plain. Where soil rich in humus has accumulated on rocks or in cavities and crevices, this fern may be sought. The leaves are evergreen, hence are frequently found in winter, when they are prominent. The foliage is deep-green, the leaf-blades being particularly bright-green on the upper side, or somewhat lustrous and with a golden or coppery tint. It was discovered in North America early in the eighteenth century and was named in 1753. Its geographic range extends from Georgia to Missouri, Manitoba, Keewatin, Labrador, and Newfoundland. Being such a wide-spread and common fern it has received many common names. Some of these are: my-many-feet, golden-locks, moss-fern, sweet-fern, rock-brake. It occurs as high as 4000 feet in the local highlands and at nearly or quite 6000 feet in North Carolina, and as low as sea-level in New Jersey and Maryland. At both high and low altitudes plants occur often on moss-covered limbs and trunks of trees. This is perhaps our most abundant, or at least most wide-spread fern which is unaffected by unusual cold in winter. In the fall the tissues of the leaves become hardened in readiness for the coming winter, which it spends in immunity with its frequent associate, *Dryopteris marginalis*. Curiously enough, the tissues of the leaves of these only distantly related ferns are quite similar in texture and aspect.—The variations referred to under the specific description may be summarized as follows: *P. virginianum* f. *acuminatum* has the leaf-segments toothed near the acuminate or attenuate tips; *P. virginianum* f. *deltoideum* has the lower segments auricled at the base; *P. virginianum* f. *cambricoides* has the segments toothed or pinnatifid; *P. virginianum* f. *cristatum* has the segments once or several-times forked at the tip. —The common polypody persists when established in a

garden, and will thrive for a decade or two, showing but
little change from year to year.

2. PTERIS L.

Coarse terrestrial plants, with elongate branching rootstocks clothed with often velvety scales; sometimes
vine-like. Leaves borne singly along the elongate rootstock, which is sometimes greatly elongate and clamber-
ing or climbing: petiole continuous with the rootstock,
scaly or naked at the base: blades broad, triangular or
pentagonal in outline, ternately decompound, the leaflets
entire, toothed, or pinnatifid. Veins free, simple or
forked. Sori marginal, linear, continuous, borne on a
slender receptacle which connects the ends of the free
veins. Indusium double, the outer prominent, formed by
the reflexed margin of the leaf-blade, the inner obscure,
borne upon the vein-like receptacle and extending beneath
the sporangia.—BRACKENS.—Several species of very wide
geographic distribution.—The genus is based on *Pteris
aquilina* L. of Europe.—The name is the Greek for fern.

1. P. latiuscula Desv. Rootstock elongate, stout,
woody, horizontal, extensively spreading underground:
leaves erect, often in extensive colonies, sometimes 2 m.
tall; petioles stramineous or brownish, more or less velvety scaly at the base; blades 3–12 dm. long, triangular
to deltoid-ovate in outline, usually subternate, the three
divisions each 2-pinnate, the ultimate segments lanceolate
or ovate (linear and more or less elongate as well as
glabrous or nearly so in *P. latiuscula pseudocaudata*),
usually approximate and connected at their bases: veins
mostly twice or thrice-forked. [*P. aquilina* Michx., not
L. *Pteridium aquilinum* Kuhn.]—(BRACKEN.)—Open
woods, hillsides, mountain slopes and open sandy places,
various provinces, throughout our range.—Spores mature,
July to September.

This bracken is one of the common ferns throughout
eastern North America, except the extreme north and
south, occurring in varying forms in all the plant provinces. It goes to the extremes in altitude. On dry
mountain sides it forms extensive colonies, often appro-

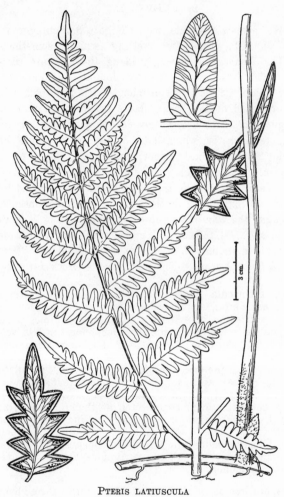

PTERIS LATIUSCULA

priating areas almost to the exclusion of other vegetation. On the other hand, this is one of the few northern ferns that approach or really intrude into a tropical fern-flora. It occurs fully as far south as the latitude of the Lake Okeechobee region in Florida. It appears to grow about equally well in woods and in open sandy places. In the latter habitat it often takes possession of large areas, spreading extensively by its long and strong rootstocks, and grows luxuriantly to the exclusion of nearly all other plants. In our area it occurs up to at least 2300 feet altitude; southward, its range increases up to 5000 feet in North Carolina, while northward it tapers down to less than 2000 in New England. Unlike most other ferns it is tolerant of fire, its strong underground stem-system enabling it to reassert its aerial growth promptly. The present fern vies with the common polypody for first place in abundance and wide geographic distribution. However, it usually occurs in drier localities and poorer soils. It seems to need but little humus for vigorous growth. Although easily recognized even by the novice, there is considerable variation in the forms of the foliage, both broad and narrow leaf-segments appearing. The amount of pubescence is also a very variable character. The more pubescent forms may have been known as *P. latiuscula lanuginosa.*—The common bracken is a beautiful fern for the large garden. Being a rampant grower, it is difficult to control in a small place.

3. **ADIANTUM** L.

Delicate or graceful wood-plants inhabiting rich soil or moist cliffs. Leaves erect or pendulous, single or tufted on the rootstocks: petiole and its divisions black or dark, shining or dull, sometimes pubescent: blades pinnately or pedately compound, with the petiole continuous into the rachis or forked at the top. Leaflets sometimes prominently jointed to the rachis or to the ultimate stalks, very inequilateral, with the midrib wanting or marginal and the veins mostly flabellate, forking, free. Sori short or laterally extended, appearing marginal on the back of the leaflets, borne at the ends of the veins. Indusium formed by the more or less altered and reflexed edges or lobes of the leaflets.—MAIDENHAIR-FERNS.—About one hundred and seventy-five species, most abundant in tropical America.—The genus *Adiantum* was based on *A. Capillus-Veneris* L., a widely distributed species, as the type.— The name is from the Greek and means unwetted, the foliage shedding rain.—Extremes of altitude are represented in this genus.

1. A. pedatum L. Rootstock slender, often elongate, mostly horizontal: leaves numerous in colonies; petioles 2–4.5 dm. long, dark chestnut-brown, polished and shining; blades reniform-orbicular to reniform, mostly 2–4 cm. broad, with the larger divisions 1.5–4 dm. long; the leaflets rather numerous, various, the blades generally oblong or somewhat lanceolate about the middle of the pinna, obliquely reniform to obliquely deltoid at the base, and the terminal one flabellate, all short-stalked, glabrous, the lower margin entire, the upper margin toothed, cleft, or lobed: sori transversely linear-oblong to reniform or linear on the ends of the leaflet-lobes.—(MAIDENHAIR. MAIDENHAIR-FERN.)—In rich woods and damp rocky banks, various provinces, throughout our range, except the pine-barrens and contiguous regions.—Spores mature, July to September.

Many of the typically tropical fern genera have pushed either one or a few representatives up into the colder latitudes of the north. The genus *Adiantum*, with numerous species in tropical America, is represented in the continental United States by five species, but the one under consideration has alone extended its range into Canada. It is frequent in eastern North America from Georgia and Louisiana northward, and in varying forms to the Pacific coast. Another species, *A. Capillus-Veneris*, ranges as far north as Virginia and Missouri in the East. The others reach only the latitude of Florida and Texas in eastern North America. This maiden-hair fern has a wide geographic distribution, as indicated above, and consequently occurs in many geographic forms showing

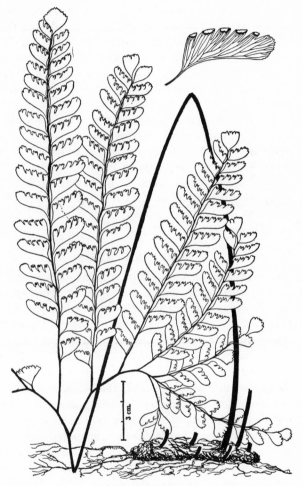

ADIANTUM PEDATUM

slight variations. However, considering the great variation in latitude, longitude, and altitude, and also in habitat, the plants are astonishingly uniform in characters. The species was botanically named in 1753, based on specimens that had been collected in Canada and Virginia earlier in the eighteenth century. It occurs up to 3000 feet altitude in our area; southward its range extends to over 5000 feet in North Carolina; northward the altitudinal range again increases. The plant is also sometimes known as LOCKHAIR-FERN.—The maidenhair-fern, if planted on a sloping bank, makes a fine showing year after year, and usually increases by the spreading of its rootstocks.—The type species of the genus, *A. Capillus-Veneris*, has been reported as growing naturally in our area. So far reports seem to be untrustworthy. However, this species has an erratic range, and may yet be found at some out of the way station in the Pocono or Catskill plateaus.

4. **CHEILANTHES** Sw.

Low, mostly small, usually rock-inhabiting and evergreen plants, with usually horizontal or creeping, often wiry rootstocks, typically with more or less pubescent or variously scaly foliage. Leaves uniform: blades 2- or 3-pinnate, rather finely divided and usually lace-like: petiole and rachis wiry: leaflets relatively broad, deeply pinnatifid or incised with the midrib central. Veins oblique to the midrib, forked, the veinlets thickened at the tips. Sori terminal on the veins, marginal, roundish and distinct, or confluent. Indusium formed by the reflexed usually modified leaflet-margins, separated or sometimes continuous. Sporangia often obscured by the hairy or scaly covering.—LIP-FERNS.—Comprises more than one hundred species widely distributed in temperate and tropical regions.—The genus *Cheilanthes* was founded on *C. micropteris* Sw. of the West Indies.—The name is from the Greek, referring to the marginal sori.—In this genus the leaves are often bent in vernation, not coiled.

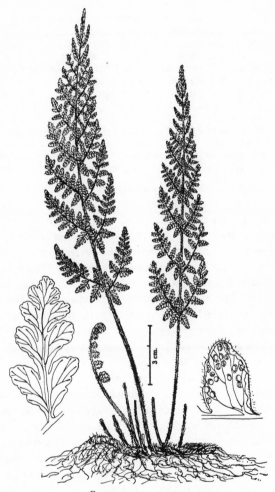

3 cm.

CHEILANTHES LANOSA

1. C. lanosa (Michx.) Watt. Rootstock copiously chaffy with pale rusty-brown scales: leaves more or less closely tufted on the short-jointed, often contorted root-stock, 1–3.5 dm. tall; petioles wiry, chestnut-brown, villous-hirsutulous; blades herbaceous, linear to lanceolate or oblong-lanceolate, usually longer than the petioles, villous-hirsutulous, gradually attenuate to the apex, 2-pinnate, the leaflets somewhat distant, ovate to ovate-lanceolate or lanceolate-deltoid, usually somewhat glandular, the ultimate lobes close, roundish or ovate, obtuse: indusium interrupted, brown, herbaceous. [*Nephrodium lanosum* Michx. *C. vestita* Sw.]—(HAIRY LIP-FERN.)— Ledges, cliffs, rocky ridges, and rocky woods, various provinces, chiefly in the medial parts of our range, except southern New Jersey, but locally distributed; in New Jersey especially frequent on trap-rock, but sometimes on shale and sandstone.—Spores mature, July to September.

Although the lip-ferns delight in the tropics for the most part, more than a dozen species range into or occur in temperate North America. Unlike some of the typically tropical fern genera which do not migrate much beyond the ancient limits, the extratropical lip-ferns have migrated or developed to a greater extent in western North American than on the eastern side of the continent. The species under consideration holds the record for "far north" (Connecticut) in the eastern United States. Its general range is from Georgia to Texas, Kansas and Connecticut. The states of Maryland, Pennsylvania, New Jersey, and New York intervene between the northern limit of the other lip-fern, *Cheilanthes tomentosa*, which has followed the leader up from the south. As contrasted with *Cheilanthes alabamensis*, another southern species, the plants of the present species prefer non-calcareous soils. This fern was discovered in the mountains (perhaps the Blue Ridge) of Tennessee and North Carolina about the beginning of the past century and named in 1803. Like its relatives, it has a considerable range in altitude. It occurs from sea-level up to nearly 3000 feet. In the southern mountain region its altitude does not seem to increase. Many of our ferns bear scales of one kind or another, either on subterranean or aerial parts. However, the foliage of this lip-fern is more copiously supplied with fine glistening hair-like scales than any other of our ferns.—Rock ferns may be grown, or at least tried, on different kinds of rock in a garden. In a case where the hairy lip-fern was tried in two different positions, one on limestone, the other on broken trap-rock, both plants flourished, but the one on the limestone ledge became much the larger; this is all the more remarkable in that under natural conditions in our region it strictly avoids calcareous rocks.

5. **PELLAEA** Link.

Stiff, usually low, rock-inhabiting plants, relatively small, with stout, often horizontal, densely scaly rootstocks, the foliage glabrous, or inconspicuously pubescent. Leaves uniform on mature plants, often simple or less divided on young plants: petioles usually wiry, often polished: blades 1–3-pinnate; leaflets commonly jointed at the base, the blades various, entire or hastate-lobed, those bearing spores usually slightly narrower than the others. Veins oblique, forked, the veinlets not thickened at the immersed tips. Sori borne at or near the ends of unconnected veins, intramarginal, at length confluent laterally in a broad submarginal line. Indusium formed by the reflexed margins of the spore-bearing leaflets, these often somewhat modified or even membranous. Sporangia evident or nearly concealed by the revolute leaflet-margins.—CLIFF-BRAKES.—Embraces about fifty species of wide geographic distribution, most abundant in North America.—The genus *Pellaea* was founded on *Pteris atropurpurea* L., the Linnean name of the first enumerated species.—Name is from the Greek, referring to the dark-colored petiole and rachis of the leaf.

Petiole, rachis, and petiolules more or less clothed with crisped hairs. 1. *P. atropurpurea.*
Petiole, rachis, and petiolules glabrous or nearly so. 2. *P. glabella.*

1. P. atropurpurea (L.) Link. Rootstock with very short congested branches, clothed with slender scales

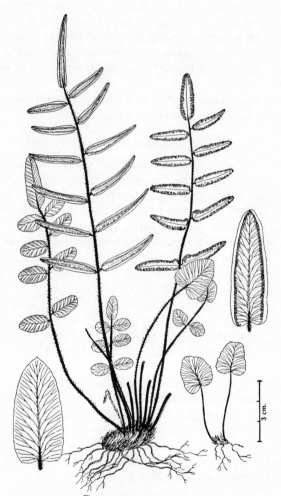

PELLAEA ATROPURPUREA

which are pale or white when young, but red at maturity: leaves various, but rather loosely tufted, the early ones simple or mostly 3–5-foliolate, the blades broad, mostly reniform, deltoid, or ovate, erose-crenate, rather slender-stalked; the later leaves several together, larger and more compound, mostly 8–40 cm. long, the leaflets thickish, the lower ones usually pinnate, the upper simple, the blades varying from linear to ovate, often more or less auricled at the base, pale-green, short-stalked, curved: indusium hyaline, erose: sori red or brown. [*Pteris atropurpurea* L.]—(CLIFF-BRAKE.)—Exposed or sheltered rocks, preferring limestone, various provinces, throughout our range, except southern New Jersey.—Spores mature, June to September.

This cliff-brake is a cool-climate fern, occurring in Canada; it reaches northern Florida on the south only by a southern extension of its range along limestone outcrops. One of the more widely distributed ferns of North America. It has also a wide longitudinal range which extends throughout a large part of the United States, from the Atlantic Ocean southwest to Arizona. It has even been collected in Mexico, but has not yet been detected in the West Indies. Its altitudinal distribution, too, is extensive. Although it occurs only up to somewhat less than 3000 feet in our area, it ranges from near sea-level to over 4000 feet in the Appalachian mountain system, and even higher elevations in the Rocky Mountains. So far as we definitely know, this fern was discovered in Virginia on the banks of the Rappahannock River about the beginning of the eighteenth century. It was well described as early as 1743, but it was not botanically named under the genus *Pteris* until 1753. The plants of this fern are commonly evergreen. They thus represent one of the few ferns that may be collected in winter as well as in summer. In fact, it is often more evident during the winter season, because then there is not as much competition of color from other growths about the plants to hide them or distract one's attention. The clusters of leaves are characterized by a glaucous hue.—The cliff-brake is not difficult to establish in an artificial habitat. It may be grown as a potted plant, in which case the

PELLAEA GLABELLA

leaves often become larger than they do in their natural haunts.

2. P. glabella Mett. Rootstock with short congested branches, densely clothed with bright-red very slender scales: leaves various, several or many together in a dense but not compact tuft, the early ones mostly 5–7-foliolate, the blades of the leaflets rather broad and thinnish; the later leaves, 5–25 cm. long, are usually once or rarely twice-pinnate, the leaflets thick, the lower ones usually 3-foliolate, short-petioled, and with the leaflets sessile or nearly so, elliptic-linear to lanceolate; the upper ones simple, the blades mostly linear or lanceolate, rarely auricled at the base, pale- or deep-green, sessile or nearly so: veins once- or twice-forked, curved: indusium entire: sori mostly brown.—(SMOOTH CLIFF-BRAKE.)—Dry rocks, bluffs, and cliffs, almost invariably of limestone, throughout our range, except the Coastal Plain.—Spores mature, June to September.

Most of the species of *Pellaea* have what might be called a decidedly marked generic likeness. The present species closely resembles the more widely distributed *Pellaea atropurpurea*. However, the plants are normally smaller in stature. A gross character is frequently at hand in the peculiar 3-lobed or 3-foliolate pairs of leaflets at the base. These are sessile or nearly so, and similar ones often extend well to the tip of the blade, giving the whole blade a narrower form than in the case of the related species. The leaflets also lack the auricle at the base. The typical dense tufts have a grayish hue. The species was named in 1809, the specimens having been collected near St. Louis, Missouri. It seems to be rare in the more northern part of the United States and southern Canada. In our range it reaches an altitude of about 700 feet in New Jersey.—The smooth cliff-brake may also be cultivated. It may be grown as a pot plant, but although it thrives in such artificial habitat, it still retains the proportionate (small) size of leaves.

6. CRYPTOGRAMMA R. Br.

Rather lax, small, slender, more or less wiry rock-plants, with slender horizontal or sometimes creeping

rootstocks, the foliage glabrous or nearly so. Leaves
dimorphous, the sporophyls taller than the foliage leaves;
petioles slender and wiry, dull or polished: blades 2- or
3-pinnate; leaflets not jointed at the base, the blades
various, those of the sporophyls narrow, those of the foliage leaves broad. Veins free, forked, the veinlets not
thickened at the tips. Sori borne near the ends of the
veins or veinlets, thus intramarginal, and at length confluent with a submarginal line. Indusium formed by the
reflexed scarious margins of the sporophyls which close
over to the midrib. Sporangia concealed until the indusia unroll.—CLIFF-BRAKES.—Embraces four species, 2
American and 2 Eurasian.—The genus is based on
Cryptogramma acrostichoides R. Br.—The name is
Greek, alluding to the hidden sori, prior to maturity.

1. C. Stelleri (S. G. Gmel.) Prantl. Rootstock slender, often branched, somewhat scaly: leaves solitary or
clustered, mostly 0.5–1.5 dm. long; petioles very slender,
stramineous or brownish especially near the base where
they are also sparingly scaly; blades mostly ovate in outline, the leaflets various, those of the foliage leaves
mostly cuneate to ovate, those of the sporophyls mostly
lanceolate to linear: veins few: indusium scarious.
[*Pteris Stelleri* S. G. Gmel. *Pellaea gracilis* Hook.]—
(SLENDER CLIFF-BRAKE.)—On limestone and trap-rock,
various provinces, very rare in Pennsylvania, northern
New Jersey, New York, and Connecticut.—Spores mature,
August and September.

Here a species belonging to a boreal group enters
the northern edge of our range. As in the case of many
of our boreal species, this fern ranges across northern
North America and it also occurs in Asia where it was
discovered in Siberia, and was named in 1768. Within
our area this fern shows little altitudinal range, notwithstanding the fact that it is a typically northern species.
The general geographical range in North America covers
the area from northern New Jersey and Pennsylvania to
Wisconsin, Iowa, Colorado, Alaska, and Labrador. It is
an interesting fact that so many boreal ferns, and many
other plants of Europe and Asia, enter our local flora

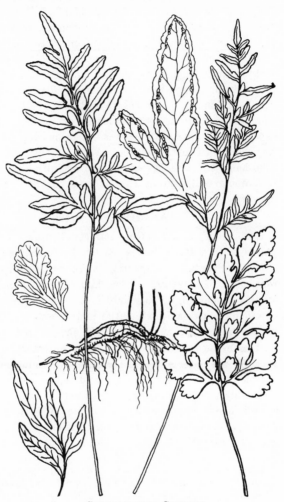

CRYPTOGRAMMA STELLERI

range, for this area lies hundreds of miles south of the
boreal regions of Europe and Asia. Notwithstanding the
fact that this fern is a boreal plant, in our area, it
occurs only at moderately high altitudes, 2000 feet in
the Catskills being the maximum. It reaches its
southern limit in northern New Jersey. Although this
fern is quite suggestive of the genus *Pellaea*, it may
promptly be recognized by the strongly dimorphous leaves
which are much less rigid than those of the pellaeas.
The leaves also lack the paleness or decided glaucous
aspect of the generic relatives.—The slender cliff-brake
may be grown in the garden. It, apparently, is slow to
take hold, but after a year or two of initiation it seems
to become well established. It must be kept cool and
moist.

7. **ANCHISTEA** Presl.

Herbaceous, coarse, erect, terrestrial swamp or marsh
plants, with uniform leaves scattered or clustered on the
stout, horizontal or creeping, more or less branching
rootstocks. Leaves erect or arching: blades pinnate, the
leaflets pinnatifid. Veins united to form a single series
of elongate areolae next to the midrib and its branches
in the segments, elsewhere free, simple and forking.
Sori borne on each side of the midrib on transverse veins
forming the outer sides of the areolae. Indusium opening on the side away from the midrib, persistent.—Contains only the following species, *Blechnum virginicum* L.,
on which the genus is based, native of eastern North
America.—The name is Greek in allusion to the alliance
with *Woodwardia*.

1. A. virginica (L.) Presl. Rootstock stout, usually
horizontal, often greatly elongate, branching: leaves erect
or arching, 1.5 m. long or less, or rarely more; petioles
stout, usually purple and shining, or partly green above;
blades lanceolate to elliptic-lanceolate or ovate-lanceolate
in outline, the leaflets separate, mostly 1–2 dm. long, the
blades lanceolate to linear-lanceolate, acuminate or merely
acute, pinnatifid, sessile, the segments ovate to lanceolate
or elliptic with a very narrow obscurely toothed pale bor-

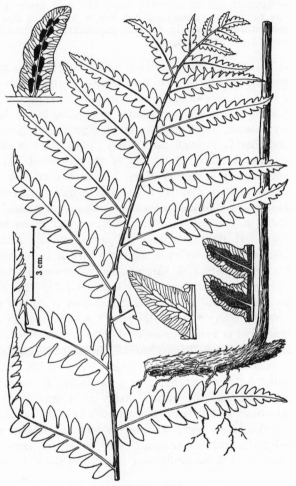

ANCHISTEA VIRGINICA

der: veins beyond the areolae simple and forked: indusium mostly 2–2.5 mm. wide. [*Blechnum virginicum* L. *Woodwardia virginica* Smith.]—(VIRGINIA CHAIN-FERN.) —Swamps, ponds, marshes, bogs, and acid prairies, various provinces, throughout our range, but more abundant southward, especially in the pine-barrens.—Spores mature, June and July.

This chain-fern, sometimes called Virginia chain-fern, a northern type, like the related netted chain-fern, *Lorinseria areolata,* is distributed over the eastern United States, from the states contiguous to the Mississippi River, reaching Canada through various provinces and Florida through the Coastal Plain, where it extends southward nearly to the tip of the peninsula. It does not reach the Florida Keys, but does reach the West Indies in Bermuda. It is common in many parts of our range, and it often occurs in and about low places, especially in the Coastal Plain; it sometimes grows in the open, but it thrives best in partial shade. Although discovered in America in the early part of the eighteenth century or before, in Virginia, this plant was not botanically named until many years later, in 1771. The chain-fern is a typical lowland plant. It does not attain much altitude in our range. However it does invade the highlands and is known to occur at 1200 feet in New Jersey and 2000 feet in Pennsylvania. Unlike *Lorinseria,* which is sometimes included in the genus *Woodwardia,* although quite different in habit and in technical characters, *Anchistea* has the general habit of a true or typical *Woodwardia,* but is easily separated by technical characteristics in the leaf; the most evident and reliable mark being the series of areolae formed by the uniting of the veins between the medial row of sori and the leaf-margin.

8. LORINSERIA Presl.

Succulent, rather tender plants, with erect, dimorphous leaves scattered along the horizontal, somewhat woody rootstock, the foliage ones shorter than the sporophyls. Foliage leaves with deeply pinnatifid blades, the few segments finely toothed and more or less undulate, with copiously anastomosing veins, which form large transverse areolae along the midrib and smaller oblique areolae gradually diminishing toward the margin. Sporophyls rigidly erect, the segments narrower than those of the foliage leaves, with a single series of elongate costal areolae and a few short excurrent veinlets. Sori in a single row on each side of the midrib, linear to elliptic, borne on transverse veins which form the outer side of the areolae, superficial, sometimes appearing immersed. Indusium opening on the side away from the midrib, persistent, scarcely reflexed with age.—Contains only the following species, *Acrostichum areolatum* L., native of North America.—The genus is named for Gustav Lorinser, an Austrian physician and botanist.

1. **L. areolata** (L.) Presl. Rootstock relatively slender, horizontal, chaffy, often widely branched: leaves gregarious, 1 m. tall or less; foliage leaves less rigid than the sporophyls, the blades ovate or deltoid-ovate, broadest at or near the base, acuminate, with the petiole and rachis mostly green, the segments succulent-membranous, elliptic to lanceolate, serrulate, sometimes undulate, rarely pinnatifid on individual plants, spreading, mostly acute or acuminate, connected by a rather broad rachis-wing; sporophyls taller than the sterile leaves, the blades deeply pinnatifid, borne on brown or black petioles 3–6 dm. long, the rachis like the petiole, mostly black, the segments contracted, separate or distant, mostly ascending or erect, their bases usually connected by a slight wing along the rachis: sori usually absent from the leaf-segments near the rachis, mostly 2.5–6 mm. long. [*Acrostichum areolatum* L. *Woodwardia angustifolia* Smith. *W. areolata* Moore.]—(INTERRUPTED CHAIN-FERN. NETTED CHAIN-FERN.) — Bogs, acid swamps, especially along streams, and ditches, various provinces, nearly throughout our range, lacking, however, northward; especially abundant in the pine-barrens.—Spores mature, August to October.

This cool-climate and primarily coastal fern is widely distributed over the eastern United States, not ranging to Canada like its generic associate, *Anchistea;* but extending to Florida and the other Gulf States mainly

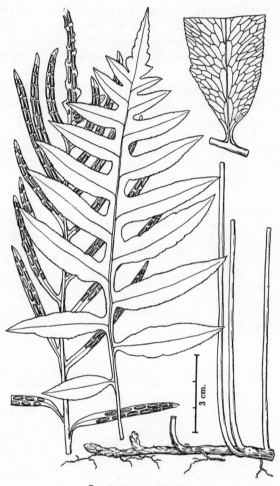

LORINSERIA AREOLATA

through the Atlantic Coastal Plain. It has about the same general distribution southward as that of its relative, *Anchistea virginica*, except that it apparently does not grow as far south in the Florida peninsula, but, curiously enough, it has been found on Big Pine Key of the Florida Keys. Its typical home is in the Coastal Plain from Texas to Florida and in New England Lowland to southern Maine. As in the case of some other typically Coastal Plain plants, it also occurs in Michigan and locally in the Piedmont and the highlands. The specimens on which the species was founded were collected in Virginia and Maryland early in the eighteenth century and botanically named in 1753, under the genus *Acrostichum*. It usually shows but little altitudinal range in our region, but it may be found as high as 2000 feet in the Pocono region. There is a curious similarity between the foliage leaves of this chain-fern and those of the sensitive-fern (*Onoclea*), as well as in the habit of growth. However, in spite of this resemblance the two need not be confused, for the leaf-segments of the present fern are placed alternately on the rachis. Curiously enough, *Lorinseria* seems to have become much more stabilized in its characteristics than the sensitive-fern, for there are fewer intergrading examples between the foliage leaves and sporophyls.

9. ASPLENIUM L.

Delicate and either small or large terrestrial, or sometimes epiphytic, often wood-plants or rock-plants, with short erect or elongate horizontal or creeping rootstocks. Leaves clustered or tufted on the rootstock, erect, arching, or prostrate, uniform or dimorphic, evergreen: blades coriaceous or membranous, simple, entire, toothed, or pinnatifid, or 1- or several-pinnate, the leaflets or segments entire, toothed, incised, or pinnatifid. Veins free, more or less forked, or individually united into areolae. Sori linear to elliptic, or rarely broader, straight, borne apart on the free ultimate veins, oblique to the midrib. Indusium present, lateral, usually mem-

branous.—SPLEENWORTS.—Fully six hundred species of
wide geographic distribution.—The genus was based on
Asplenium Trichomanes L.—The name is Greek, the
plants being a supposed remedy for diseases of the
spleen.—The foliage leaves and sporophyls are sometimes different in shape and in position.—The spores
mature, for the most part from June to October.

Blades of the leaves or leaflets thick-coriaceous : rachis green
and flat nearly throughout.   I. PINNATIFIDA.
Blades of the leaves thin-coriaceous :
rachis brown and terete at least
below.   II. PLATYNEURA.

I. PINNATIFIDA

Leaf-blade pinnatifid.   1. *A. pinnatifidum.*
Leaf-blade once or twice pinnate, at
least below.
  Leaf-blade once pinnate; leaflets
  toothed.   1a. *A. Trudelli.*
  Leaf-blades twice pinnate or pri-
  marily pinnate and secondarily
  pinnatifid.
    Blades of the leaflets ovate to
    lanceolate, the ultimate seg-
    ments lobed or coarsely toothed. 2. *A. montanum.*
    Blades of the leaflets cuneate to
    cuneate-flabellate, the ultimate
    segments finely toothed at the
    apex.   3. *A. cryptolepis.*

II. PLATYNEURA

Leaf-blades pinnatifid or with several
leaflets at the base : rachis brown
below.   4. *A. ebenoides.*
Leaf-blades pinnate nearly throughout.
  Plants with uniform leaves, all spore-
  bearing, ascending or spreading.
    Rachis brown for about half its
    length : leaflets coarsely serrate,
    or the lower ones pinnatifid or
    again pinnate, auriculate.   5. *A. Bradleyi.*
    Rachis brown throughout : leaflets
    crenate or dentate, cuneate or
    truncate at the base.   6. *A. Trichomanes.*
  Plants with dimorphic leaves, the
  foliage leaves small, spreading or
  prostrate, the sporophyls larger,
  erect : leaflets obscurely or sometimes prominently serrate, auricu-
  late, truncate at the base.   7. *A. platyneuron.*

    1. A. pinnatifidum Nutt. Rootstock short, copiously
chaffy and leafy: leaves tufted, sometimes densely so,
mostly 0.5–4 dm. long; petioles blackish, rather dull,
sparingly chaffy below, green above; blades lanceolate
to broadly lanceolate, firm, acuminate, often tapering to
a long narrow tip, pinnatifid or sometimes pinnate mainly

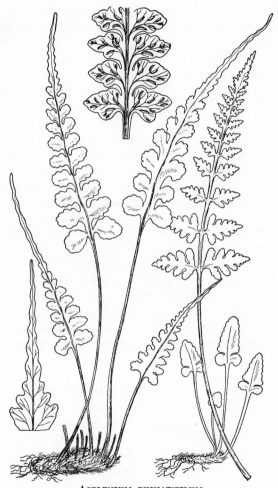

ASPLENIUM PINNATIFIDUM

at the base, one or more lower segments or leaflets coarsely toothed or lobed and sometimes prolonged into a slender tip like the apex of the blade, the typical segments variable in shape, usually obtuse or rounded at the apex and bluntly toothed or lobed and bluntly auricled at the base, sessile: veins mostly twice or thrice forked and some partially anastomosing: sori elliptic or oval, rather close to the midrib.—(LOBED-SPLEENWORT.)— Rocks and cliffs, both igneous and sedimentary, but lacking lime and yielding acid soils, various provinces, local in our range, only outside the Coastal Plain, not collected outside of southeastern Pennsylvania, except in one locality in Warren County, New Jersey.

The rock-ferns are usually quite different in aspect from the wood-ferns. Their leaves, in our range, are of a different pattern, usually less divided, and smaller. The lobed-spleenwort belongs with the more unusual-appearing rock-ferns. It is also to be classed among the rarer ones. However, it is not as rare as it was thought to be up to a half century ago. This fern seems to have been first noticed about the beginning of the nineteenth century. Its entrance into botanical literature, however, was made under the generic name of *Camptosorus*, a fern somewhat similar in habit, but different in technical characters. In 1818 the plant was placed in its proper genus, *Asplenium*, the specimens involved having been found on the banks of the Schuylkill River at Philadelphia, Pennsylvania. Although growing only on rocks this fern shows considerable variation in leaf-form and in habit. In fact, the form with especially pinnate leaf-blades has been given a distinctive name, *viz.*, *Asplenium Trudelli*. The plants of this fern grow in crevices in cliffs and boulders, taking distinctive habits according to the amount of available moisture. When a good supply is available the leaves grow strong and erect; where moisture is scant, the plants are smaller and the leaves lie more or less closely appressed to the rock-surface. The known geographic range has now been extended to cover an area bounded by Georgia, Oklahoma, Missouri, and western New Jersey. Connecticut was formerly included in the range, but the specimens involved proved to be *Asplenium ebenoides*. The altitudinal range in our region where it is very rare, extends from near sea-level to a few hundred feet, while a maximum of 4000 feet is attained in the Blue Ridge. In addition to its peculiar habit which somewhat resembles that of *Camptosorus*, these and *Asplenium ebenoides* are our only simple-leaved true ferns. Extreme well developed forms may be pinnate or nearly so, but only or mainly at the base of the blade. Its typically pinnatifid tapering leaf-blade with rounded lobes sets it off sharply from all our other species of *Asplenium*. However, it should be noted that the basal lobes are occasionally prolonged into slender tips. This fern and *Asplenium ebenoides* are our only spleenworts that propagate by the vegetative method. As in the case of *Camptosorus* sometimes a leaf taking root at the tip will form a new plant. If the usual habitat of these plants was of a damper character, this feature would doubtless be more common.

The plant designated as *Asplenium Trudelli* is interesting and is a good subject for further study. It is clearly closely related to *Asplenium pinnatifidum*, but the leaflets are so intriguingly suggestive of those of *A. montanum*, on a large scale, although much less deeply cut, that a mixture of the blood of *A. pinnatifidum* and of *A. montanum* is more than vaguely hinted. Where the writer has found *A. Trudelli* in southern Pennsylvania and southward, both *A. pinnatifidum* and *A. montanum* were present, but in our local area this seems not to be the case. (See large leaf at right hand side of figure.) However, this suggestion should be followed up experimentally just as was the case of suspected and later proved hybridity of *Asplenium ebenoides*.

2. **A. montanum** Willd. Rootstock short, the congested branches dark-brown, scaly. Leaves tufted, mostly 0.5–2 dm. long, evergreen; petioles naked, slender, dark-brown on the lower portion, naked or sparingly scaly at the base; blades lanceolate to ovate-lanceolate or deltoid-lanceolate, 1–2-pinnate, firm, the primary divisions short-

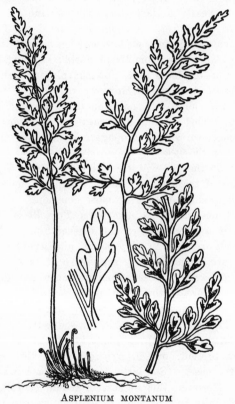

ASPLENIUM MONTANUM

stalked or sessile, the leaflets deltoid to ovate in outline, pinnatifid, or the lower ones especially, pinnate, the lobes or segments ovate or oblong: veins obscure, simple or twice or thrice forked; sori few, short, elliptic, more or less confluent at maturity: indusium thin-membranous.— (MOUNTAIN-SPLEENWORT.)—Rocks in woods, cliffs and crags, igneous and sedimentary, but giving rise to acid soils, various provinces, except Coastal Plain, especially widely distributed in the northern part of our range.

Although not a conspicuous fern, the mountain-spleenwort was among those discovered in the early days of botanical study in the United States. It is thus unlike *Asplenium Bradleyi*, its frequent associate, which escaped detection until nearly a century later. Like its associate, however, the mountain-spleenwort has a wide geographic distribution. Although it grew in the vicinity of many of the older towns and cities of the eastern states, it seems first to have been recognized in the high mountains of the Carolinas, late in the eighteenth century, and was named in 1810. It was soon found to have an extensive geographic range, extending from Georgia and Alabama to Kentucky, Ohio, and Massachusetts. As compared with the preceding species the leaf-form may be described as a fine lace-work. This structure is especially pronounced in well-developed leaves. The altitudinal range extends from near sea-level to nearly 4000 feet in our area and up to nearly 6000 feet in the Blue Ridge. In more southern latitudes the present species and *Asplenium pinnatifidum* are often associates as they frequent the same kind of habitats and rocks. In our range this feature apparently does not exist on account of the rarity of *A. pinnatifidum*. The leaf of the present fern is interesting because of the regularity of the divisions and lobes of the leaflets, and also the uniformity of all the leaves.—The mountain-spleenwort apparently does not take kindly to cultivation. Specimens planted for several years remain diminutive.

3. **A. cryptolepis** Fernald. Rootstock short, the branches congested, brown, scaly: leaves tufted, mostly 0.5–1.5 dm. long, evergreen; petioles naked or minutely

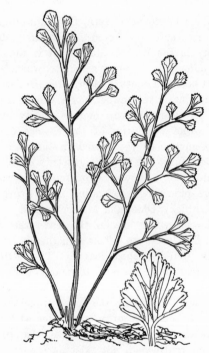

ASPLENIUM CRYPTOLEPIS

scaly at the base, green or brown; blades rhombic to deltoid-ovate in outline, glabrous, 2–3-pinnate, or pinnatifid above, lax, the primary leaf-divisions slender-stalked, the leaflets stalked, variable, cuneate to cuneate-flabellate and commonly rhombic or obovate, mostly obtuse, finely toothed at the apex: veins flabellate, simple or twice- or thrice-forked: sori few, linear-oblong, strongly confluent at maturity; indusium membranous, delicate. [*A. Ruta-muraria* Michx., not L.] — (RUE-FERN.   WALL-RUE.) — Cliffs, bluffs, and rocks in woods, almost exclusively on limestone, occasionally on stone walls, various provinces, more northern parts of our range.

As a result of the geographic position and the geologic structure of the eastern part of the United States, a much varied fern association has been established through the more recent ages and maintained there.   The highlands at the North and the tropics at the South combine to give the fern student in a midway region a more abundant assemblage of species and a greater variety in pattern of leaf than is to be found in any area of similar extent in North America.   The leaf of the present fern forms a rather coarse lace-work.   Up to a few years ago this fern was confused with the European *Asplenium Ruta-muraria*.   Although it was discovered in the early days of botanical activity in this country, it received its present name as late as 1928.   Limestone areas from Alabama to Missouri, Michigan, Ontario, and Vermont, harbor this fern.   The altitudinal range extends from near sea-level to over 3000 feet in our range and up to about 3000 feet in the southern highlands. The leaves of this fern are quite regularly divided, but the blades, for some reason, do not give the impression of regularity that is shown by those of *A. montanum*. However, the slender petiolules, the spaced leaflets, often broadened upward, and the finely toothed apex give the leaf a very individualistic aspect.   It is thus readily separable from *Asplenium montanum*.—The American rue-fern usually grows indifferently in cultivation, and may remain undersized for a long time or permanently.

4. A. ebenoides R. R. Scott.   Rootstock short or somewhat elongate, chaffy, sometimes copiously leafy.

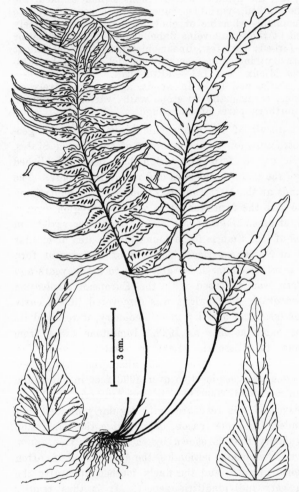

3 cm.

ASPLENIUM EBENOIDES

Leaves tufted, mostly 1–3 dm. long; petioles purplish-brown, shining, sparingly chaffy at the base; blades lanceolate to deltoid-lanceolate, often irregular and variable, firm, tapering to a slender acuminate apex, pinnatifid, or commonly pinnate near the base, the segments lanceolate to deltoid-ovate, frequently irregularly narrow and broad on the same leaf, obtuse, acute or long-acuminate at the apex, entire or irregularly and shallowly toothed, more or less broadly auricled at the base, sessile: veins mostly once to thrice forked: sori linear to elliptic, rather close to the midrib.—(SCOTT'S-SPLEENWORT.)—Rocks, and rocky banks, various provinces, rare in our range, known definitely from a few stations in northern New Jersey, Pennsylvania, New York, and Connecticut.

Most of our spleenworts were known to botanists before the middle of the past century. Some, however, escaped detection or recognition until in the latter half of the nineteenth century. Scott's-spleenwort, like the lobed-spleenwort, belongs with those of the less usual kinds. Its habit and habitat have caused quite an unusual reaction among fern students for many years. The banks of the Schuylkill River at Philadelphia were again destined to furnish a new fern. This discovery occurred about a half century after the launching of *Asplenium pinnatifidum*, and the fern in question, *Asplenium ebenoides*, was named in 1866. On account of its comparative rarity, the irregular pattern of the leaves, and its repeated occurrence only in company with two well known ferns, *Camptosorus rhizophyllus* and *Asplenium platyneuron*, hybridity was assumed to be responsible for its origin. The suspected natural hybrid origin finally was proved by the successful artificial crossing of the two presumable parents. The plants found from time to time at widely separated localities, either as single specimens or few individuals at the most, seemed not to be self-perpetuating. Finally the fern was found in great abundance at Havana Glen, Alabama, where the plants are unquestionably self-perpetuating by their spores. The geographic range is bounded by Alabama, Missouri, Vermont, New Jersey and Virginia. The alti-

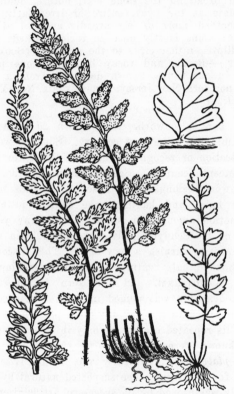

ASPLENIUM BRADLEYI

tudinal range is only up to about 800 feet in New Jersey, and rather slight generally compared with some of our other spleenworts, ranging from near sea-level to about 2000 feet in the southern mountains. This fern has some resemblance to the preceding species in its leaf-form, but the lobes are typically acute or acuminate, except rounded ones near the tip of the leaf-blade. Vigorous plants show a more irregularly jagged leaf-outline. It is very rare, but seems seldom misidentified when it is found.

5. **A. Bradleyi** D. C. Eaton. Rootstock short, erect or ascending, with narrow dark-brown scales. Leaves tufted, 0.5–3.5 dm. long, mostly spreading; petioles stoutish, like the rachis grooved above, rich chestnut-brown; blades lanceolate, oblong-lanceolate, or broadly linear in outline, acuminate, scarcely if at all narrowed at the base, the leaflets short-stalked or sessile, ovate to deltoid-ovate, or rarely oblong, or the lower leaflets often deltoid, mostly 1–2.5 cm. long, all pinnatifid or the lower ones pinnate, with obtuse lobes, segments, or leaflets which are toothed at the apex: veins except the basal ones simple or once or twice forked: sori few, near the midrib. — (BRADLEY'S-SPLEENWORT.) — Precipitous cliffs, igneous or metamorphic, or sedimentary, giving rise to intensely acid soils, various provinces, rare in our range, known definitely only from north of the moraine, in Carbon County, Pennsylvania, Warren County, New Jersey, and the Shawangunk Mountains, New York.

Several of our more interesting ferns, now known to have a wide geographic range, escaped detection for many years. Curiously enough, this fern is widely distributed in the regions where the more active botanical collecting was in progress during the many years preceding its discovery. The vicinity of large cities—Baltimore, Maryland and Little Rock, Arkansas, not to mention many smaller ones, and historic spots, such as Kings Mountain and Crowders Mountain, North Carolina, of Revolutionary War activities, and Lookout Mountain, Tennessee, of Civil War operations, are now well known localities for the Bradley-spleenwort. The first collection seems to have been in the Cumberland Mountains of Tennessee, in 1870. The species was named after the

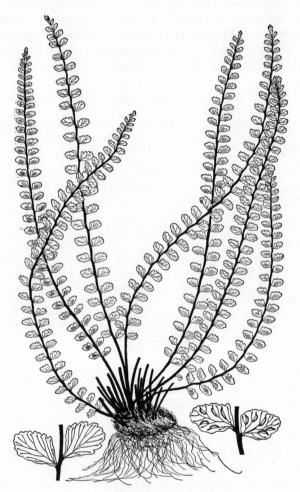

ASPLENIUM TRICHOMANES

discoverer in 1874. Its known geographic range may be stated as from Georgia and Alabama to Oklahoma, Missouri, and New York. No great altitude has been recorded for this fern. It ranges from about 2000 feet in our area as it does on Lookout Mountain, Tennessee, to near sea-level on the Atlantic seaboard. The size and dividing of the leaf-blades depend largely on the supply of moisture available. Plants growing in crevices of rocks where water is scarce or the supply irregular have small once-pinnate leaves that lie flat against the rock, while plants that have a steady and generous water-supply grow with the leaves erect and the blades often more or less completely twice-pinnate. At present this fern may be rated the rarest spleenwort in our range. It is an elegant plant. The leaves, typically pinnate, are evenly and regularly developed; the sessile or nearly sessile leaflets being uniformly toothed, while the basal ones, which on vigorous plants are sometimes pinnate, set this plant off distinctly from all its associates.

6. A. Trichomanes L. Rootstock short, nearly erect, or ascending, branched, the branches congested, with blackish scales. Leaves densely tufted, numerous, mostly spreading, 0.5–3 dm. long, evergreen; petioles purplish-brown, shining; blades linear, pinnate, the rachis purple-brown, the leaflets oval or roundish-oblong, inequilateral, rounded at the apex, crenate or dentate, especially on the upper edge, cuneate to truncate at the base: veins mostly once or twice forked: sori 2–6 pairs, elliptic.—(MAIDEN-HAIR SPLEENWORT. ROCK-MAIDENHAIR.)—Rocks, mostly sheltered, or if exposed, rather moist, various provinces, throughout our range, except southern New Jersey.

As a result of its very wide geographic range and its relative abundance, the maiden-hair spleenwort, in spite of its rather diminutive size, is one of the more early fern acquaintances of young botanists generally. In North America it has a much wider distribution, east and west and north and south, than any of the related small-leaved spleenworts, for example, *Asplenium resiliens, A. heterochroum,* and *A. platyneuron.* It occupies the United States and southern Canada. The plants, too, are able to withstand a greater variety of adverse climatic conditions, and considering their small root-system, small rootstocks, and limited supply of food and water, often produce a prodigious number of leaves. The name of the species published in 1753, referred to the plants growing in Europe. The species ranges in altitude from near sea-level to moderate elevations in our area and to 4000 feet in the Blue Ridge. There is great variety in the leaves of our spleenworts. The uniform leaves of the present plant are the plainest among the pinnate species, composed merely of numerous small, short, quite similar leaflets with shallowly toothed, non-auriculate blades, borne along the very slender rachis.—The maidenhair-spleenwort will grow in a garden, but changes little from year to year. A small plant will remain almost the same for a decade, except for the addition of a few sporelings.

7. A. platyneuron (L.) Oakes. Rootstock short, erect or ascending, scaly. Leaves tufted, few or several conspicuous ones erect, these sporophyls however accompanied by a rosette of small spreading leaves at the base; petioles purplish-brown, shining, like the rachis, slightly grooved above; blades linear or linear-oblanceolate in outline, or gradually narrowed at the base, firm, pinnate, the rachis chestnut-brown, the leaflets 20–40 pairs, lanceolate, or linear-lanceolate, or the diminishing ones below the middle of the blades gradually smaller and broader, elliptic, ovate, or triangular, subfalcate, alternate or partly so, crenate, or serrate, (or incised-serrate in *A. platyneuron serratum* and pinnatifid in *A. platyneuron incisum*), sessile, auricled on the upper side at the base and sometimes below: veins simple or once-forked, or the basal pair several times forked: sori 8–12 pairs, elliptic, crowded or rather approximate. [*Acrostichum platyneuros* L. *Asplenium ebeneum* Ait.]—(EBONY-SPLEEN-WORT. BROWN-STEM SPLEENWORT.)—Woods, roadside-banks, sand-dunes, and rocky slopes, various provinces, throughout our range, less common southward, more common northward.

The ebony-spleenwort may well be considered a northern type. Nowhere does it reach the Tropic of Cancer. Its range does extend southward into Florida, but it has never succeeded in achieving even the southern part of

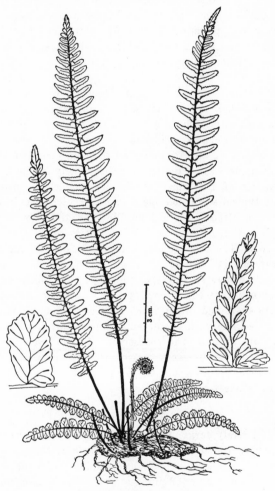

ASPLENIUM PLATYNEURON

the peninsula. It is widely distributed and usually common east of the Rocky Mountains, except in the extreme north. However, it is rather less frequently seen in the Coastal Plain than in the higher regions, and is less abundant, perhaps, in the Gulf States than in the states further north. In the South it differs somewhat from the northern plants in the form and toothing of the leaflets. Within our range it grows from sea-level to over 2000 feet altitude, and reaches 4500 feet in the Blue Ridge. It prefers to grow in partial shade. This fern was first found in Virginia in the early part of the eighteenth century and named in 1753. A fern growing over so wide an area is bound to show variations. These divergences from the type consist chiefly in the different cutting of the edges of the leaf-segments; instead of the typical serration, one may find leaflets deeply incised or pinnatifid. Various peculiarities are shown by this spleenwort. It is our only species with dimorphous leaves. The primary leaves are small, sporeless, and prostrate at the base of the plant. The secondary ones are erect, elongate, and spore-bearing. As compared with the next preceding species the leaves are outstanding, with short and broad, much reduced leaflets on the lower part of the rachis, and longer, narrower leaflets above. All are auricled and coarsely toothed or even incised.— The ebony-spleenwort thrives well in a garden if not crowded by other plants. It prefers the tops of banks and ledges for a habitat.

10. **ATHYRIUM** Roth.

Relatively large, terrestrial plants with horizontal or creeping rootstocks. Leaves erect or arching, not evergreen: petioles greenish or reddish, succulent: blades herbaceous, 2- or 3-pinnate or 2- or 3-pinnatifid, the ultimate segments herbaceous-membranous, irregularly toothed or incised, relatively broader and blunter than the leaflets. Veins free, simple or sparingly forked, running nearly or quite into the teeth of the leaf-segments. Sori usually curved when young, elliptic to linear-elliptic, or crossing the vein and recurved, thus vaulted, part way or all the way to the base. Indusium shaped like the sorus and opening as a whole along the side facing the midrib, or rarely vestigial and concealed. [*Asplenium* L. in part.]—LADY-FERNS.—Comprises about eighty-five species, most abundant in the tropics.—The genus is founded on *Polypodium Filix-foemina* L.—The name is Greek, meaning without a shield, of doubtful application here.— The following species have usually been treated as conspecific with *Athyrium Filix-foemina* (L.) Roth.—The spores mature from July to September.—The number of vaulted sori is variable. Sometimes they are scattered on the leaflets, other times their development is essentially complete.

Rootstock creeping, not densely clothed with old petiole-bases: leaf-blades broadest near the base: indusia with gland-tipped cilia: spores blackish.   1. *A. asplenioides.*

Rootstock horizontal or somewhat oblique, completely covered with the bases of spent petioles: leaf-blades broadest near the middle: indusia with lobes or glandless cilia: spores yellow-brown.   2. *A. angustum.*

1. A. asplenioides (Michx.) Desv. Rootstock relatively slender, copiously chaffy: leaves 3.5-11.5 dm. tall; petioles tufted, stramineous, brownish, or reddish, coarsely scaly at the base; blades broadly elliptic-ovate to elliptic-lanceolate, or lanceolate, broadest near the base, acuminate, 2-pinnate, except towards the apex (or pinnate and with pinnatifid segments in depauperate forms), the leaflets lanceolate, acuminate, short-stalked or the upper ones sessile, 1-2 dm. long, the ultimate divisions elliptic, oblong-lanceolate, or lanceolate, coarsely toothed, serrate, incised, or pinnatifid with their lobes or teeth often again toothed, sometimes decidedly auricled at the base: sori short, curved when young, oblique to the midrib: indusium with gland-tipped cilia. [*Nephrodium asplenioides* Michx.]—(LOWLAND LADY-FERN.)— Moist hammocks, wet woods, creek-banks, and shaded bluffs, various provinces throughout our range, but less common in the Coastal Plain.

The temperate and boreal parts of the Northern Hemisphere are girdled by the geographic range of this species and its near relatives, Europe and Asia as well as nearly

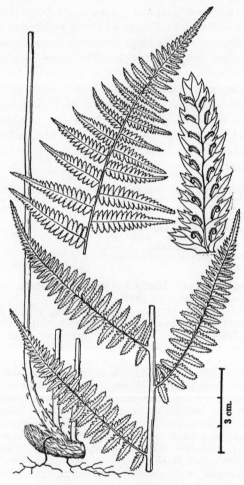

3 cm.

ATHYRIUM ASPLENIOIDES

all parts of the United States and southern Canada being in their range. It is a cool-climate plant, common in the north and reaching only as far south as northern Florida. The present sparse representation southward may be the mere relic of a more generous growth when the climate was cooler. Where this plant is more plentiful than in the Gulf States it presents numerous forms. In the southern mountains it occurs nearly or quite to the summits of the higher peaks and often grows luxuriantly on the moist, often cloud-bathed mountain tops. Within our range it is quite constant in its form of growth and in the technical characters which set it off from *A. Filix-foemina* of Europe, with which it has often been confused. When this species was named in 1803, it was said to range from New England to Canada. However, it actually grows chiefly farther south. This helps to account for much minor variation in the cutting of the leaf-blade. Some forms show much more lacy patterns than others. The altitudinal distribution is extensive, reaching from sea-level to nearly 4000 feet in our area, and to about 6600 feet in the Blue Ridge.

2. **A. angustum** (Willd.) Presl. Rootstock short, horizontal or somewhat oblique, completely covered with the bases of spent petioles: leaves 4–11 dm. tall, sometimes dimorphic; petioles somewhat tufted, stramineous, the scales with narrow dark-walled cells; blade somewhat elliptic in outline, at least broadest near the middle, 2-pinnate, the leaflets lanceolate, acuminate, sessile or nearly so, mostly 1–1.5 dm. long, the ultimate divisions lanceolate to elliptic-lanceolate or ovate-lanceolate, doubly serrate, not auricled at the base: sori rather short, often strongly curved, oblique to the midrib: indusium with glandless cilia. [*Aspidium angustum* Willd.]—(UPLAND LADY-FERN.)—Wet woods, moist banks, wooded hillsides, rocky streams, and sandy bogs, various provinces, throughout our range, except the Coastal Plain.

As noted under the preceding species, this plant and its relatives girdle the globe. The several species now recognized as distinct were formerly included under the Linnaean specific name *Filix-foemina*. Some of the

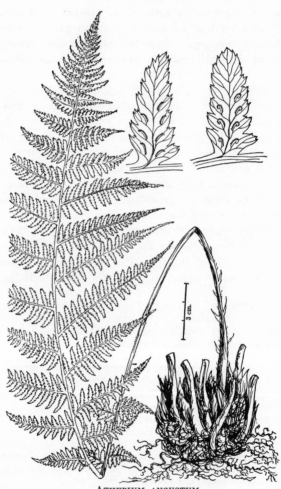

ATHYRIUM ANGUSTUM

present-day segregations grow as far south as the Gulf of Mexico, but the species prefer a cool climate and are more wide spread north of the latitude of the Mason and Dixon line. When the species was named in 1810, it was said to grow in Canada. Today it is known to range from Pennsylvania to Arkansas, South Dakota, Ontario, Quebec and Newfoundland. Its altitudinal distribution in our range seems to be limited by the 4000 foot contour.—Several varieties and forms of this unstable species have been proposed and described. They seem to fall into two primary groups: One with dimorphic leaves, the blades of the sporophyls coriaceous, contracted, with the sori confluent and thus covering the segments. Here belong the typical form and *A. angustum elatius.* The leaflets of the former are relatively small, (5–12 cm.) with the segments of the foliage leaves obtuse, and only slightly toothed or lobed. The leaflets of the form *elatius* are larger (12–25 cm.) with the segments strongly toothed or pinnatifid. *Athyrium angustum rubellum* represents the form with uniform leaves whose blades are membranous and not contracted, the sori spaced and not confluent at maturity. In some cases this seems to pass into the preceding species.

11. DIPLAZIUM Sw.

Large terrestrial plants, with horizontal or erect rootstocks which are scaly at the tips. Leaves in a crown, resembling those of *Athyrium* but less divided, and like them not evergreen: petioles succulent, more or less scaly at the base: blades 1-pinnate (in our species), broad, the leaflets numerous, rather broad, pinnatifid, the ultimate segments toothed or incised. Veins free, simple or sparingly forked, running almost or quite into the teeth of the leaf-segments. Sori elongate, double, at least in part, borne back to back on a vein, but not crossing it. Indusium covering the sorus, opening in opposite directions when double.—Consists of about three hundred and fifty species, mostly tropical.—The genus is based on

Asplenium plantagineum L.—The name is Greek, alluding to the double indusia.

1. D. acrostichoides (Sw.) Butters. Rootstock sinuous, copiously chaffy: leaves 6–12 dm. tall; petioles ultimately stramineous, coarsely scaly at the base; blades lanceolate, acute or acuminate at the apex, decidedly narrowed at the base, 1-pinnate, the leaflets lanceolate to linear-lanceolate, mostly 0.5–1.5 dm. long, sessile, acuminate, deeply pinnatifid into numerous oblong, obtuse, or subacute, or sometimes truncate, finely crenate or serrate-crenate segments: sori crowded, slightly curved, or straight, the lower ones often double: indusium light-colored, lustrous when young. [*Asplenium acrostichoides* Sw. *Asplenium thelypteroides* Michx. *Athyrium thelypteroides* Desv. *Diplazium thelypteroides* Presl.] — (SILVERY-SPLEENWORT. SILVER-FERN.) — Rich, moist woods, shaded banks, river-flats, and swamps, various provinces, throughout our range, except southern New Jersey.—Spores mature, July to October.

There are two relatively large ferns that the young plant collector and the amateur encounter in almost any wooded region in eastern North America. One of them is the plant commonly called silvery-spleenwort and its generic relative, the so-called lady-fern. The plants of these two ferns have the same general habit, but by the more compound structure of the leaf in *Athyrium asplenioides* and the less compound structure in *Diplazium acrostichoides* the two may be distinguished from each other at a glance. The present fern is much less lace-like than the lady-fern. The simply pinnate blade and the less deeply cut segments give the leaf a less elegant appearance. The plant has nearly as wide a geographic distribution in eastern North America as those of the preceding genus, but the altitudinal distribution seems to be less extensive. About 4000 feet in our range and 5000 feet in the Blue Ridge seem to be maximum. When the plant was named *Asplenium acrostichoides* in 1801, no locality was given for the origin of the specimens. The plant was again named *Asplenium thelypteroides* in 1803, the specimens said to have come from the moun-

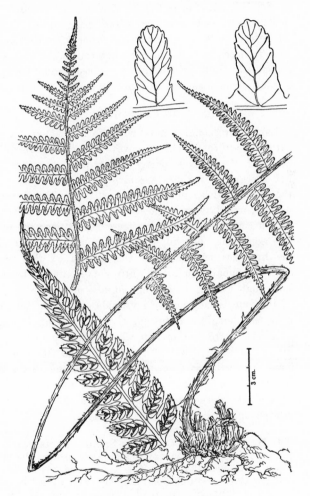

DIPLAZIUM ACROSTICHOIDES

tains of Virginia and North Carolina. As is the case in many species of *Diplazium* the double sori do not predominate on the leaflets. They are often more abundantly developed near the distal part of the leaflets. Therefore, as in the case of *Homalosorus* careful observation is necessary in order to determine the genus correctly.—The silvery-spleenwort thrives under rather dry garden conditions and spreads freely by its rootstocks.

12. **HOMALOSORUS** Small.

Large terrestrial plants with horizontal or creeping, rather stout rootstocks. Leaves in a crown, resembling those of *Nephrolepis,* partly foliar, partly spore-bearing, not evergreen: petioles succulent, more or less scaly at the base: blades 1-pinnate, narrow, the leaflets numerous, narrow, undulate or shallowly toothed, sometimes slightly auricled at the base. Veins free, forked near the midrib and sometimes beyond, or partly simple in sporophyls, the branches running into the sinuses of the margin. Sori occasionally double, slightly curved, linear, becoming somewhat turgid, extending mainly on upper branches of the vein, sometimes on both sides, from the midrib to near the margin. Indusium closely covering the sorus, opening toward the midrib when single, or in opposite directions when double.—Consists of the following species.—The name is from the Greek, alluding to the regular lines of sori.—The double sori are often imperfectly or sparsely developed. Where well-developed they are located on the basal part of the leaflet.

1. **H. pycnocarpus** (Spreng.) Small. Rootstock stoutish, creeping or horizontal: leaves in a crown, the sporophyls usually taller than the foliage leaves, 4–13 dm. long; petioles 2–3 dm. long, slightly scaly at the brownish base, green above; foliage-blades lanceolate to elliptic-lanceolate, pinnate; leaflets numerous, the blades lanceolate to linear-lanceolate, acuminate or attenuate at the apex, entire or crenulate, obtuse, truncate or subcordate at the base, with or without basal auricles: sporophyls and their leaflets narrower than the foliage leaves: sori 20–60 pairs, linear, approximate or crowded. [*Asplenium*

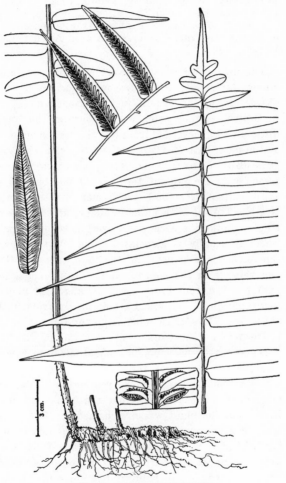

3 cm.

Homalosorus pycnocarpus

angustifolium Michx., not Jacq. *Asplenium pycnocarpum*
Spreng. *Athyrium pycnocarpum* Tidestrom. *Diplazium
angustifolium* Butters.]—(GLADE-FERN. DAGGER-FERN.)
Moist, rich woods, shaded ravines, rocky hillsides, and
talus at the base of cliffs, various provinces, scattered in
the more northern parts of our range, except in New
Jersey where rare.—Spores mature, August and September.

The narrow-leaved spleenwort may be associated with
either *Asplenium*, *Athyrium* or *Diplazium* by technical
characters, or the genera just mentioned might likewise
be united, as they often are. However, this fern is so
different in general habit and in the leaf structure, gross
and minute, that if *Athyrium* and *Diplazium* may be held
generically distinct from *Asplenium* there is no good
reason why the present fern should not be held generically distinct from both its former book associates. It
is a wood plant with annual foliage, and in every other
respect unlike the coriaceous, evergreen spleenworts with
which it usually is associated. The even branching of
the veins in the leaflets and the termination of the veins
and veinlets in the sinuses on the leaflet edge, together
with the numerous oblique sori arranged in almost perfectly parallel order, set it off distinctly from its former
associates. It stands alone in general habit as well as
in technical characters. The altitudinal distribution
appears not to be wide, but about 4000 feet has been
recorded in our range, while only the 3500 foot contour
seems to be its limit in the southern mountains. The
original specimens came from the banks of the Ohio
River, and the plant was first named in 1803. The geographic range extends from Georgia to Louisiana, Missouri, Wisconsin, and Quebec. The glade-fern or dagger-
fern has no counterpart so far as technical characters
are concerned, but in habit it resembles the Boston-fern
and the sword-fern (*Nephrolepis*) of peninsular Florida.
It should be remembered that the double sori are not
always numerous, and often absent.—The glade-fern,
contrary to its usual or normal moist habitats, thrives
well in rather dry garden conditions, which may be any-

thing but swampy, and spreads freely by its branching
rootstocks.

13. CAMPTOSORUS Link.

Slender plants with short, erect or ascending, somewhat
scaly rootstocks. Leaves approximately clustered, diffuse: petioles very variable in length, naked or nearly
so: blades narrow and tapering, simple, entire or lightly
sinuate, truncate or cordate at the base. Veins forking
and anastomosing. Sori linear or oblong, several times
longer than broad, irregularly scattered on either side of
the reticulate veins or sometimes crossing them, partly
parallel to the midrib and partly oblique, the outer ones
sometimes approximate in pairs, with the two indusia
opening face to face, or confluent end to end, thus forming crooked or bent lines of sori. Indusium thin, narrow.
Two species, the following and one in Asia.—WALKING-
FERNS.—The genus is based on *Asplenium rhizophylla*
L.—The name is Greek, alluding to the curved or bent
sori.

1. **C. rhizophyllus** (L.) Link. Rootstock short, chaffy:
leaves diffuse, prostrate, or arching, mostly 1–4 dm.
long; petioles light-green above the brown or purple base,
tufted; blades thin, but somewhat coriaceous, lanceolate,
simple, prolonged at the apex into a caudate-attenuate
tip which often takes root at the apex, undulate to sinuate, usually cordate and auriculate, sometimes hastate,
with the basal auricles occasionally much elongate and
caudate-attenuate: veins slender, some of the veinlets
running to the margin, others vanishing in the tissues:
sori irregular in size, shape, and position. [*Asplenium
rhizophylla* L.]—(WALKING-LEAF. WALKING-FERN.)—On
damp, often mossy rocks and stony banks, preferring
limestone, but frequent on many other kinds of rock,
various provinces, throughout our range, except southern
New Jersey.—Spores mature, July to October.

As in the case of some flowering-plants, certain ferns
have made doubly sure of holding their own, not only
through sexual reproduction but by vegetative propagation as well. The walking-leaf is an unusual fern in the
general and varying pattern of the leaf. It is well de-

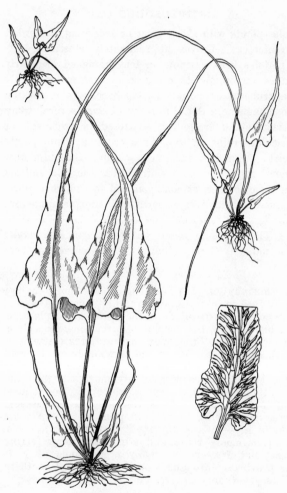

CAMPTOSORUS RHIZOPHYLLUS

signed for increasing away from the parent plant, by a
series of short leaps, as it were, and spreading in all directions. The greatly elongate tip of the leaf arches to
the ground, and from the apex which takes root, it sends
up a new plant. Then from the tip of each leaf of the
resulting plant a new individual may arise. Thus by a
few generations of vegetative propagation, many new
complete plants may appear at a considerable distance.
This fern shows instability in its leaf-form. Whether
this is the result of innate characteristics assumed in its
ancestral history or due to modern individual chance
hybridization cannot be determined. Of course, we do
know that at times the walking-fern hybridizes with the
ebony-spleenwort to make *Asplenium ebenoides*. The
walking-fern was named in 1753, as *Asplenium rhizophylla*, the specimens being said to have come from Virginia and Canada. The geographic range now includes
an area within a boundary indicated by Georgia and
Alabama to Kansas, Minnesota, and Quebec. The altitudinal distribution ranges from about sea-level to nearly
4000 feet in our range and to about 3000 feet in the
Blue Ridge. This and the one fern—*Asplenium pinnatifidum*—that resembles it in habit, more than any of our
other ferns, have a great deal in common, both in habit
and pattern. In addition to the similarity in general
shape of the leaf, the tip is often elongate and the basal
lobes are sometimes elongate and acuminate instead of
rounded. The rooting of the leaf-tip is frequent in
Camptosorus but rare in *Asplenium pinnatifidum.*—The
walking-fern may be established on a shady limestone
ledge, but it is difficult to keep birds from pulling and
scratching it to pieces.

13. **THELYPTERIS** Schmidel.

Rather slender, typically wood, marsh, or bog plants.
Leaves erect or nearly so, usually clustered or colonized
on the rootstock, dimorphic, not evergreen: petioles not
jointed to the rootstock, slender, scaleless or nearly so:
blades narrow, 1-pinnate, the leaflets membranous, pin-

natifid, the segments usually entire. Sori nearly or quite orbicular, borne on the back of the somewhat modified leaf-blade or a division of it. Indusium orbicular or reniform-orbicular, attached near the center. [*Aspidium* Sw. in part.]—SHIELD-FERNS.—About one hundred species, of wide geographic distribution. The genus is based on *Acrostichum Thelypteris* L.—The name is Greek, meaning female-fern.—The spores mature from July to September.

Leaf-blades conspicuously narrowed toward the base, the lower
  leaflets much reduced, sometimes
  very small and remote.   1. *T. noveboracensis.*
Leaf-blades not conspicuously nar-
  rowed at the base, the lower
  leaflets not at all or not much
  reduced in length, not widely
  separated.
Veins of the segments of the foliage leaves forked or with simple
  veins intermixed, or those of the
  sporophyls forked or simple.   2. *T. Thelypteris.*
Veins of the segments of the foli-
  age leaves and sporophyls simple.   3. *T. simulata.*

1. T. noveboracensis (L.) Nieuwl. Rootstock slender, wide-creeping, somewhat scaly: leaves about 1 m. tall or less, erect; petioles rather short, sparingly if at all scaly; blades lanceolate or elliptic-lanceolate, tapering both ways from near the middle, long-acuminate, 1-pinnate, the leaflets membranous, lanceolate or linear-lanceolate, sessile, long-acuminate, deeply pinnatifid, pilose on the midribs and veins, especially beneath, 3–7 dm. long, the lower ones gradually smaller and very short, distant and deflexed, the segments flat, oblong, obtuse, entire or crenate, the basal often slightly enlarged: veins simple, or those of the basal segments occasionally forked, in 4–8 pairs: sori submarginal, not confluent: indusium minute, delicate, glandular. [*Polypodium noveboracense* L. *Dryopteris noveboracensis* A. Gray.]—(NEW-YORK FERN.)—Rich woods, bogs, ravines, and moist pastures, in rather acid soil, various provinces, throughout our range except that it barely enters the pine-barrens.

For some reason comparatively few ferns have States for namesakes. East of the Mississippi River there are only seven species distinguished by such names. These are as follows, Florida (one), Alabama (two), Louisiana (one), Carolina (one), Virginia (one), and New York

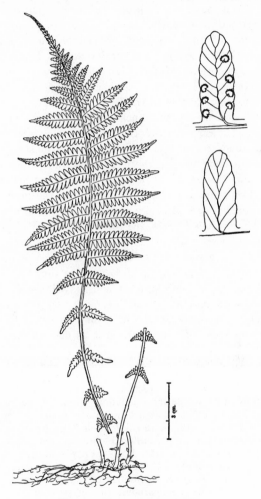

THELYPTERIS NOVEBORACENSIS

(one). One of our Florida ferns is also named for Panama and another for a minor area, the Bay Biscayne region in southern Florida. Linnaeus inaugurated the geographic designation of species by states by the publication of the fern under consideration and also the fern-relative *Lycopodium carolinianum*. This shield-fern is characteristic of the inland and more elevated plant provinces, and occurs as high as 4000 feet in our range and up to 5000 feet in the Blue Ridge. It may be recognized at once by the much reduced and distant leaflets on the lower part of the rachis. The structures are sometimes reduced to mere scales. Curiously enough, it has a counterpart in the Coastal Plain of southern peninsular Florida, for *Dryopteris panamensis* has the same kind of reduced and distant leaflets in the lower part of the blade, and although a distinct species with larger and coriaceous leaflets, the technical characters that separate the two relatives are slight. The original specimens of *T. noveboracensis* are said to have come from Canada. The species was named in 1753. Its range is wide, extending from Georgia to Arkansas, Minnesota, Ontario, and Newfoundland.—The New York fern is easily grown almost anywhere, even in sunny places. It spreads rapidly from the rootstocks just as does the marsh-fern.

2. T. Thelypteris (L.) Nieuwl. Rootstock rather slender, horizontal or widely creeping, black, glabrous or nearly so: leaves erect, 1.5 m. tall or less, in colonies, not evergreen; petioles slender, glabrous or nearly so, purple or purplish toward the base; blades lanceolate or elliptic-lanceolate, with the rachis glabrous or finely pubescent, short-acuminate, 1-pinnate, the leaflets membranous, numerous, the larger ones 4–8 dm. long, the blades lanceolate to linear-lanceolate, slightly acuminate, sessile or nearly so, pinnatifid, the segments ovate to ovate-lanceolate or ovate-elliptic, mostly obtuse, more or less revolute: veins of the segments of the foliage leaves 1-forked or occasionally twice-forked near the base: sori about medial, numerous, sometimes confluent: indusium s m a l l, delicate, glabrous. [*Acrostichum Thelypteris* L. *Dryopteris Thelypteris* A. Gray.]— (MARSH-FERN.)—Marshes, swamps, bogs, damp woods,

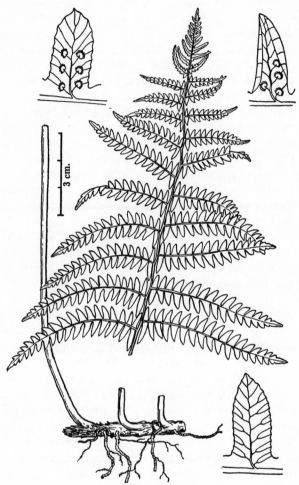

3 cm.

THELYPTERIS THELYPTERIS

and ditches, various provinces, throughout our range, but very rare in the pine-barrens.

Various ferns show the results of environmental experiences in the past ages. There are great differences in their geographic distribution. The area occupied by some species is vast; that of others is very localized. The former may represent a species that has reached its maximum development in geographic distribution, while the latter may be either a species that has had its maximum geographic development long ago and is now on the wane or it may be just starting on its career. How many ferns have thus reached their acme and then gradually passed out of existence we will never know. The present fern is distributed in Europe and North America. In Atlantic North America it ranges from southern Florida to southern Canada, and thence approximately to the Rocky Mountain region. It is not among those ferns, paired as it were, that have a counterpart southward or northward as the case may be. It is somewhat distinctive among ferns of similar habit by its general port, but it may be known definitely by the forked veins of foliage leaves. The original specimens were from Europe and were named in 1753. This fern seems to prefer the lowlands, not reaching the altitude achieved by its associates; however, it ranges up to 2000 feet in our range and 2500 feet in the interior highlands. This is one of our ferns that was known to Linnaeus from European specimens. Aside from its technical character of forking veins, there are gross earmarks that may be partially relied on for separating it from the related *Thelypteris simulata*. The leaflets on the lower part of the rachis are not narrowed at the base, the lowest pair of segments often being longer than the others. The segments of the sporophyls are tightly revolute when the sporangia are mature, making them lanceolate or narrowly ovate and giving the sporophyl quite a different aspect from the foliage leaf.—The marsh-fern will grow almost anywhere in a garden, and sporelings from the parent plant soon appear far and wide. If in too shady a place foliage leaves only appear. It makes a good rock fern and will cling to crevices where there is little soil, but spreads rapidly by rootstocks.

3. T. simulata (Davenp.) Nieuwl. Rootstock slender, widely creeping, sparingly if at all scaly: leaves erect, mostly 3–11 dm. long, sometimes clustered; petioles slender, stramineous above the dark very sparingly scaly base, otherwise glabrous; blade lanceolate to elliptic-lanceolate in outline, acuminate at the tip, like the rachis glabrous or nearly so, 1-pinnate, the leaflets lanceolate to elliptic-lanceolate, mostly 3–9 cm. long, membranous, approximate or separated, mostly spreading or the lower ones reflexed, pinnatifid, the segments ovate to oblong-ovate, obtuse, entire or sometimes obscurely crenate: veins simple, oblique: sori few to several, usually 4–12 on a segment, submarginal: indusium minutely glandular. [*Dryopteris simulata* Davenp.] — (BOG-FERN.) — Moist acid woods and bogs, various provinces, throughout our range, more abundant in the Coastal Plain, but, in general, much rarer than the two preceding species.

The present fern is a conspicuous example of how a fairly abundant and wide-spread plant may escape detection for many years in a region of rather intense botanical activity. Our native ferns have been studied by both professional and amateur botanists, continuously for a century or more, yet it was not until 1894 that this one was brought to light and named. The type specimens were collected at Seabrook, New Hampshire, in 1880. By the outline of the leaflets and the general habit it is related to the next preceding species. This fern apparently reaches less altitude in its distribution than the preceding species both in our range and in the interior highlands. The simple veins of the leaflets of this species are diagnostic. However there are gross characters that may be relied on as a general rule. The lower leaflets in this species are somewhat narrowed to the base as a result of the shortening of the lower segments, and the segments of the sporophyls are not tightly revolute, thus leaving them but little different from those of the foliage leaves. The reduced basal leaflets may be

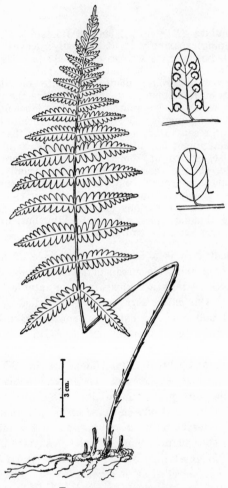

THELYPTERIS SIMULATA

considered as indicating a transition to *Thelypteris nove-boracensis* or at least a closer relationship to this species than to *T. Thelypteris*. *T. noveboracensis* also has mostly simple veins.—The bog-fern is quite adaptable to almost any habitat, if the soil is acid and sterile. It will even grow in dry sandy soil, but naturally prefers some moisture and shade. It spreads rapidly by its branching rootstocks.

14. **DRYOPTERIS** Adans.

Coarse or delicate typically terrestrial wood, frequently humus, plants. Leaves erect, spreading, or drooping, usually clustered on the rootstock, often somewhat dimorphic, mostly evergreen: petioles not jointed to the rootstock: blades narrow or broad, 1- to 3-pinnate or dissected; leaflets subcoriaceous or firm-herbaceous, the segments usually toothed, lobed, or pinnatifid. Veins simple or forked, usually free, the tips running to the margin remote from the sinus. Sori nearly or quite orbicular, borne on the back of the unmodified leaf-blade or its divisions, on the veins or rarely at their tips. Indusium orbicular-reniform, attached at the center or at or near the sinus. [*Aspidium* Sw. in part.]—SHIELD-FERNS. WOOD-FERNS.—About two hundred species, of wide geographic distribution.—The genus is based on *Polypodium Filix-mas* L.—The name is Greek, meaning oak-fern.— The spores mature, for the most part, from May to September.

Leaf-blades 1-pinnate or if 2-pinnate with the segments toothed.	I. MARGINALES.
Leaf-blades 3-pinnate or if 2-pinnate with the segments pinnatifid.	II. SPINULOSAE.

I. MARGINALES

Sori submarginal: petioles copiously and densely scaly at the base.	1. *D. marginalis.*
Sori medial or toward the midrib: petioles not copiously and densely scaly at the base.	
Leaflets at the base of the blade often shorter and relatively broader at their bases than those above.	
Sori medial.	
Indusium glabrous: leaflets pinnatifid.	2. *D. cristata.*

Indusium   glandular-pubescent:
  leaflets pinnate.   3. *D. Boottii.*
Sori against or near the midrib.   4. *D. Clintoniana.*
Leaflets at the base of the blade not
  much shorter nor broader than
  those above.   5. *D. Goldiana.*

II. SPINULOSAE

Indusium glandular: leaflets usually at
  right-angles to the rachis: the lowest
  pair   inequilaterally   lanceolate-tri-
  angular, or ovate-lanceolate.   6. *D. intermedia.*
Indusium glabrous or nearly so: leaflets
  oblique to the rachis: the lowest
  pair of leaflets inequilaterally
  broadly ovate to deltoid.
Sori terminal on the veinlets: indusium glabrous: leaflets flat, de-
  current.   7. *D. spinulosa.*
Sori subterminal on the veinlets: in-
  dusium glabrous or with a few
  glands: leaflets concave, some of
  them not decurrent.   8. *D. campyloptera.*

1. D. marginalis (L.) A. Gray. Rootstocks stout,
woody, ascending, with bright-brown shining scales:
leaves in a crown, up to 1 m. long, evergreen; petioles
stout, chaffy and with a dense mass of scales below;
blades ovate-oblong or ovate-lanceolate, 1- or 2-pinnate,
acuminate, slightly narrowed at the base, the leaflets
coriaceous, numerous, nearly sessile, glabrous, the blades
5–15 cm. long, the lower unequally triangular-lanceolate,
those above lanceolate to oblong-lanceolate, all pinnatifid,
with the sinuses reaching nearly or quite to the midrib,
the segments oblong or lanceolate, falcate, subentire,
crenate, or pinnately lobed, partially adnate or the lowest
merely sessile: sori few to several, distant, 1.5–2 mm. in
diameter, close to the margin: indusium relatively large,
firm, glabrous. [*Polypodium marginale* L.]—(EVERGREEN
WOOD-FERN.   MARGINAL SHIELD-FERN.)—Rocky woods,
swamps, and bluffs, various provinces, throughout our
range except the pine-barrens and the region south of
them.

Just as the Christmas fern is the cosmopolitan species
of the genus *Polystichum* in eastern North America,
the marginal shield-fern or this wood-fern is the almost
cosmopolitan species of *Dryopteris*. Like the Christmas-
fern, whose leaves are also evergreen, it prefers the
rocky woods, banks, and ravines for its habitats. It is
true that several species of our wood-ferns have an extensive geographic distribution, but none of those that range

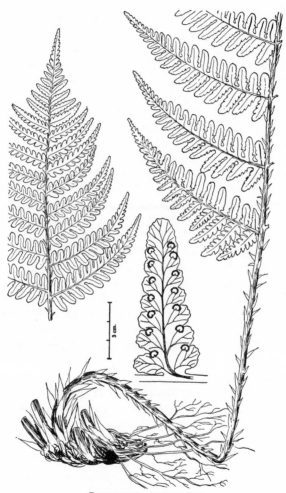

DRYOPTERIS MARGINALIS

from the Atlantic Coast to the Pacific ranges as far
north in eastern North America as does *Dryopteris marginalis*. This rather outstanding fern is frequently an
associate of the common polypody (*Polypodium virginianum*), consequently it is one of the larger evergreen
ferns that the beginner in plant studies is apt to become
acquainted with in the field. It may be collected in
the winter as well as in the summer. Rocky woods are to
its liking. It grows equally well in the rich, deep soil
of the forest or in accumulations of soil on rock or in
crevices of rocks or cliffs. It is an elegant fern. The
deep-green upper side of the leaf-blade, the pale under
side, and mass of buff scales on the lower part of the
petiole all together make the leaf very attractive. This
species has a greater south and north distribution than
any of its taxonomic associates, *Dryopteris Goldiana,
D. cristata, D. Clintoniana,* and *D. floridana,* running
from the mountains of Georgia up into Canada where the
original specimens were collected and subsequently named
in 1753. The altitudinal range is also extensive. In our
area it achieves about 4000 feet, while in the Blue Ridge
it is not rare even up to 6000 feet. The leaves of this
species are, perhaps, the most hardy of those among the
species of *Dryopteris* in our range. By the time winter
approaches the leaf-tissues have become firm and
hardened to such an extent that the most severe winter
weather does not affect them seriously. Curiously enough,
there is a striking similarity between the leaf-tissues of
this plant and the evergreen common polypody, *Polypodium virginianum.*

2. **D. cristata** (L.) A. Gray. Rootstock stout, creeping, densely brown-chaffy: leaves erect or spreading, up
to 1 m. long, yellowish-green, evergreen, the foliage ones
smaller than the sporophyls; petioles stramineous above
the base, sparsely scaly or sometimes copiously so at the
base; sporophyls rigidly erect, the blades linear-oblong
or lanceolate, acuminate, pinnate; the leaflets spaced, the
lower ones deltoid or ovate, those above oblong-lanceolate
to lanceolate or linear-lanceolate, deeply pinnatifid, the
segments oblong to ovate or triangular-oblong, obtuse,

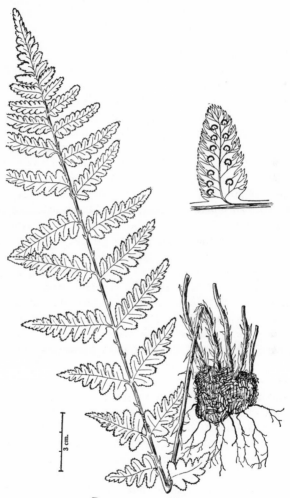

DRYOPTERIS CRISTATA

finely serrate: sori nearly medial: indusium glabrous. [*Polypodium cristatum* L.]—(CRESTED SHIELD-FERN.)— Low woods, swamps, and boggy thickets, various provinces, including the Coastal Plain, throughout our range.

The plants of this genus in coming down from the primitive ancestral form have traveled along several rather definite lines. These lines are now represented by groups of species, as indicated in the main divisions of the key to the species. The group with leaves of rather thick or subcoriaceous texture is represented over a wide geographic area. Most of the species prefer more northern regions or the highlands. Only one, *Dryopteris floridana*, not only prefers but is confined to the southeastern Coastal Plain. Curiously enough, there is a very close relationship between the species under consideration and *D. floridana*. In fact, although the extremes of the geographic ranges of the two are widely separated, specimens, for example from Florida (*D. floridana*), and from Ohio (*D. cristata*), are difficult to separate even by the technical characters. The questions suggested are: Did *Dryopteris cristata* and *D. floridana* have a common ancestor, or is one an offshoot from the other? The plant was named in 1753, the name being based on European specimens. The geographic area occupied extends from North Carolina to Arkansas, Nebraska and southern Canada. The altitudinal range extends from near sea-level to over 2500 feet in the Pocono region, and to moderately high points in the Blue Ridge. This fern represents the narrow extreme of the group, *Dryopteris Goldiana*, *D. Clintoniana*, and *D. cristata*. The leaves are smaller and conspicuously narrower, while the shortened leaflets at the base of the rachis are very broad in proportion to their length.—The crested shield-fern although an inhabitant of low grounds or wet woods, will sometimes thrive high up on dry shaded banks in a garden, in a healthy condition, but does not reach as large a size as on the lower part of banks where there is more moisture. The yellowish-green hue of the foliage is very evident in the garden.

3. D. Boottii (Tuckerm.) Underw. Rootstock stout, horizontal and ascending at the tip: leaves erect or ascending, up to 1 m. tall, evergreen, the sporophyls larger than the foliage leaves; petioles stramineous above the purple base, with pale-brown scales, especially near the base; blades lanceolate to narrowly oblong-lanceolate in outline, acuminate, 2-pinnate, except sometimes toward the apex, the leaflets somewhat spaced, subcoriaceous, the lower ones pinnate, triangular, those above triangular-lanceolate to lanceolate, acuminate, short-petioluled, the segments narrowly triangular to lanceolate, oblong, or ovate, evidently spinulose-serrate, but with the teeth mostly directed forward or somewhat incurved, acute or acutish: sori distinct, medial or rather nearer the midrib: indusium glandular. [*Aspidium Boottii* Tuckerm.]— (BOOTT'S SHIELD-FERN.)—Low woods, swamps, and moist hillsides, various provinces, nearly throughout our range.

Some ferns have had a quiet existence in literature, others like the present one have stirred up controversy. The main disputed points are as to whether or not it is of hybrid origin and its presumable parents. The leaf is intermediate in some respects, between *Dryopteris cristata* and *D. intermedia*. It stands between the two in shape, texture, and cutting of the leaf. These two supposed parents are often associated in the field where *Dryopteris Boottii* is found, and are frequently associated with it in fern literature. However, theoretically considered, *Dryopteris Clintoniana* would be a more likely parent than *D. cristata*. This fern was discovered before the middle of the past century and named in 1843. Later it was made a variety of *Dryopteris spinulosa*, and also considered a hybrid, several alleged parents being involved. At any rate it is an elegant fern with the leaf combining the laciness of the *spinulosa* group and the regular clean-cut form of the *cristata* group, irrespective of its hybrid or non-hybrid origin. Its natural range is from Virginia and West Virginia to Minnesota and Nova Scotia. It occurs from sea-level to 2000 feet in the Pocono Plateau in Pennsylvania; perhaps at higher altitudes in the Catskills. Plants referable to *Dryopteris Boottii* have quite regular leaves in regard to the pinnate blades

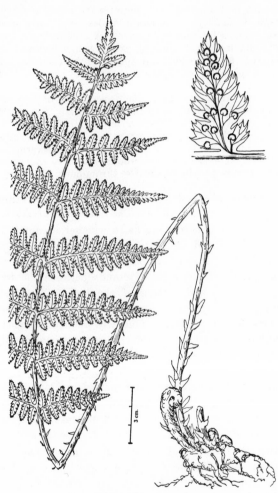

DRYOPTERIS BOOTTII

and the cutting of the ultimate leaflets or segments. If a hybrid it does not show the very erratic leaf-forms of other hybrid ferns.—A list of described hybrids between species of ferns growing in our area is given at the end of this generic treatment.—The Boott's shield-fern is a beautiful subject for the garden, easy to grow and to keep healthy. The same may be said about the various hybrids of the wood-ferns.

4. D. Clintoniana (D. C. Eaton) Dowell. Rootstock stout, creeping, densely brown-chaffy: leaves erect or ascending, up to 1.5 m. long, bluish-green, evergreen; petioles stramineous or brownish, sparsely scaly or copiously so at the dark base; blades triangular-lanceolate or ovate-oblong, acute or short-acuminate, 1-pinnate, the leaflets somewhat separated, the lower ones triangular to triangular-lanceolate, those above lanceolate, sometimes broadly so, deeply pinnatifid, the segments oblong to ovate, usually obtuse, serrate, or the basal ones pinnately cut: sori near the midvein: indusium glabrous. [*Aspidium cristatum Clintonianum* D. C. Eaton. *Dryopteris cristata Clintoniana* Underw.] — (CLINTON'S-FERN.) — Swamps, low woods, and bogs, various provinces, throughout our range, rare in the Coastal Plain.

The present species, though fairly common, was nearly as long-neglected as *Thelypteris simulata,* and then first became known to the botanical public as a subspecies. Attached to *Dryopteris cristata,* it posed in a subordinate way for nearly four decades before it was given specific standing. In spite of its claim to specific rank, it has been often confused with *Dryopteris Goldiana.* Accompanying the original description, a note records that this is "A showy fern, unlike any European form of [*Aspidium*] *cristatum,* and often mistaken for *A. Goldianum.*" Wood-ferns growing in abundance in our higher altitudes and latitudes are, perhaps through former hybridization, liable to present taxonomic difficulties until thoroughly and carefully studied. The plants of this species often grow in company with *Dryopteris Goldiana* and *D. cristata.* If these were its associates ages ago, one would be justified in considering the pres-

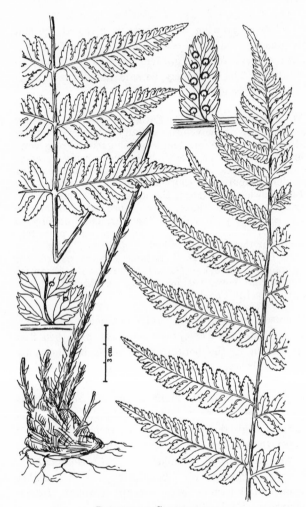

Dryopteris Clintoniana

ent species to be of hybrid origin. Of the two it more resembles *D. Goldiana,* but the narrower leaf-blade, the usually horizontal leaflets which are broadest at the base, and the scarcely falcate segments easily separate it from that species. The petiole too is less scaly and the scales paler. The plants are typically larger than those of *D. cristata.* The leaf-blade is broader, the leaflets slender pointed, and the petiole more scaly. A diagnostic character is the more medial position of the sori. This plant was described as a subspecies of *Dryopteris cristata* in 1867. At that time its range was given as New England to New Jersey, New York and westward. Now, it is known to grow from North Carolina to Wisconsin, Ontario and Maine. The altitudinal range extends from near sea-level to at least 1000 feet in our area, and to nearly 5000 feet in the Blue Ridge. — The Clinton's shield-fern is adaptable to garden culture like the crested shield-fern. Its bluish-green foliage holds in cultivation just as it does in its native swamps and partly shaded bogs.

5. **D. Goldiana** (Hook.) A. Gray. Rootstock stout, woody, horizontal and ascending, chaffy: leaves erect or ascending, up to 1.7 m. long; petioles stramineous, scaly and densely covered near the base with large lanceolate, usually dark, lustrous scales; blades ovate to oblong, nearly glabrous except the scaly rachis, dark-green above, 1-pinnate, the leaflets broadly lanceolate to oblong-lanceolate, broadest above the base, 1.5–2.5 dm. long, deeply pinnatifid, the segments as high as 20 pairs, oblong, oblong-linear, or ovate, subfalcate, serrate, the teeth appressed: sori 6–10 pairs, near the midrib, close but distinct, large; indusium orbicular, glabrous. [*Aspidium Goldianum* Hook.]—(GOLDIE'S-FERN. GIANT WOOD-FERN)— Rich woods, swamps, mossy mountain slopes, sometimes on rotting logs, various provinces throughout our range, except the Coastal Plain.

The leaves of the group of *Dryopteris* represented by *D. cristata, D. floridana, D. Clintoniana, D. marginalis,* and the one under consideration vary greatly in the proportion of the width to the length of the blade. In some

DRYOPTERIS GOLDIANA

species the leaf-blades are narrow, in others they are broad. In addition the outline of the leaf-blades of each species is distinctive. In the case of the present one the leaf is large, very broad, and rather abruptly short-acuminate; the leaflets are also broad and are separated sufficiently at the rachis to stand out like so many spreading feathers. The lower pair or several pairs of leaflets, scarcely reduced in size, are not spore-bearing. *Dryopteris Goldiana* was named in 1822, the specimens having been collected at Montreal, Canada. The geographic area has been found to be wide, extending from North Carolina and Tennessee to Iowa, Minnesota, and New Brunswick. The altitudinal range extends from sea-level to nearly 4000 feet in our area and to between 5000 and 6000 feet in the Blue Ridge. Curiously enough, a closely related fern occurs in the Dismal Swamp region of eastern North Carolina and Virginia. This Coastal Plain plant has been described as *Dryopteris celsa* or *Dryopteris Goldiana celsa*. However, the technical characters ascribed to it do not seem to be constant. This plant is not yet well understood. Suffice it to say here, the sorus characters of some leaves place it with *Dryopteris Goldiana*, while those of other leaves associate it with *D. Clintoniana.*—The Goldie's-fern grows well in cultivation, even in rather dry locations. It responds to fertilization by an increase in vigor.

6. D. intermedia (Muhl.) A. Gray. Rootstock creeping or ascending at the tip, chaffy: leaves equal, up to 1 m. long, spreading in a complete crown, evergreen; petioles with light-brown concolorous or darker-centered scales; blades mostly lanceolate, sometimes broadly so, in outline, glandular-pubescent when young, the leaflets usually at right angles to the rachis, the lower ones at least pinnate, lanceolate to ovate-lanceolate, the upper ones lanceolate to oblong, acuminate, the segments convex, oblong or lanceolate, acute, the largest not decurrent, pinnately divided nearly at right angles, the ultimate segments dentate, usually straight: sori submarginal, not quite terminal: indusium glandular. [*Polypodium intermedium* Muhl. *Dryopteris spinulosa intermedia* Underw.] —(AMERICAN SHIELD-FERN.)—Moist banks or rich upland

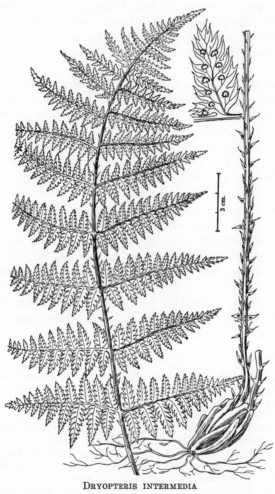

3 cm.

D<small>RYOPTERIS</small> <small>INTERMEDIA</small>

woods or rarely swamps, various provinces, throughout our range, except the pine-barrens.

Although this fern and the following species belong to the thicker-tissued group, collectively they form a subgroup characterized by more divided leaf-blades whose ultimate divisions end in spine-tipped teeth. The three species of the so-called *spinulosa* group of shield-ferns are somewhat difficult to understand taxonomically. One of the species, *D. spinulosa*, is cosmopolitan in the Northern Hemisphere, while the present one and *D. campyloptera* are American. They enter our geographic range from the north and pass on southward to the Blue Ridge of North Carolina and Tennessee. The present species was described from specimens collected in Pennsylvania and named in 1810. This fern probably has the same altitudinal range as its two associates which follow. However, up to the present time it seems not to have been found much above the 2000 foot contour in the highlands of our range. In the New England mountains this plant and its associates range up to 5000 feet, while in the southern Blue Ridge they have been found more than 6500 feet above sea-level. The geographical range extends from North Carolina and Tennessee to Wisconsin and Newfoundland. Plants of this fern cannot be determined casually by habit alone, for the leaves often closely simulate those of members of a very distinct genus, particularly those of *Athyrium asplenioides* and *A. angustum*. The shape of the leaf, the toothing or incising of the leaf-segments and the scales at the base of the petiole are very similar.—The American shield-fern, like its two relatives, *Dryopteris spinulosa* and *D. campyloptera*, does well in gardens in shady positions. Sporelings are produced in shady nooks and crevices.—Frequently furnishing the ''fancy-fern'' of the cut-flower trade.

7. D. spinulosa (Muell.) Kuntze. Rootstock stout, erect, chaffy: leaves in an incomplete crown, up to 1 m. long, the taller erect, the others spreading, mostly not evergreen; petioles with pale-brownish concolorous scales; blades ovate-lanceolate to oblong, acuminate, deeply

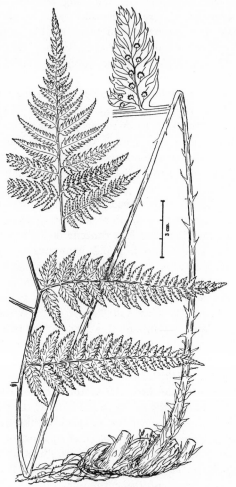

DRYOPTERIS SPINULOSA

2-pinnate, the leaflets oblique, the lower ones unequally triangular, deltoid, or deltoid-ovate, those above lanceolate to oblong, acuminate, the segments flat, oblong to lanceolate, acute, decurrent, pinnately cut almost to the midveins, the ultimate segments somewhat incised, the teeth mucronate, falcate, somewhat appressed: sori submarginal, terminal on veinlets: indusium without glands. [*Polypodium spinulosum* Muell.]—(TOOTHED WOOD-FERN. SPINULOSE SHIELD-FERN.)—Moist or low wet woods, often in rocky places, more northern provinces in our range, and lowland swamps of the Coastal Plain, except the southern tip.

There is no mistaking the plants of the three spinulose ferns as far as their group relationship is concerned. The peculiar texture of the leaf and the spinulose teeth of the segments being very evident at all times. This species represents the spinulose group as it occurs in eastern North America and in the Old World. Its taxonomic associate, *Dryopteris intermedia,* occurs in both the highlands and the lowlands in our area. However, this species is found mainly in the highlands where it ranges up to almost 4000 feet above sea-level. The geographical range is large, extending from North Carolina and Tennessee to Idaho and Labrador. It also occurs in Europe. The leaves of *Dryopteris spinulosa* are more hardy than those of *D. campyloptera,* but less so persistent than those of *D. intermedia.* At least the non-spore bearing leaves remain green all winter, whereas those of *D. campyloptera* wilt and turn brown when the temperature reaches freezing point or slightly lower.

8. D. campyloptera (Kunze) Clarkson. Rootstock horizontal and creeping, very chaffy: leaves equal, up to 1.5 mm. long, spreading in a complete crown, not evergreen; petioles copiously scaly, especially toward the base, with dark-brownish, often darker-centered, scales; blades triangular to ovate or broadly oblong, acuminate, 2- or 3-pinnate, the leaflets variable, the lower ones broadly and unequally ovate or triangular, those above lanceolate to oblong, acute or acuminate, at least the lowermost pinnately divided, the segments convex, broadly oblong to lanceolate, acute, the largest not decurrent, pinnately divided, the ultimate segments pinnately lobed, the teeth

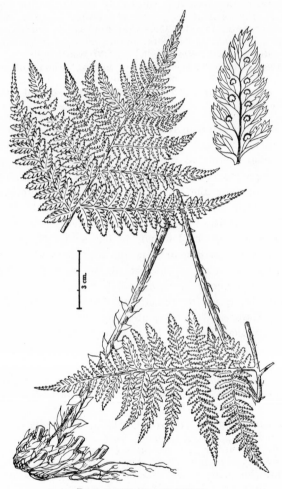

DRYOPTERIS CAMPYLOPTERA

mucronate, usually not appressed; sori mostly submarginal; indusium glabrous or with a few glands. [*Aspidium campylopterum* Kunze. *Aspidium spinulosum americanum* Fischer. *Dryopteris dilatata* A. Gray, in part.]—(SPREADING SHIELD-FERN.)—Moist, rocky woods, more northern provinces, highlands north of the terminal moraine.

There has been and is much difference of opinion as to the specific or subspecific standing of this and the two preceding plants. However, the present one seems to be thoroughly worthy of specific standing. From its closest relative in eastern North America it differs in the horizontal rootstock, the less-evergreen leaves, and the very broad basal leaflets with their more or less diminutive odd-leaflet near the rachis. For many years it was almost universally confused with *Dryopteris dilatata*, a species of the Old World and western North America. However, two attempts to give it separate standing were made, but were slow in taking root, so to speak. This plant probably reaches the limit of the higher altitudes in our range, at least it is known to occur at over 4000 feet above the sea in the Catskills and at 2000 feet in the Poconos. Its altitudinal distribution increases southward until about 6000 feet are achieved in the Blue Ridge. The present geographic area of this plant extends from North Carolina and Tennessee to Newfoundland.

SOME RECORDED HYBRIDS BETWEEN SPECIES OF
Dryopteris

(Some of the following have also appeared under the generic names *Aspidium* and *Nephrodium*)

Dryopteris Clintoniana × *Goldiana* Dowell.
Dryopteris Clintoniana × *marginalis* Slosson.
Dryopteris Clintoniana × *spinulosa* Benedict.
Dryopteris cristata × *Goldiana* Benedict.
Dryopteris cristata × *intermedia* Dowell.
Dryopteris cristata × *marginalis* Davenport.
Dryopteris cristata × *spinulosa* C. Chr.

Dryopteris Goldiana × *intermedia* Dowell.
Dryopteris Goldiana × *marginalis* Dowell.
Dryopteris Goldiana × *spinulosa* Benedict.
Dryopteris intermedia × *marginalis* Benedict.
Dryopteris marginalis × *spinulosa* Slosson.

14. **POLYSTICHUM** Roth.

Tufted, coarse, and usually rigid terrestrial plants, with chaffy, short, erect or horizontal rootstocks, often with chaffy foliage. Leaves clustered, mostly evergreen: petioles firm, not jointed to the rootstock: blades 1–6-pinnatifid or pinnate, the foliage leaves and the sporophyls usually similar, but the sporophyls and the spore-bearing leaflets relatively narrower than the foliage ones, the leaflets with toothed or pinnatifid blades. ‸Veins once- to several-times forked, free. Sori orbicular, usually borne on the backs of the veins. Indusium superior, centrally peltate, orbicular, without a sinus, opening all around.· [*Aspidium* Sw. in part.]—HOLLY-FERNS.—Approximately one hundred species widely distributed, but most abundant in temperate regions.—The genus is founded on *Polypodium Lonchitis* L.—The name is Greek, alluding to the many rows of sori in some species.

Leaf-blades 1-pinnate: leaflets somewhat reduced at the base of the blade: sori confluent.   1. *P. acrostichoides.*
Leaf-blades 2-pinnate: leaflets much reduced at the base of the blade: sori not confluent.   2. *P. Braunii.*

1. **P. acrostichoides** (Michx.) Schott. Rootstocks stout, often short, densely chaffy: leaves evergreen, several or many together, 2.5–8 dm. tall; petioles stout, rusty, often copiously chaffy; blades lanceolate in outline, or sometimes in the case of foliage ones elliptic-lanceolate, 1-pinnate, the leaflets somewhat coriaceous, linear-lanceolate to lanceolate or elliptic-lanceolate, and half-hastate, 3.5–7 cm. long, more or less falcate, with appressed or oblique bristly teeth: sporophyls somewhat contracted above, the reduced leaflets forming a conspicuous narrow tapering apex to the leaf, bearing many mostly contiguous sori, which sometimes nearly cover the lower surface: veins in the sterile leaflets twice to five times forked, in the sorus-bearing leaflets simple: sori

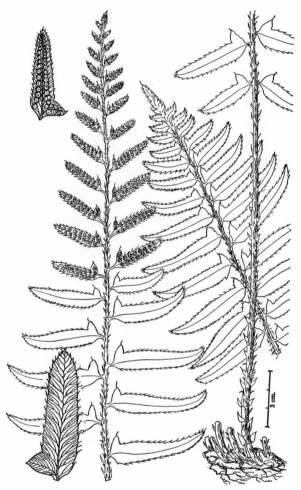

POLYSTICHUM ACROSTICHOIDES

about 1 mm. in diameter, confluent in age: indusium glabrous, entire. [*Nephrodium acrostichoides* Michx. *Dryopteris acrostichoides* Kuntze.]—(CHRISTMAS-FERN. DAGGER-FERN.)—Rocky, sandy, or rich soil, ravines, stream-banks, hillsides, bogs, and woods, various provinces, throughout our range, except the pine-barrens.—The form with deeply toothed, incised, or pinnatifid leaflets has been described as *P. acrostichoides Schweinitzii* (*Aspidium acrostichoides incisum*).—Spores mature, June and July.

The Christmas-fern is generally distributed in eastern North America. It is a frequent associate of its distant relative the marginal shield-fern (*Dryopteris marginalis*) and like it, is in season the year round, the leaves of both being evergreen. The Christmas-fern is a northern type but, curiously enough, the plants growing near the Gulf of Mexico and those growing in Canada are identical in habit and in evergreen leaves. The rigors of the ice-age may have been the chief agent in pushing the ancestors of the Christmas-fern from the more northern regions almost to the shores of the Gulf. Although this is one of the more common ferns east of the Mississippi River, it extends only into northern Florida. In the highlands of our local area it ranges up to 2500 feet above sea-level. Since it is a really cold climate fern, we are not surprised to find plants in the Blue Ridge up to at least 5000 feet. When the plant was named in 1803, it was said to grow in ''Pennsylvania, Carolina, and Tennessee.'' Its geographic range is Florida to Texas, Wisconsin, Ontario, and Nova Scotia. There is considerable instability in the build of the leaves of the Christmas-fern. Sometimes one or more leaves of a cluster or occasionally whole plants will have the leaflets incised or even pinnately parted. This character may represent a reversion to a former normal condition or an indication of a character the plant may be developing for future ages.—The Christmas-fern is one of the most satisfactory ferns for the garden. It always looks well without requiring special care or watering, and moreover, it keeps within bounds. It will continue to thrive for many years.

2. P. Braunii (Spenner) Fée. Rootstock short, stout, ascending or suberect, densely chaffy: leaves evergreen or partly so, several in a cluster, 2–7 dm. long; petioles short, sometimes very short, copiously brown-scaly, often coppery; blades elliptic to lanceolate in outline, 2-pinnate, the leaflets usually numerous, ovate on the lower part of the blade, lanceolate to elliptic-lanceolate above, the ultimate segments mostly ovate, with appressed bristly teeth: sporophyls not distinct from the foliage leaves: sori 1 mm. or a little more in diameter, not confluent, nearer the midrib than the margin: indusium glabrous, entire. [*Aspidium Braunii* Spenner. *Dryopteris Braunii* Underw.]—(HOLLY-FERN. PRICKLY-FERN.)— Rocky and mossy woods, cliffs, and talus, various provinces, mountains of Pennsylvania north of the terminal moraine, and Catskill Mountains, New York.—Spores mature, August and September.

While the Christmas fern is cosmopolitan in eastern North America, the holly-fern, treated here, is a boreal species whose range extends southward only into two regions of the northern part of our local floral area. Like many boreal ferns the leaves of this plant are more or less shaggy, particularly on the petiole and the rachis, with scales of various shapes and sizes. Within our range this fern not only stays north of the glacial moraine, but there is confined to the higher mountains. The original specimens came from Switzerland and were named in 1825. Before this date however, specimens had been discovered in the mountains of Vermont, where they were found up to 4000 feet in altitude. In our area the species occurs between about 1400 and 4000 feet above sea-level. It is a wide-spread plant growing from New York and Pennsylvania to Michigan, British Columbia, Alaska, and Nova Scotia; also in Europe. Apparently this fern is more highly developed than the common Christmas-fern. Its leaf is both more complex and more stable in form. The most noticeable variation in the structure occurs where the leaflets, sometimes the upper ones on the

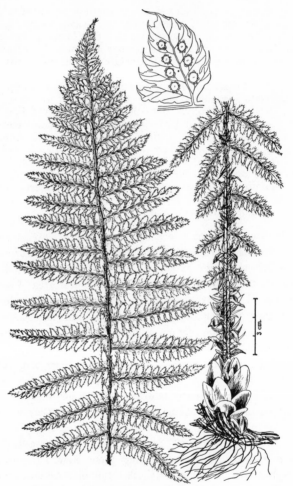

POLYSTICHUM BRAUNII

rachis, are slightly more separated than usual from each other.—The holly-fern is healthy and hardy like the Christmas-fern and like it, keeps within bounds, not interfering with its associates. However, it can not stand as much drought or summer heat.

15. PHEGOPTERIS Fée.

Rather small and usually slender wood plants, with elongate, slender, horizontal, scaly rootstocks. Leaves erect, rather tender, usually not clustered, but often occurring in colonies, uniform: petioles continuous with the rootstock, stramineous, often scaly, particularly near the base: blades broad, pinnatifid or pinnate, sometimes truncate, the leaflets sessile or stalked. Veins free, usually forked. Sori orbicular, borne on the veins back of the tip or in the middle of the veinlets. Indusium wanting. [*Aspidium* Sw. in part.]—BEECH-FERNS. OAK-FERNS.—About one hundred species widely distributed.—The genus is based on *Polypodium Phegopteris* L.—The name is Greek, signifying beech-fern.—The spores mature mostly in July and August.

Leaflets sessile or decurrent on the rachis thus forming wings : leaf-blades 1- or 2-pinnate.

Leaf-blade as wide as long or wider : lower pair of leaflets almost pinnate.	1. *P. hexagonoptera.*
Leaf-blade decidedly longer than wide : lower pair of leaflets pinnatifid.	2. *P. Phegopteris.*
Leaflets, at least the lower ones stalked : leaf-blades subternate.	3. *P. Dryopteris.*

1. P. hexagonoptera (Michx.) Fée. Rootstock horizontal, chaffy, somewhat fleshy, often elongate: leaves mostly 4–8 dm. long; petioles stramineous above the base, weak, naked except at the base; blades triangular, often broader than long, slightly pubescent, often glandular beneath, acuminate, deeply pinnatifid, the leaflets adnate at the base, as it were, making an irregularly winged rachis, acuminate, the upper and middle ones lanceolate, with numerous obtuse, oblong segments, the lowest ones unequally ovate to lanceolate or lanceolate-ovate, with some of the segments spaced and often deeply pinnatifid: veins few, mostly twice- or thrice-forked: sori mostly near the margin, separated. [*Polypodium hexagonop-*

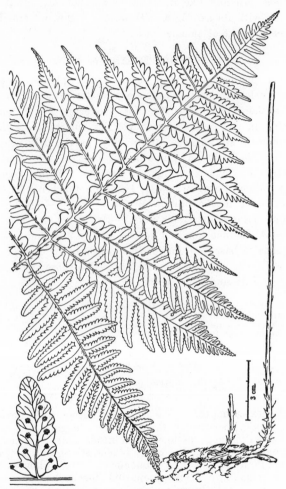

PHEGOPTERIS HEXAGONOPTERA

terum Michx. *Dryopteris hexagonoptera* C. Chr.]—
(BROAD BEECH-FERN. TRIANGLE-FERN.)—Rich, often
open, rocky or dry woods and shaded banks, various
provinces, throughout our range, except the pine-barrens.

This beech-fern is widely distributed in temperate
North America east of the Mississippi Valley. However,
it is rare southward beyond the highlands, the extreme
southeastern corner of its geographical range being
northern Florida. It is an inhabitant of deciduous
woods where it grows in large but not dense colonies by
the extensively creeping rootstocks. The pinnatifid leaf-
blade, indicated by the portions of the blade still adnate
to the rachis, sets this fern off from the other species of
Phegopteris and those of the related genera—*Dryopteris*,
Goniopteris, *Polystichum*, and others. The plant was
named in 1803 when its distribution was given as Canada
and Virginia. This fern is mainly a cool climate plant
and reaches more than 4000 feet of altitude in our highlands, somewhat more than its generic associates attain.
The geographic range extends from Florida to Oklahoma,
Kansas, Minnesota, Ontario and Nova Scotia. In addition to the characters given in the key, this species may
be separated from *Phegopteris Phegopteris* by additional
leaf-characters. Typically, the blades of the lower pair
of leaflets are longer and much broader than those of the
contiguous pair. The breadth is the result of the greater
length of the segments about the middle of the blade.—
The beech-ferns and oak-ferns make attractive additions
to the fern garden. The broad beech-fern introduced in
a garden as a small clump will increase into such a
colony that in a short time it may have to be limited.

2. **P. Phegopteris** (L.) Keyserl. Rootstock horizontal, slender, chaffy near the tip: leaves solitary or
clustered along the rootstock, 2.5–6 dm. long; petioles
slender, stramineous, or purplish at the chaffy base:
blades triangular or ovate-triangular, long-acuminate,
more or less short-hairy beneath, the leaflets elliptic to
lanceolate, more or less adnate at the base, obtuse, acute
or acuminate, pinnatifid, usually close together, or the
lower one somewhat separated and often reflexed: veins

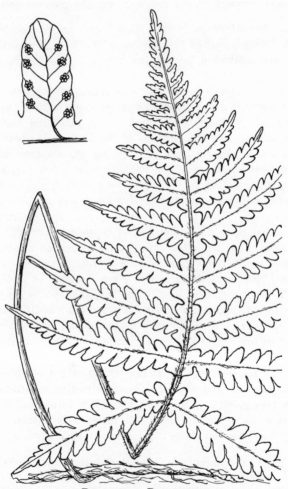

PHEGOPTERIS PHEGOPTERIS

few, usually once-forked: sori almost on the margin, separated. [*Polypodium Phegopteris* L. *Phegopteris polypodioides* Feé. *Dryopteris Phegopteris* C. Chr.]— (LONG BEECH-FERN.)—Low woods, wet cliffs, and shaded banks, various provinces, more northern parts of our range, away from the coast.

The four species of *Phegopteris* in eastern North America are associated by technical characters in pairs, yet they may also be divided geographically. One species, *P. Robertiana*, which is one of the Oak-ferns, does not fall within our area. The relationship of the present species with *P. hexagonoptera* seems to be reflected in their ranges too, for both the present and preceding species which are the two beech-ferns, extend further south than the two oak-ferns, *Phegopteris Dryopteris* and *P. Robertiana*. The original specimens of *Phegopteris Phegopteris* were said to have come from Europe and Virginia, and were named in 1753, under the genus *Polypodium*. In our range the altitudinal record is about 4000 feet. The geographic area is from the Smoky Mountains of Tennessee to Michigan, Washington, Alaska, and Newfoundland; also in Greenland, Europe, and Asia. Here, as in the case of the preceding species, the lower pair of leaflets usually furnishes a diagnostic character. As compared with the preceding species, the blades of the lower pair of leaflets are often shorter and scarcely if any wider than those of the contiguous pair.

3. **P. Dryopteris** (L.) Feé. Rootstock horizontal, elongate, often branched, scaly: leaves mostly borne singly along the rootstock, 2–5 dm. long; petioles stramineous with often purplish and sparingly scaly bases, very slender; blades deltoid or nearly so, or pentagonal, 2-pinnate, subternate, the two slender-stalked lateral inequilateral divisions and the terminal slender-stalked, equilateral division subequal, the ultimate leaflets sessile, lanceolate or elliptic-lanceolate, 1-pinnatifid, glabrous or nearly so, the few distal leaflets adnate at the base: veins mostly forked: sori submarginal. [*Polypodium Dryopteris* L. *Dryopteris Linneana* C. Chr. *Dryopteris Dryopteris* Britton.] — (OAK-FERN. TRIPLET-FERN.) — Moist, often

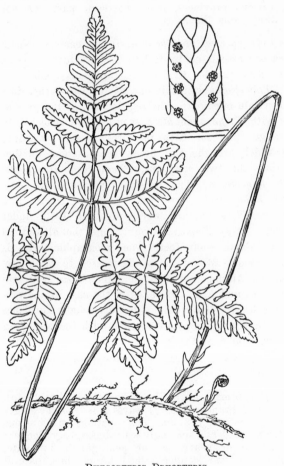

PHEGOPTERIS DRYOPTERIS

boggy or rocky woods, ravines, stream-banks, and cliffs, more northern parts of our range; adventive in the pine-barrens.

The beech-ferns and oak-ferns (*Phegopteris*) in eastern North America show two tendencies in their geographic distribution. Three species, the present one, *P. Phegopteris*, and *P. Robertiana*, have an extensive range eastward and westward, from one side of the continent to the other, especially up toward the Arctic regions. The broad beech-fern (*P. hexagonoptera*) on the other hand, ranges westward only as far as the Mississippi Valley, but extends from the lower boreal regions all the way down to the Gulf of Mexico. This oak-fern was originally found in Europe, and named in 1753. The altitudinal range extends up to nearly 4000 feet in our highlands. The geographic range extends from Virginia to Colorado, Oregon, Alaska, and Labrador; also in Greenland, Europe, and Asia. It must be conceded that the two preceding ferns are closely related species. However, a plant of the present species should not be confused with either of its relatives even by the most careless observer. The lower leaflets with slender stalks and pinnate blades are unvarying diagnostic characters.—The oak-fern thrives under cultivation and if protected soon forms green mats of its numerous leaves. As a rule the smaller ferns are the more difficult to keep, because they are so easily destroyed or damaged by birds and quadrupeds. For example, thrushes and catbirds, in their search for grubs, pick and scratch them to pieces, and squirrels hiding nuts dig them up.

16. **CYSTOPTERIS** Bernh.

Delicate plants inhabiting moist rocks, cliffs, talus, or grassy places, with short, branching rootstocks. Leaves erect or pendent, often several together or clustered, sometimes bulblet-bearing, not evergreen: petioles slender, scaly at the base, at least when young: blades 1- or 2-pinnate; leaflets spreading, more or less spaced, the lower ones at least 1-pinnate, the ultimate leaflets coarsely toothed or pinnatifid. Veins rather few, sparingly forked. Sori roundish, each borne on the back of a vein. Indusium membranous, hoodlike, attached by a broad base on its inner side and partly under the sorus, early thrust back by the expanding sporanges, thus partially concealed. [*Filix* Adans. not Ludwig.]—BLADDER-FERNS. —About ten species mostly of temperate regions.—The genus is founded on *Polypodium bulbiferum* L.—The name is Greek, meaning bladder-fern.

Leaf-blades somewhat narrowed at the base, not bulblet-bearing, not long-attenuate at the apex, the lower pair of leaflets shorter than those above them. 1. *C. fragilis.*

Leaf-blades broadened at the base, bulblet-bearing, long-attenuate at the apex, the lower pair of leaflets longer than those above them. 2. *C. bulbifera.*

1. C. fragilis (L.) Bernh. Leaves erect, rather firm, tufted, 1–4 dm. long; petioles very slender, mainly stramineous; blades lanceolate, oblong-lanceolate, or ovate in outline, slightly narrowed at the base, mostly 1–2 pinnate, the leaflets thin, lanceolate-ovate to ovate, irregularly pinnate or pinnatifid, the segments bluntly or sharply toothed, without bulblets: indusium acute. [*Polypodium fragile* L. *Filix fragilis* Underw.]—(BRITTLE-FERN.)—Moist rocks and cliffs, ledges and stream-banks, and in moist grassy woods, various provinces, throughout our range except the pine-barrens and coastal parts.—Almost cosmopolitan in distribution and very variable in leaf-pattern.—Spores mature, May to July.

The brittle-fern belongs with those that have quite delicate leaves, both in regard to texture and pattern. That such a frail plant should have made itself almost cosmopolitan in the Northern Hemisphere is rather remarkable. In North America it thrives almost up at the arctic Circle and down near the Gulf of Mexico. In the North the active foliar stage is comparatively short, for the plants usually grow in damp places or even on dripping rocks so that the early heavy frost or freezing weather strikes down the tender leaves. On the other hand, in the South the mild frosts and perhaps absence of freezing weather allow the leaves to complete more

CYSTOPTERIS FRAGILIS

nearly an annual cycle. This fern was first studied in
Europe and named in 1753. The altitudinal range extends from near sea-level to almost 4000 feet in our highlands, and to about the same contour in the Blue Ridge.
The geographical range is extensive: Georgia to Alabama,
Kansas, Arizona, California, Alaska, Labrador, and Newfoundland; also in Greenland, Europe, and Asia. Although
the leaves of the brittle-fern have no mark of distinction
such as the bulblets of *Cystopteris bulbifera,* the small
pair of leaflets at the base of the only slightly tapering
blade and the acute indusium make confusion of the two
species, though possible, remote. Two kinds of rootstocks
are exhibited by the plants of this species; the one is
short and relatively stout, while the other is elongate and
slender. These differences may be due to ecological
conditions.

2. C. bulbifera (L.) Bernh. Leaves weak, often
tufted, decumbent, prostrate, or pendent, up to 1 m.
long; petioles slender, mainly purplish; blades lanceolate,
sometimes elongate-lanceolate, from a broad base and
frequently long-attenuate, 1- or 2-pinnate, the leaflets
coarsely toothed or pinnatifid, commonly bearing underneath, in the axils of the leaflets and segments, fleshy
bulblets (these early deciduous and giving rise to new
plants), the segments toothed or incised: indusium
truncate. [*Polypodium bulbiferum* L. *Filix bulbifera*
Underw.]—(BLADDER-FERN.)—Moist rocks, wet ledges,
mossy cliffs, talus, shaded stream-banks, often on limestone, various provinces, more northern part of our
range.—Spores mature, June to August.

The bladder-fern, unlike the preceding species of
Cystopteris which reproduces by spores alone, reproduces
by spores and also by bulblets which are borne on the
backs of the leaflets. Yet the present species has a relatively restricted area of distribution within North
America, whereas the brittle-fern is widely known. It
may be that this fern once had a more extensive distribution, or it also may be that it is now expanding its
geographic area. The original specimens were collected
in Canada, and named in 1753. In altitudinal distribu-

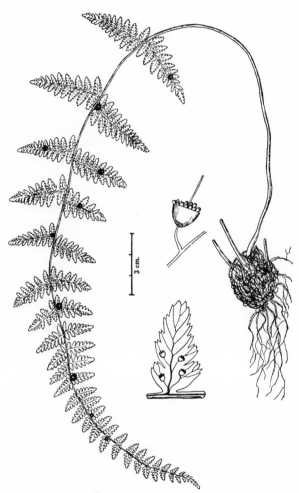

CYSTOPTERIS BULBIFERA

tion its range falls short of that of its generic associate, about 2500 feet being the recorded maximum. The geographic range too falls within that of *Cystopteris fragilis*, viz., Georgia to Oklahoma, Manitoba, Ontario, and Newfoundland. Both the habitat and the habit of this fern indicate the possibility of its being a creeping-fern or walking-fern, after the manner of *Goniopteris reptans* of Florida and tropical America. However, the greatly elongate leaf-tips and the inviting moist habitats do not seem quite to bring about this form of vegetative propagation. But the plant does have a distinctive vegetative method of increasing itself in the form of bulblets borne on and dispersed from the rachis at the axils of the leaflets as mentioned at the beginning of this paragraph. —The bladder-fern takes promptly to garden conditions and produces an abundance of sporelings and new plants from the bulblets. It often becomes a weed if not promptly removed from places it is not wanted. Like some of the larger ferns it would soon crowd out the less rampant species.

17. **WOODSIA** R. Br.

Small or medium-sized plants inhabiting exposed rocky places and cliffs, with branching but usually congested and thus tufted rootstocks. Leaves often evergreen, erect, clustered: petioles often jointed above the base and finally separating: blades 1- or 2-pinnate. Veins few, mostly once-forked. Sori round, borne on the simply forked free veins. Indusium inferior, either roundish and soon cleft into irregular lobes, or deeply stellate, the broad or filiform divisions partially concealed under or inflexed over the sporanges.—CLIFF-FERNS.—About twenty-five species mainly of cold and temperate regions. —The genus is based on *Acrostichum ilvense* L.—The generic name is in honor of Joseph Woods, an English architect and botanist.—The spores mature mostly from June to August.

Leaf-blades 1-pinnate: petioles jointed near the base: indusium small and inconspicuous, the lobes very narrow, filiform or nearly so, often inflexed over the sori.

Leaf-blades lanceolate; leaflets longer than wide, chaffy beneath, pinnatifid; petioles pubescent and scaly.   1. *W. ilvensis.*

Leaf-blades linear or nearly so; leaflets about as wide as long, glabrous, crenately lobed; petioles glabrous and scaleless.   2. *W. glabella.*

Leaf-blades 2-pinnate: petioles not jointed near the base: indusium ample, the lobes broad jagged-toothed, more or less spreading.   3. *W. obtusa.*

1. W. ilvensis (L.) R. Br. Leaves tufted, often copiously and densely so, 1-4 dm. long; petioles stramineous or purplish, slender, scaly, jointed near the base; blades lanceolate in outline, glabrous or nearly so above, more or less covered with rusty chaff beneath, the leaflets approximate or crowded, sessile, pinnatifid or pinnately parted, the crowded segments oblong to ovate, obscurely crenate: sori near the margins, confluent with age: indusium minute, largely concealed beneath the sorus, its filiform segments inflexed over the sporanges. [*Acrostichum ilvense* L.]—(RUSTY CLIFF-FERN.)—Exposed rocks, cliffs, and talus, various provinces, throughout the more northern parts of our range.

The woodsias are among the smaller ferns. Taxonomically they are situated close to the genus *Cystopteris.* The plants, too, are often quite similar in habit, except that the woodsias are generally more copiously and densely tufted. The leaf-tissues of the plants of the two genera, however, are distinctive. In the case of *Cystopteris* the leaf is quite delicate, the petiole and the rachis slender and the blade thin, but in drying these parts are not particularly fragile; while in *Woodsia*, although the leaf is of firmer tissues, when dry the various parts are quite fragile and tend to crack and separate at almost any point. The present species is very widely distributed in North Temperate regions. Being partial to cold climates, it occurs up to almost 4000 feet in our highlands. It reaches southward only in the mountainous regions where, in the Blue Ridge, specimens have been found at an altitude of at least 4000 feet. The plants on which the name was based, in 1753, came from Europe. The geographical range extends from western North Carolina to Minnesota, Alaska, Ontario, and Labra-

WOODSIA ILVENSIS

dor; also in Greenland, Europe, and Asia. Considering the wide geographic distribution of this species in our range the leaves are remarkably constant in pattern and size, with very little variation in the shape and cutting of the leaflets.—The rusty cliff-fern prefers the exposed tops of banks and cliffs in the fern garden and there grows to its ordinary stature.—Plants of the rusty cliff-fern are long persistent as is evidenced by the frequent tufts of stubble, the remains of former leaf-petioles.

2. W. glabella R. Br.   Leaves sparingly tufted, 0.5–1.5 dm. long; petioles stramineous, nearly filiform, glabrous and scaleless, jointed above the base; blades linear or nearly so, glabrous or essentially so, the leaflets deltoid to orbicular-ovate, approximate or the lower ones separated, sessile, crenately lobed, the lobes few, entire; sori few, near the margins, separated or sometimes confluent with age: indusium minute, partly concealed beneath the sorus, its few (6–10) filiform segments inflexed over the sorus or spreading. — (SMOOTH CLIFF-FERN.) — Exposed, moist, often mossy rocks and cliffs, Catskill Mountains.

The rusty cliff-fern is among our smaller ferns, but it is rarely so reduced in stature as the smooth cliff-fern. Two features, the diminutive size and the subalpine distribution have operated against general acquaintance with the plant in our local range.   In fact, its occurrence in the state of New York was doubted or overlooked for many years.   However, it is certain now that the fern was found many years ago at Haines Falls in the Catskill Mountains.   In 1895 it was re-discovered at the same locality, and in 1921 collected there for the third time.   Regarding the latest finding of this fern the collector records that, "In the latter part of August, 1921, while collecting in Greene County, New York, near Haines Falls, I explored a deep ravine where sheer dripping cliffs with the talus extending almost to the bank of the stream formed an agreeable prospect.   Here I found on the rocks the slender cliff-brake (*Cryptogramma Stelleri*). . . . Growing near the slender cliff-brake were bleached specimens of the long beech-fern (*Thelypteris Phegopteris* (L.) Slosson) and, almost concealed in the fissures, a

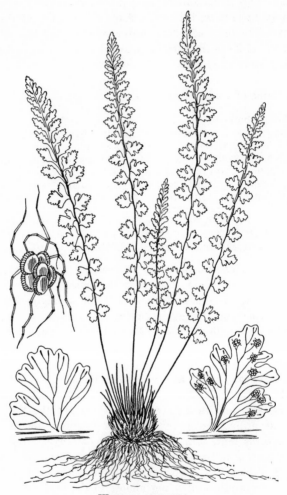

WOODSIA GLABELLA

small fern in some abundance at this particular spot, which I at first supposed might be *Asplenium viride* Huds. A glance at the text-books and manuals, however, soon assured me that I had found the smooth Woodsia. . . ." The geographic distribution of this woodsia extends from New York to British Columbia, Alaska, Greenland, Labrador, and New Brunswick. It prefers limestone or calcareous shale, and is found within this range only where such rocks occur. The altitude at which it occurs in this area is about 2500 feet.

This cliff-fern was discovered on the journey to the shores of the Polar Sea by Sir John Franklin between 1819 and 1822. It was found in the wooded country between 54° and 64° north latitude, and was named in 1823. Later it was found to be distributed in arctic and alpine Europe and Asia.—The cliffs and crags of the Catskills, upon further exploration, may conceivably yield *Woodsia alpina,* a close relative both in habit and technical characters, though apparently requiring even colder conditions.

3. **W. obtusa** (Spreng.) Torr. Leaves clustered, 1–4 dm. long; petioles stramineous in drying, or purplish, often scaly, not jointed; blades broadly lanceolate or elliptic in outline (or broadly linear and with correspondingly narrow leaflets in *W. obtusa angusta*), minutely glandular-pubescent, 1- or 2-pinnate at least below, the leaflets spaced, ovate, triangular-ovate, or broadly lanceolate, pinnately parted or pinnatifid, the segments obtuse, crenate-dentate: sori nearer the margin than the midvein: indusium conspicuous, splitting into several broad jagged lobes. [*Polypodium obtusum* Spreng.] —(CLIFF-FERN.)—Rocks, cliffs, sandy banks, and stone walls, various provinces, nearly throughout our range.

As in the case of the two common species of *Cystopteris, C. fragilis* and *C. bulbifera,* there is considerable difference in the geographic distribution of our two more common eastern species of *Woodsia,* and there is a certain similarity of distribution between these pairs of representatives of the two genera. The first species, *Woodsia ilvensis,* ranges far north in North America, and

WOODSIA OBTUSA

also like *Cystopteris fragilis*, is found in Europe and Asia. On the other hand, the present species, like *Cystopteris bulbifera*, ranges less extensively into boreal regions, but further south in eastern North America. Furthermore, as in the case of *Cystopteris bulbifera*, it is not native in the Old World. Instead of stopping in the mountains of Virginia and Tennessee, this fern ranges southward to the highlands of Georgia and through the higher parts of the Gulf States. The original specimens came from a geographically intermediate point on the Atlantic seaboard, namely Pennsylvania, and were named in 1804. The highest altitude recorded for this woodsia in our range is over 4000 feet, while in the Blue Ridge it is also known up to at least 4000 feet. The geographical range extends from Georgia to Texas, Wisconsin, British Columbia, Alaska, and Maine. The plants of this fern are, withal, larger than those of the preceding species, and they are less densely and copiously tufted. Although growing within a small geographic area, the leaves are more variable in pattern, particularly in the shape and proportion of the leaflets. In some cases these are lanceolate in outline, in others triangular.—The cliff-ferns are easy to grow. The southern cliff-fern (*Woodsia obtusa*) thrives and increases by sporelings so that a colony soon encroaches on smaller ferns to such an extent that it must be occasionally reduced in size.

18. **DENNSTAEDTIA** Bernh.

Medium-sized or large terrestrial wood or hammock plants, with wide-creeping, scaly rootstocks. Leaves more or less clustered or colonized, but somewhat distant on the horizontal rootstock, erect, or arching; petioles glabrous, not jointed to the rootstock: blade ample, broad, 2–4-pinnate, the leaflets or ultimate segments generously toothed or lobed, giving the leaf a lacy appearance. Veins free, simple or pinnately branched. Sori marginal, solitary, terminal on the free veinlets. Indusium cup-like or pouch-like, formed in part of a more or less modified recurved segment of the leaf-margin.—Consists of about

seventy-five species, mostly of tropical regions.—The
genus is based on *Trichomanes flaccidum* Forst. — The
name is in honor of August Wilhelm Dennstaedt, a Swed-
ish botanist.

1. D. punctilobula (Michx.) Moore. Rootstock very
slender, rather extensively creeping, finely scaly, sometimes much-branched: leaves clustered or in colonies, up
to 1 m. long; petioles slender, except at the base when
young, dull, chaffless, pale-brown; blades lanceolate to
deltoid-lanceolate, acute to long-attenuate, 2-pinnate,
the leaflets thin and delicate, numerous, lanceolate, acute
or acuminate, (or forked at the tip in *D. punctilobula
schizophylla*) the ultimate leaflets very numerous, elliptic
to ovate, finely toothed or pinnatifid, the teeth or lobes
oblique; rachis and under leaf-surface minutely glandular
and pubescent: veins forked, very fine: sori minute, each
on or at the base of a recurved toothlet, usually one at
the upper margin of each lobe: indusium pouch-like, as
long as wide. [*Nephrodium punctilobulum* Michx. *Dicksonia pilosiuscula* Willd. *Dicksonia punctilobula*
A. Gray.] — (HAY-SCENTED FERN. BOULDER-FERN. PAS-
TURE-FERN. GOSSAMER-FERN. FINE-HAIRED FERN.)—
Open hillsides, poor and often acid soil in coniferous or
deciduous woods, rocky bluffs, and pastures, various
provinces, throughout our range except the pine-barrens.
—Spores mature, June to August.

Ferns may rarely be detected by the sense of smell. Of
course, many of them have a slight amount of the peculiarly "ferny" odor, especially when bruised or in drying; but few species give off naturally the amount of
fragrance characteristic of the hay-scented fern. In addition, one of its outstanding characteristics is the rather
delicate and lacy appearance of the leaf-blade as a
result of the numerous and finely cut segments. Although
widely distributed, this fern prefers the more northern
and higher plant-provinces. Stony hillsides and pastures
and edges of woods are its favorite haunts. In our range
its altitudinal distribution is known to extend up to 2000
feet. It occurs high up in the Blue Ridge, approximately
to 6000 feet altitude. The original specimens came from
Canada, and were named in 1803. The geographical
range now is known to extend from Georgia to Arkansas,

3 cm.

DENNSTAEDTIA PUNCTILOBULA

Minnesota, Ontario, Quebec, and Nova Scotia. Within our area the hay-scented fern stands alone in the group *Davallieae*. Its technical isolation often leads one to think specimens are easily recognized on sight. However, unless the sori are developed, leaves may easily be mistaken for those of the two species of Athyrium: *A. angustum* or *A. asplenioides*. The shape and toothing of the leaflets are similar to those of these lady-ferns.— The hay-scented fern is very satisfactory for the garden, remaining always fresh and green, even in dry weather. It spreads rapidly, however, and is liable to crowd its neighbors.

19. ONOCLEA L.

Succulent, tender plants with widely creeping black scaleless rootstocks. Leaves dimorphic, erect, borne singly or several together upon the rootstocks. Foliage leaves conspicuous, the blades broad, pinnatifid into few, undulate, toothed, or lobed segments. Veins forming numerous areolae, which are larger toward the midrib and smaller towards the margin. Sporophyls less conspicuous than the foliage leaves, rigidly erect, the segments tightly contracted and bipinnatifid, the ultimate divisions round, berry-like, completely concealing the sori, finally dehiscent, but persistent. Sori roundish, on elevated receptacles, partially covered by delicate hood-shaped indusia fixed at the base.—The genus consists of only the following species.—The name is classical Greek, but was not originally associated with this plant.

1. **O. sensibilis** L. Rootstocks widely spreading, thus forming colonies of leaves: foliage leaves 3–13 dm. high; blades triangular to ovate in outline, deeply pinnatifid, the segments few, irregularly lanceolate-elliptic, lanceolate, broadly linear, or ovate, entire, undulate, or sinuate-pinnatifid, the teeth or lobes obtuse or rounded, (the form with bipinnatifid leaf-blades and rounded lobes is *O. sensibilis obtusilobata*): sporophyls rigid, 3–7 dm. high, the contracted divisions separated, borne in a narrow panicle and resembling a cluster of tiny berries, ascending or appressed to the rachis. Intermediate forms between foliage leaves and sporophyls occur.—

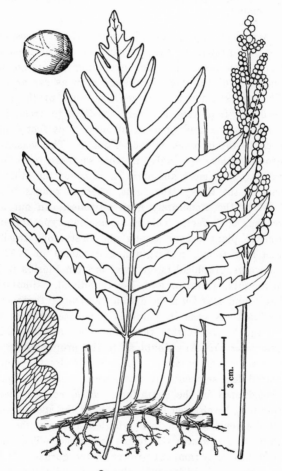

ONOCLEA SENSIBILIS

(BEAD-FERN. SENSITIVE-FERN.)—Moist soil in woods, stream-banks, river-bottoms, meadows, hillsides, fence-rows, and bogs, various provinces, throughout our range except the pine-barrens.—Spores mature, October and November.

A cool climate is most favorable, if not necessary, for the best growth of the sensitive-fern. The ice-age may have been responsible for extending the range of the ancestors of this fern southward even as far as Florida. The leaves are not evergreen like some of the northern ferns, in fact, they are very sensitive to frost, but the rootstocks or underground stems are perfectly immune even to the extreme cold of Canada. The sensitive-fern grows rather sparingly in the southern part of our range. It is more abundant in many of the other states east of the Rocky Mountains, where it ranges from sea-level to the moderately high altitudes. In our area it reaches 2000 feet. This is an ancient type of fern. A similar plant occurs among the Cretaceous fossils. It was first found in Virginia, and named in 1753. The known geographical range extends from Florida to Texas, Minnesota, Ontario, and Newfoundland. Similarity in habit and leaf-form in distinctly related ferns is often striking. A case in point is the close likeness of the foliage leaves of this fern and those of the chain-fern (*Lorinseria*). Any doubt as to the proper identification of one or the other may be removed by the oppositely placed leaf-segments of this species and the alternately placed ones in the chain-fern. Also, certain identification may be effected by the rachis of the sporophyl alone. In the sensitive-fern it is wingless between the leaflets, while in *Lorinseria* the rachis is winged.—The sensitive-fern may be a rampant grower in the garden. It is best to plant it where it can be by itself and thus more easy to control.

20. **PTERETIS** Raf.

Large and elegant lowland plants with stout branching rootstocks. Leaves dimorphic, tall, erect or ascending, borne in a circular crown. Foliage leaves very broad, conspicuous, the blades 1-pinnate, the leaflets numerous, pinnatifid, elongate, the segments entire. Veins free, straight. Sporophyls much shorter than the foliage leaves, within the crown of which they are borne, rigidly erect, the leaflets closely contracted into necklace-like or pod-like divisions, which completely conceal the sporangia, but ultimately dehisce and free the spores. [*Matteuccia* Todaro.]—Three species, the following on which the genus is based, and two Asiatic.—The name is Greek, derived from pteris, a fern.

1. P. nodulosa (Michx.) Nieuwl. Rootstock stout, ascending, giving off slender stolons: foliage leaves 4–18 dm. long; petioles dark and scaly at the base; blades oblanceolate or elliptic-oblanceolate in outline, deep-green, the leaflets numerous, approximate on the channeled rachis, lanceolate to linear-lanceolate, or reduced to triangular rudiments at the base of the blade, acuminate, glabrous or minutely pubescent, sessile, deeply pinnatifid, the segments entire, obtuse: sporophyls 3–5 dm. long, ascending and more or less curved, crenate-beaded, with the sori included, crowded and confluent. [*Onoclea nodulosa* Michx. *Onoclea Struthiopteris* D. C. Eaton, not Hoffm. *Struthiopteris germanica* Beck, not Willd.]—(Ostrich-fern.)—Alluvial woods and stream-banks, various provinces, rare on the Coastal Plain, more northern part of our range.—Spores mature, August and September.

Outside of certain species of the subtropical parts of Florida, *Pteretis* is one of the taller and more bulky ferns in eastern North America. The ostrich-fern is a northern type, in this way differing from its relative, the sensitive-fern (*Onoclea*), which claims both the north and the south in its geographical distribution. This is one of the ferns like *Phegopteris Dryopteris*, for example, that pass southward over the Mason-Dixon line, far into Virginia, but do not appear, as yet, in the floristics of North Carolina. The plants seem to delight especially in the talus of partly shaded rocky river-banks where the good soil has been washed down and collected among the rocks, especially where moisture seeps down or out from higher

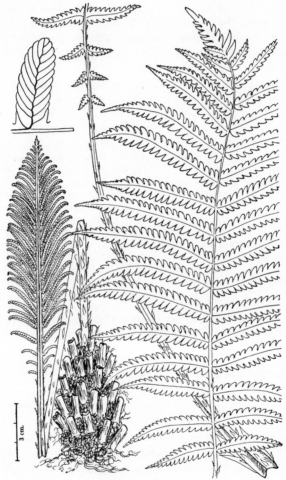

3 cm.

Pteretis nodulosa

up the banks. The general geographic distribution
ranges from Virginia to Iowa, British Columbia and
Nova Scotia; also in Europe and Asia. In altitudinal
distribution it reaches only to about the half-way mark
of the local maximum, about 2300 feet in our highlands.
There are two cases among our ferns of a complete distinction between the foliage leaf and sporophyl — the
present species and sensitive-fern, *Onoclea sensibilis*.
The chain-fern (*Lorinseria*) is a close third, but its
sporophyl is only partially set off by the degree of
dimorphism. The sporophyl of the sensitive-fern is, on
the other hand, set off to the second degree by the pinnate leaf-blade and the compound or pinnate, berry-like
leaflets. Although this fern is by some considered con-
generic with *Onoclea*, it is abundantly distinct. Besides
having more technical differences, *Onoclea* is more of a
wanderer, the leaves, foliage, and sporophyls being carried over considerable areas springing up from the elon-
gating and branching underground stems. On the other
hand, *Pteretis*, although it may travel by underground
stems, does not scatter itself as much and springs up
with the foliage leaves in a crown supporting the one
or more sporophyls in the center of the group.—Of the
larger ferns, the ostrich-fern in spite of its elegant port
when at its best and strong rootstock system seems not
to be satisfactory as a garden subject. It spreads
widely by the rootstocks, but in late summer the foliage
looks brown and shabby, and the leaves die down early
in the fall.

FAMILY 2. **SCHIZAEACEAE**

CURLY-GRASS FAMILY

Erect and rigid or climbing (twining), mainly terrestrial plants, sometimes tufted. Leaves with simple,
pinnate or dichotomous and palmate-lobed blades.
Sporophyls borne on the ordinary leaves or on
specialized leaves. Sporangia borne in double rows
on narrow specialized leaf-lobes or leaf-segments,
ovoid, sessile, naked or indusiate, provided with a

transverse apical ring, opening vertically by a longitudinal slit. Prothallia green.—Comprises six genera or more. Besides the following another genus, *Actinostachys,* is represented in southern Florida.

KEY TO THE GENERA

Plant erect, dwarf: leaves not twining, dimorphic; leaflets
    with a single vein.   1. SCHIZAEA.
Plant climbing, greatly elongate: leaves twin-
    ing, not dimorphic; leaflets with many
    forking veins.   2. LYGODIUM.

1. SCHIZAEA J. E. Smith

Dwarf, erect, wiry, tufted plants with very small, usually short rootstocks. Leaves dimorphic, usually inconspicuous: foliage leaves slender, often filiform, simple (in our species) or dichotomously lobed. Sporophyls erect, commonly exceeding the foliage leaves, long-petioled, 1-pinnate (in our species). Sporangia relatively large, ovoid, borne in two rows on the single vein of the leaflet. Indusium continuous, formed by the reflexed margin of the leaflet.—About twenty-five species, widely distributed, but most abundant in the tropics.—The genus is based on *Acrostichum dichotomum* L. —The name is Greek, in allusion to the prominently lobed leaf-blades of some species.

1. S. pusilla Pursh. Rootstock short, but slender and creeping: leaves tufted, but inconspicuous; foliage leaves very slender, narrowly linear, somewhat flattened, more or less crisped and curled, 2–4 cm. long; sporophyls very slender, but strict, 6–12 cm. long, the petiole elongate, wiry-filiform, the blade mostly 0.5–1 cm. long, with 3–6 pairs of approximate leaflets forming a spike-like tip on the petiole: sporangia ovoid or pyriform, partly concealed by the recurved margins of the leaflet.—(CURLY-GRASS.)—Swamps and bogs, pine-barrens and contiguous areas, New Jersey. Spores mature, August.

This species is one that has become celebrated and widely known on account of its rarity. It has been a lure for botanists for over a century, an incentive for doing field work. Accompanying the original description (1815), the author records: "In barren sand but moist

SCHIZAEA PUSILLA

grounds: New Jersey, Burlington County, near a place
called Quaker Bridge. . . . This singular little fern is
very scarce, and so small that it generally escapes the
notice of the botanist, unless accident points it out.''
Later in the past century the fern was discovered in
Nova Scotia and Newfoundland. This is a case of a
curiously localized distribution. It is, without much
doubt, a result of the far reaching effects of the Ice
Ages, but whether the present localities for the fern
represent areas that escaped destruction when the glaciers
covered most of the region north of northern New Jersey
or a redistribution from a plant reservoir after the Ice
Ages we do not know. At any rate, the fern has a wide
range of resistance to extremes of temperature—heat in
southern New Jersey; cold in Newfoundland. In modern
times, however, it has attained but little altitudinal range.
The size and aspect of this plant has little to classify
it on first sight, as a fern. The common name indicates this. Both size and habit place this and its family
associate, the climbing-fern, far apart. Only technical
characters bring them close together. The retiring habit
of the curly-grass may account for its very restricted
geographic range. Now that *Lycopodium carolinianum* has
been discovered on Long Island, careful search for
schizaea should be made wherever that lycopod grows.—
The curly-grass is one of the more difficult ferns to grow.
Of two plants set out in a carefully prepared acid soil
bed, one was soon uprooted by the birds, the other protected by wire survived over one winter, but disappeared
during the following summer.

2. **LYGODIUM** Sw.

Vines with elongate climbing or twining leaves, the
rachis wiry, pliable, and more or less flexuous. Rootstock
elongate, horizontal or often creeping. Leaves uniform,
greatly elongate, consisting of stalked, lobed, pinnate, or
pinnately compound secondary divisions arising in pairs
from alternate slender or short, naked stalks, which are
the primary petiolules. Leaflets mostly lobed. Veins

several times forked, mostly free, the midvein mostly zigzag. Sporophyls terminal, the leaflets usually narrower. Sporangia obovoid, borne in a double row upon the contracted and more or less revolute segments. Indusium scale-like or clamshell-like, hooded, fixed by its broad base to a short oblique veinlet, opening antrorsely.— CLIMBING FERNS.—Comprises nearly thirty species which are most abundant in the tropics.—The genus is based on *Ophioglossum scandens* L.—The name is Greek, alluding to the pliable rachis.

1. L. palmatum (Bernh.) Sw. Rootstock slender, wide-creeping: leaves 5–15 dm. long, narrow, vine-like; foliage leaflets simple, orbicular to broadly reniform in outline, 2.5–6 cm. long, 3–8 cm. broad, dichotomously pedatifid ½ to ⅔ the distance to the cordate base into 4–8 spreading unequal lobes, thus subpalmate, the outer lobes small, rounded or emarginate at the apex, the main ones elliptic to lanceolate, obtuse or obtusish: sporophyl leaflets usually numerous, 3- or 4-pinnate, the divisions narrowly linear or linear-lanceolate, covered beneath with the scale-like indusia, somewhat revolute: indusium 0.6–0.7 mm. wide, the free edge uneven. [*Gisopteris palmata* Bernh.]—(CLIMBING-FERN.)—Low woods, shaded banks, meadows, and pastures, various provinces, scattered in various parts of our range.—Spores mature, September and October.

Whatever its remote history may have been, this fern is now localized in the eastern United States. Thus it is a temperate region plant. Its distribution in latitude is not as great as that of many of our ferns. At the North it does not reach Canada. It apparently reaches Florida from the north—its ancestors, perhaps, driven southward during the reign of the Ice Age. It is somewhat local in its general area of distribution, but occurs from Florida to New Hampshire, Kentucky, Tennessee, Ohio, and Massachusetts. It is most abundant in the last named State. High soil-acidity is most favorable to it. The original specimens were collected in Pennsylvania, and the species was described in 1801. In our range it is sometimes found at an altitude exceeding 2100 feet.

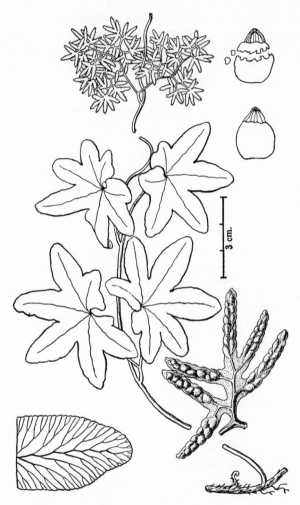

Lygodium palmatum

Its maximum altitude, however, is reached in North Carolina, between 3000 and 4000 feet, whence it extends to sea-level. Besides climbing-fern, it is known as creeping-fern, Hartford-fern, and the Windsor-fern, the geographical apellations referring to the cities near which the plant was found. A fern in the form of a vine is unique in our range. It has no fern associates which might be confused with it. In fact, it has little on first sight to associate it with the ferns. The climbing-fern was observed and described many years before it was properly named, having been erroneously asssociated with the European climbing-fern then known as *Pteris scandens*. The following notice and description appears in Bartram's Travels in 1791: ''Observed near Combelton [North Carolina] a very curious scandent fern (*Pteris scandens*) rambling over low bushes, in humid situations; the lower larger fronds were digitated, or rather radiated, but towards the tops or extremities of the branches they became trifid, hastated, and lastly lanceolate: it is a delicate plant, of a yellowish lively green, and would be an ornament in a garden.''—The climbing-fern thrives in an acid bog garden and will continue to grow for many years with little attention, provided the soil remains strongly acid and sterile.

Family 3. OSMUNDACEAE

Cinnamon-fern Family

Tall leafy terrestrial plants, with creeping, suberect, or erect rootstocks. Leaves erect or spreading: blades 1- or 2-pinnate, the veins free, mostly forked, extending to the margins of the leaflets: petioles winged at the base. Sporophyls occupying a whole leaf or combined with a foliage leaf. Sporangia naked, large, globose, mostly stalked, borne on modified contracted leaflets, or in clusters (sori) on the lower surface of the leaflets, opening in 2 valves by a longitudinal slit; ring few-celled or wanting. Prothallia green.—There are three genera in this family, the following, and two others in the Old World.

1. **OSMUNDA** L.

Leaves in large crowns, erect, from a thickened, creeping or erect rootstock: blades once-pinnate or twice-pinnate, some wholly or some partly, either near the middle or at the apex, spore-bearing, the spore-bearing leaflets very much contracted and devoid of chlorophyl (red or brown). Sporangia short-stalked, thin, reticulate, opening in halves, a few parallel thickened cells near the apex representing the rudimentary transverse ring. Spores copious, greenish.—Besides the following, one other species grows in North America, and four or five additional ones occur in other parts of the world.—The genus is based on *Osmunda regalis* L.—The name is Saxon for the god Thor.

Foliage leaves with 2-pinnate blades, some of them terminating in a compound sporophyl: veins mostly twice-forked.   I. REGALES.
Foliage leaves with 1-pinnate blades: sporophyls various, either occupying the middle part of a foliage leaf or a complete separate leaf, in either case 2-pinnate: veins mostly once-forked.   II. CINNAMOMEAE.

I. REGALES

Leaves borne in a crown on the rootstock, the leaflets (pinnules) separated, decidedly serrulate.   1. *O. regalis.*

II. CINNAMOMEAE

Sporophyls and foliage-leaves wholly different, the spore-bearing pinnae cinnamon colored: leaflets of the foliage leaves with a tuft of tomentum at the base.   2. *O. cinnamomea.*
Sporophyls partly different from the foliage-leaves, the green and ultimately brown spore-bearing pinnae, borne on the middle of the rachis, with normal foliage pinnae below and above them: leaflets of the foliage leaves without a tuft of tomentum at the base.   3. *O. Claytoniana.*

1. O. regalis L. Rootstock erect, at least partly so, often forming a tussock: leaves clustered, erect, often stiffly so, 6–20 dm. tall, the foliage leaf and sporophyl combined; blades 2-pinnate, broad and open, the leaflets separated, elliptic to linear-lanceolate, 1.5–8 cm. long, serrulate and sometimes crenately lobed near the base, sessile or slightly stalked, oblique at the base: spore-

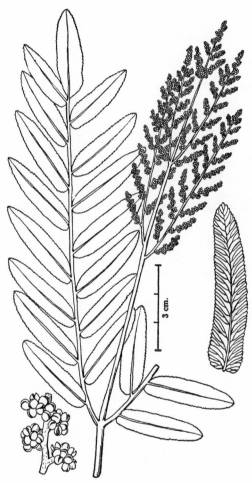

OSMUNDA REGALIS

bearing portion of the leaf when present terminal, the pinnae fewer than in the foliage portion: sporophyl panicle-like, thrice-pinnate, the divisions somewhat separated, linear-cylindric, greenish before maturity, red-brown or dark-brown and withering with age. [*O. spectabilis* Willd.]—(ROYAL-FERN.)—Wet and moist grounds, woods, swamps, bogs, thickets and rarely in pinelands, various provinces, throughout our range.—Spores mature, May and June.

This is a cosmopolitan fern. It is to be found in the greater part of North America, except the extreme north, including Mexico, to South America and the West Indies; also in Europe, Asia, and Africa. It was botanically named from European specimens, in 1753. At the North the leaves are not persistent the year round, but in places near the Gulf of Mexico they are evergreen, and often have more than one ''fruiting'' season in each year. The royal-fern also has a wide range of habitats. At the North it occurs in marshes, swamps, and low woods; southward it is most common in and about low hammocks and especially in cypress swamps and cypress-heads. There it often forms stem-like tussocks a foot and a half high. Sometimes it grows in the open Everglades especially near streams and sloughs, often occurring in patches acres in extent; occasionally it may be found in colonies in high pineland. It ranges from sea-level to 2000 feet in our highlands and to 3000 feet in the southern mountains. The extensive geographic distribution has, naturally, allowed this fern to accumulate a rather large number of common names. Besides royal-fern, we find royal-osmund, King's-fern, flowering-fern, water-fern, tree-fern, bog-fern, ditch-fern, snake-fern, locust-fern, and others. This is an outstanding plant and is readily separable, at sight, from all our other ferns. The stiff erect stem-like petioles bearing few, large, regular, pinnate leaflets and the erect, rigid, torch-like, terminal sporophyl render it a unique fern.—The royal-fern, and its two relatives, the cinnamon-fern and interrupted-fern, are good garden subjects under ordinary conditions, providing they have shade a part of each day.

2. O. cinnamomea L. Rootstock stout, creeping: leaves clustered erect or slightly arching, one or several sporophyls borne within the crown of foliage leaves; foliage leaves 5–16 dm. tall, the blades lanceolate to oblong-lanceolate to linear-lanceolate, acute, deeply pinnatifid, glandless (or permanently glandular-scaly beneath like the rachis in *O. cinnamomea glandulosa*), the segments oblong or ovate, entire (or with the lower ones more or less pinnatifid in *O. cinnamomea incisa*), obtuse: sporophyls as tall as the foliage leaves or nearly so, twice-pinnate, spear-like, bearing several or many erect or ascending, pinnate pairs of spore-bearing leaflets maturing as they unfold and soon withering, with the clusters of sporangia crowded, cylindric, cinnamon-colored.—(CINNAMON-FERN.)—Swamps, low woods, moist thickets, and stream shores, various provinces, throughout our range.—Spores mature, May.

Judging from its latitudinal geographic range, the cinnamon-fern should be considered a southern type, for it occurs in tropical America, both continental and insular, from Brazil northward, as far as Minnesota and Newfoundland. If it did come, originally, from northern regions where it is not evergreen, it later assumed an evergreen habit in the Florida peninsula and southward where its main spore-producing season is frequently as much as six months earlier than in the North, sometimes with several ''flowering'' stages in a year. The cinnamon-fern is often plentiful in swamps and wet open woods, but it does not usually appear in such extensive areas as the royal-fern. It also occurs naturally in Europe and Asia. Forms sometimes develop with leaves intermediate between the sterile and fertile types. The original specimens came from the colony of Maryland and the species was named in 1753. The cinnamon-fern reaches a greater altitude than the other two species of *Osmunda*. Specimens occur at nearly 6000 feet altitude in the southern mountains, though in our range they grow necessarily at much lower altitudes. In different parts of its area this fern is known as swamp-brake, bread-root, or fiddle-heads. The foliage leaves of this species and those of *O. Claytoniana* closely resemble each

OSMUNDA CINNAMOMEA

other in pattern. However, they may be definitely distinguished by masses of tangled wool-like scales on the
rachis and the bases of the leaflets in the cinnamon-fern.
The osmundas are somewhat unstable in their chief characteristics as is shown by several variations from the
typical forms. In addition to the variations mentioned
in the specific description, in *O. cinnamomea frondosa*
some of the leaves are intermediate between foliar and
sporophyl, *i.e.*, sterile near the base and more or less
spore-bearing at the middle or near the apex.

3. Osmunda Claytoniana L. Rootstock stout, creeping: leaves clustered, arching, some of them spore-bearing about the middle; foliage leaves 6–30 dm. tall, the
blades lanceolate to oblanceolate in outline, 1-pinnate,
the leaves usually rather numerous, lanceolate to linear-
lanceolate, acute or acutish, deeply pinnatifid, the segments ovate to oblong-ovate, obtuse, entire or shallowly
toothed: sporophyls often taller than the foliage leaves,
bearing 1–7 pairs of spore-bearing, pinnate, ascending,
leaflets between the lower and the upper plain and longer
leaflets, the clusters of sporangia cylindric, close together, green, becoming dark-brown, brittle, early withering. [*Osmunda interrupta* Michx.]—(INTERRUPTED-
FERN. CLAYTON'S-FERN.)—Woods, thickets, and swamps,
various provinces, throughout our range, except the pine-
barrens and contiguous territory.—Spores mature, May.

Our three species of *Osmunda* fall into two very natural groups. The one contains the royal-fern (*O. regalis*)
with bipinnate leaf-blades, the other comprises the cinnamon-fern (*O. cinnamomea*) and the interrupted-fern (*O.
Claytoniana*), both of them with merely pinnate leaf-
blades. Although the royal-fern and the other two species may be readily distinguished by their foliage leaves,
the cinnamon-fern and the interrupted-fern are much
alike in their sterile leaves. However, the sporophyls
are very distinctive, as is shown in the above key to the
species. The interrupted-fern has a wide geographic distribution, but its range lies mainly east of the Mississippi
River and north of Georgia. It should be considered as
a northern type. It also occurs in Asia. In the south-

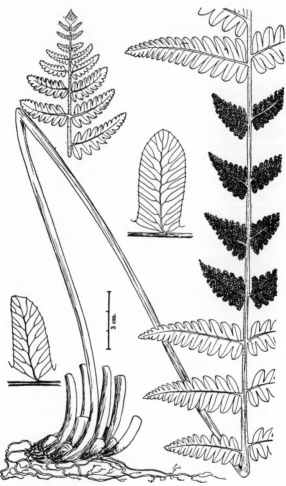

OSMUNDA CLAYTONIANA

ern mountains it ranges from near sea-level to 5000 feet altitude, but to much lower altitudes in the local area. It was named botanically in 1753, from specimens collected in the colony of Virginia. *Osmunda interrupta* is another name suggested by the peculiar structure of the sporophyl. The more restricted range and less conspicuous habit than the cinnamon-fern are reflected in the fewer popular names. Interrupted-fern and Clayton's flowering-fern are on record. The foliage leaves of this species and those of *O. cinnamomea* can scarcely be distinguished from the pattern or venation of the leaflets. However, in *O. Claytoniana* the rachis and bases of leaflets are usually glabrous or inconspicuously scaly.

Order 2. OPHIOGLOSSALES

Succulent terrestrial or epiphytic plants consisting of a short fleshy rootstock bearing several or numerous fibrous, often fleshy or tuberous-thickened roots and one or several leaves. Leaves erect or pendent, sometimes clustered, consisting of a simple, lobed, or compound sessile or stalked foliage blade and one or several, separate stalked, simple or branched sporophyls, borne upon a common stalk. Sporangia formed from the interior tissues of the leaf, naked, each opening by a transverse slit. Spores yellow, of one sort. Prothallia subterranean, usually devoid of chlorophyl and nourished by an endophytic mycorrhiza.—Comprises the following family:

Family 1. OPHIOGLOSSACEAE

Adder's-tongue Family

Terrestrial or epiphytic leafy succulent plants, the leaf straight, erect in vernation or merely inclined, from a subterranean bud which is formed within the base of the old leaf-stalk or at its side. Foliage blade sessile or stalked, entire, lobed, or much-divided, with forking or anastomosing veins. Sporophyls erect or drooping, simple and solitary or clustered, or paniculately branched. Sporangia opening horizontally.—There are five genera in this family: besides the following, another, *Cheiroglossa*, occurs in Florida; the rest are tropical.

KEY TO THE GENERA

Foliage leaf with an entire or palmately lobed blade, the veins anastomosing and with some free included veinlets: sporangia cohering or coalescent in more or less elongate spike-like clusters.   I. OPHIOGLOSSA.

Foliage leaf with 1–4-times pinnately or ternately divided blade, the veins simple or forking: sporangia distinct from each other, borne in simple or compound, sometimes congested spikes.   II. BOTRYCHIA.

I. OPHIOGLOSSA

Plants terrestrial: foliage blade relatively small, entire: sporophyl solitary, erect.   1. OPHIOGLOSSUM.

II. BOTRYCHIA

Succulent plants each with a short rootstock, a foliage leaf and a compound sporophyl.   2. BOTRYCHIUM.

1. OPHIOGLOSSUM L.

Terrestrial, low, often diminutive plants, with small erect, oblique, or horizontal fleshy, sometimes tuber-like rootstocks, and fibrous, naked roots. Leaves 1 or 2–6 together, slender, erect, consisting usually of a short, cylindric, common stalk bearing at its summit a simple, entire, broad or narrow, sessile or short-stalked foliage blade and a single erect sporophyl with a long stalk and a terminal spike of sporangia. Spike formed of 2 rows of globose coalescent sporangia: spores copious, sulphur-yellow. Bud for the following season borne at the apex of the rootstock, exposed, free.—ADDER'S-TONGUES. ADDER'S-FERNS.—Comprises about forty-five species, widely distributed. Besides the following, five or six other species occur in North America.—The genus is based on *Ophioglossum vulgatum* L. The name is Greek in allusion to the tongue-like narrow tip of the sporophyl.

1. O. vulgatum L. Rootstock subcylindric or fusiform: leaves usually solitary, 1–4 dm. tall; foliage blade

OPHIOGLOSSUM VULGATUM

near the middle or sometimes well below or above it, deep-green, glabrous, sessile, ovate to elliptic, 3–12 cm. long, rounded or obtuse at the apex, rather succulent, rather faintly reticulate, the veins very fine: areolae with few delicate veinlets within; basal veins 9–13, nearly equal: sporophyl 3–27 cm. long: spike 1–3.5 cm. long, apiculate: sporangia globose, 1.5–2 mm. in diameter, bead-like, 9–25 along each side of the rachis or rarely fewer. [Includes *O. vulgatum minus* Moore.]— (ADDER'S-TONGUE. SNAKE-TONGUE. ADDER'S-SPEAR.)— Meadows, open woods, bogs, swamps, pastures, and thickets, various provinces, throughout our range, except the pine-barrens.—Spores mature, June and July.

This adder's-tongue, like the other species of *Ophioglossum*, is little suggestive of a fern to a layman botanist. Living plants are elusive, especially when growing in turf or among shrubbery. It ranges northward from northern Florida and Texas to southeastern Canada, and occurs in Europe and Asia. Its maximum altitudinal range seems to be 2000 feet in the Pocono region. It was originally named and described from European specimens in 1753, and was discovered in America in the early years of North American botanical activity. It is a northern type of fern, and may have been forced southward during the Ice Ages, far enough to reach Florida. Its geographical range includes the various plant provinces, except the pine-barrens of the Coastal Plain, but it is usually found in distinctly acid soils. Like other ferns of this group its regular seasonal appearance in a given station is uncertain. The plants apparently live in association with a fungus, and thus the individuals of a given station may skip a season or two without appearing above ground.—A plant originally from New Jersey with leaves usually occurring in pairs or threes, with narrow acutish foliage blade with narrow areolae, has been named *Ophioglossum arenarium* E. G. Britton, but is doubtfully distinct.

2. **BOTRYCHIUM** Sw.

Fleshy, terrestrial plants, with erect rootstocks bearing clustered fleshy, sometimes tuberous-thickened roots.

Leaves 1 to 3, erect, consisting of a short cylindric common stalk bearing at its summit a 1–3-pinnately compound or decompound free-veined foliage blade and a sporophyl with long stalk and a terminal fertile spike or 1–4-pinnate panicle above the sterile blade, with numerous distinct globular sporangia in 2 rows, sessile or nearly so: spores copious, usually sulphur-yellow.—Bud for the following season at the apex of the rootstock, enclosed within the base of the common stalk, either wholly concealed or visible along one side.—Consists of about twenty species, most abundant in the temperate regions of both hemispheres. Two or three species, besides the following, occur in the eastern United States.—Moonworts. Grape-ferns.—The genus is based on *Ophioglossum Lunaria* L.—The name is Greek and refers to the grape-like bunches of sporangia.—The moonworts or grape-ferns are not often cultivated. Of their culture Mr. Dole writes as follows: "Of the botrychiums, I have tried only three. The plants show an ability to survive year after year, producing mainly only undersized foliage blades. This year (1934), however, several of the plants did better and put out full-sized blades. Two plants of *Botrychium virginianum* included also sporophyls, one plant even having two sporophyls. One plant of *B. obliquum* also produced a sporophyl. Another plant of *B. obliquum* and one of *B. dissectum* are normal in size, but have only foliage blades."

Leaf-segments succulent, crenulate, fimbriate, or serrulate, epidermal cells straight: veins several times forked: bud for the following year enclosed in the base of the common stalk.　　I. Eubotrychium.

Leaf-segments membranous, pinnatifid, epidermal cells curved: veins mostly once-forked: bud for the following year exposed along one side of the stalk.　　II. Osmundopteris.

I. Eubotrychium

Bud glabrous: foliage blade pinnately compound, sessile or short-stalked.
　　Sporophyl and foliage blade wholly or partly bent down in the bud: segments of

the foliage blade of an oblong or lanceolate type.

Foliage blade sessile, close
under the sporophyl: spo-
rophyl and foliage-blade
both bent down in the bud:
segments of the foliage
blade mostly obtuse.   1. *B. lanceolatum.*

Foliage blade stalked, remote
from the sporophyl: spo-
rophyl bent down in the
bud, with the apex of the
foliage blade bent down
and covering it: segments
of the foliage blade mostly
obtuse.   2. *B. matricariaefolium.*

Sporophyl erect in the bud, with
the foliage blade erect or
somewhat inclined over it:
segments of the foliage blade
of a cuneate, obovate, flabel-
late, or lunate type.   3. *B. simplex.*

Bud pubescent: foliage blade ternately decompound, long-
stalked, borne near the base
of the common stalk.

Segments of the foliage blade
not all of the same size, the
chief terminal divisions usually elongate, little divided:
leaf-blade herbaceous or
slightly coriaceous. Spores
maturing in September and
October.

Segments of the foliage blade
serrate or serrulate.   4. *B. obliquum.*

Segments of the foliage blade
finely laciniate.   5. *B. dissectum.*

Segments of the foliage blade
all of about the same size
and shape, ovate or ob-
ovate, the chief terminal
divisions not elongate:
blade usually succulent,
blue-green. Spores matur-
ing in August and Septem-
ber, about a month earlier
than those of the preceding.   6. *B. multifidum.*

II. Osmundopteris

Plant erect, with a thin, mem-
branous-succulent deltoid foliage blade, nearly or quite ses-
sile on the common stalk.   7. *B. virginianum.*

1. B. lanceolatum (S. G. Gmel.) Ångstr. Leaf 0.5-3
dm. high, the common stalk elongate, slender, erect:
foliage-blade closely sessile under the sporophyl, 2-6 cm.
wide and long, somewhat succulent, subternately deeply
lobed, the segments ovate to elliptic, coarsely toothed or
1- or 2-pinnatifid: sporophyl sessile or nearly so, 2-3-

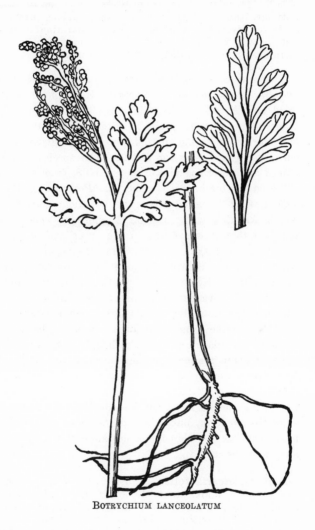

BOTRYCHIUM LANCEOLATUM

pinnate, the branches stout, the sporangia more or less separated: bud with the sporophyl bent down. [*Osmunda lanceolata* S. G. Gmel.]—Meadows, moist woods, bottoms, sandy fields, and swamps, various provinces, scattered over our area north of the terminal moraine, but usually rare and local, and very rare south of the moraine.—Spores mature, May and June.

Two species of our true botrychiums, the present one and *B. simplex,* circle the Northern Hemisphere, while a third one, *B. matricariaefolium* is also in Europe. The plants of the present species have the blade of the foliage leaf more close to the sporophyl and less stalked than in our other grape-ferns, or sessile. The species was first named and described in Europe, in 1768, from specimens collected in birch-woods about St. Petersburg, Russia. This was at a period when the botanical activities of North America were in their beginnings. The author recorded that it was found in the lower and dry places in firm ground free of turf. The geographic range in North America is wide in longitude. As recorded, it extends from New Jersey to Colorado, Washington, Alaska, and Nova Scotia, as well as in Europe and Asia. The northern character of this fern is emphasized by the fact that in the local-flora range it has not been found south of the glacial moraine, although just west of our limits it extends almost to the Maryland line in Lancaster County, Pennsylvania. In our range it attains more than 4000 feet altitude.—The American plant with narrow leaf-segments has been described as *B. lanceolatum angustisegmentum,* but this and the more typical European form occur within the same range or the same colonies in America.

2. B. matricariaefolium A. Br. Leaf 5–30 cm. high, the common stalk stout, little, if any subterranean: foliage-blade succulent, short-stalked, elliptic or ovate, or deltoid-ovate in outline, 1.5–7 cm. long, pinnate, with the segments coarsely toothed or deeply pinnatifid, or essentially 2-pinnate, with the segments separated, more or less cuneately narrowed at the base, or sometimes entire: sporophyl long-stalked, erect, 2- or 3-pinnate, the spo-

BOTRYCHIUM MATRICARIAEFOLIUM

ranges usually contiguous: bud with the sporophyl and
foliage blade bent over, the latter enfolding the former.
[*Botrychium neglectum* Wood. *B. ramosum* Rob. and
Fern., not Asch.]—Woods, sandy fields, and ravines, various provinces, in the more northern parts of our range
and rare and at scattered localities in the more southern
parts.—Spores mature, June.

A quarter of a century after *Botrychium simplex* was
described, another species was discovered in America.
This was named and described as *B. neglectum* in 1847
from specimens studied and collected in woods at Meri-
den, New Hampshire. This plant, like *B. simplex*, was
compared to *B. Lunaria* of Europe, but it was considered
by the author as "quite distinct from that species."
The original station for this plant gave it its first common name, namely Meriden-botrychium. Contrary to the
developmental idea indicated in the describing of *B.
simplex*, the author in this case, in a schedule of the
species, placed this, the more complex species, before *B.
simplex*. However, the common European form of this
fern was named three or four years earlier, so the
American name *B. neglectum* must be reduced to
synonymy. The geographic range is extensive, being
recorded as Maryland to Nebraska, South Dakota, and
Quebec; also in Europe. Within the local flora range
this species seems to be confined mainly to the more
northern provinces, where it occurs at over 4000 feet altitude.

3. B. simplex E. Hitchc. Leaf 4–15 cm. high, the
common stalk stout, partly subterranean, variable in
length: foliage-blade short- or long-stalked, spatulate,
obovate, elliptic, suborbicular, or ovate in outline, succulent, mostly 1–4 cm. long, entire or pinnately 3–7-lobed,
the lobes broad and of various shapes, approximate or
partly separated, often cuneately narrowed at the base:
sporophyl long-stalked, erect, unbranched or 1- or 2-pin-
nate, the sporangia usually contiguous; bud with the
sporophyl straight.—Hilly pastures, meadows, edges of
swamps, and rich moist woods, various provinces, more
northern parts of our range.—Spores mature, May and
June.

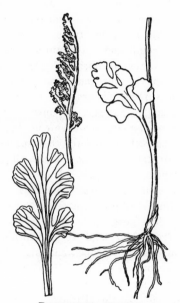

BOTRYCHIUM SIMPLEX

The little grape-fern represents one of the rather rare cases where a fern that is also native in Europe and Asia was first described in America from American specimens. *Botrychium simplex* was named and described in 1823 from specimens studied and collected in dry hilly pastures in Conway, Massachusetts. The plants were first, erroneously, associated with *Botrychium Lunaria* of Europe. The type specimens had unbranched sporophyls, for this part of the plant, is referred to as being ''a spike hardly compound, the small branches . . . —whereas in *B. Lunaria* the spike is 'twice or thrice compound.' '' By ''hardly compound'' the author refers to the fact that the sporangia are borne in glomerules at the nodes of the sporophyl, thus indicating that each cluster is borne on a suppressed branch. Curiously enough, the author had suggested, perhaps unwittingly, the developmental idea of the simple to the complex, for he records, ''If I am correct, therefore, this species will take its place as the first under the genus; all other *Botrychia* having compound fronds.'' However, in more robust plants the sporangia are sometimes borne on short branches, thus forming spike-like clusters instead of glomerules. The geographic range of the species is wide, extending from Maryland to California, Oregon, and Nova Scotia; also in Europe and Asia. In the local-flora area the distribution is not well known. On account of the diminutive size of the plants, specimens are rather rarely collected. Little altitude has been recorded. A species or a form similar to *B. simplex* in general habit, *Botrychium tenebrosum*, occurs in our range, particularly in northern New Jersey and contiguous territory. The foliage leaf is extremely tender and borne near the top of the common stalk. It is apparently best treated as a form of *Botrychium simplex*.

4. B. obliquum Muhl. Leaf 8–30 cm. high, the common stalk short, subterranean, with the bud for the following season concealed within its base: foliage-blade usually long-stalked, ovate-deltoid to broadly pentagonal, commonly 5–13 cm. broad, subternately divided, the

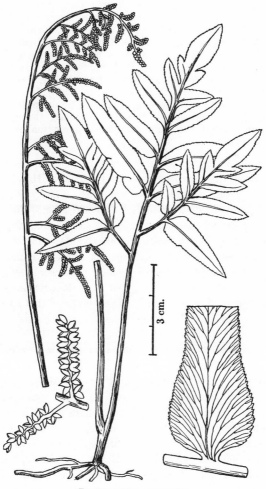

3 cm.

BOTRYCHIUM OBLIQUUM

divisions stalked, nearly equal, 1- or 2-pinnate or somewhat 3-pinnatifid in larger forms, the segments obliquely ovate to lanceolate or oblong-lanceolate, the terminal ones elongate, 1–2 cm. long (or short, broad, obtuse or rounded in *B. obliquum oneidense*), the margins throughout crenulate to serrulate: sporophyl erect, slender or stout, terminating in a very long-stalked panicle which is erect or nodding at the apex, 3- or 4-pinnate, mostly 3–13 cm. long: bud densely pilose, both portions bent in vernation. [*Botrychium ternatum* Hook. and Baker, not Sw. *B. ternatum obliquum* D. C. Eaton. *B. tenuifolium* Underw.] —(GRAPE-FERN.)—Woods, meadows, fields, pastures, riverbanks, and pinelands, various provinces, throughout our range, except the pine-barrens.—Spores mature, August to October.

The majority of the grape-ferns native in North America are also European or Eurasian. However, three of our species are American only, namely *Botrychium obliquum*, *B. dissectum*, and *B. multifidum*. The original specimens of the present species were found and studied most likely at Lancaster, Pennsylvania. The discoverer, instead of publishing the species himself, named it and sent specimens to Europe, where they were described in 1810. The type locality given with the original specimen was merely Pennsylvania. The plants of this species and the two relatives mentioned above are the larger ones of the genus as represented in our area, with the exception of the rattlesnake-fern (*B. virginianum*), which, however, belongs to a different subgenus. The range includes the United States east of the Mississippi River, the south-central states, and adjacent Canada. It is generally distributed in the local flora area, except in the pine-barrens of the Coastal Plain. Besides a wide geographic range, the altitudinal distribution extends from about 6000 feet in the Blue Ridge to sea-level, but in our range it seldom reaches 4000 feet. Its center of distribution was probably always in the more temperate regions whence it spread southward to Florida ages ago.

5. **B. dissectum** Spreng. Leaf 15–30 cm. high, the common stalk very short, subterranean, the bud pilose: foliage-blade green, long-stalked, subpentagonal, 15 cm.

3 cm.

BOTRYCHIUM DISSECTUM

wide or less, subternately divided, the divisions stalked, with the terminal division the larger, 1- or 2-pinnate, the segments lanceolate to ovate, 1–4 cm. long, laciniate, the ultimate divisions acute or acutish: sporophyl very long-stalked, far exceeding the foliage-blade, erect or nodding at the tip, 3-or 4-pinnate: bud much as in *B. obliquum*. [*B. ternatum dissectum* D. C. Eaton.]— (CUT-LEAVED GRAPE-FERN.)—Low woods, swamps, thickets, and pastures, various provinces, throughout our range, less common in the pine-barrens.—Spores mature, August to October.

Active botanists, opportunities for the study of plants, and vehicles of publication were more numerous in Europe about the beginning of the past century than they were in America. Consequently, specimens of many American plants were sent to the authorities at Old World institutions for study and for opinions as to their relationships. The present species of grape-fern was named in 1804, recorded as having been collected in Virginia, but it was described in Europe by Kurt Sprengel to whom it had been sent for identification. The geographic range of this species is nearly the same as that of its nearest relative, *B. obliquum*: or Florida to Missouri, Illinois, and Maine. Within our range the species is widely distributed, but it is less common in the pine-barrens of the Coastal Plain than in the older provinces.

6. **B. multifidum** (S. G. Gmel.) Rupr. Leaf 18–50 cm. high, sometimes twin, the common stalk short and stout, subterranean, the bud silky: foliage-blade glaucous, succulent, or subcoriaceous in drying, broadly triangular or subpentagonal in outline, 20 cm. wide or less, long-stalked, subternately divided, with the terminal division the larger, the divisions 3-pinnate, the segments numerous, obtuse or broad and rounded, crenate or sinuate: sporophyl long-stalked, stout, 2–5-pinnate, usually equaling or exceeding the foliage-blade, the branches diffusely spreading, with the sporangia contiguous. [*Osmunda multifida* S. G. Gmel. *Botrychium silaifolium* Presl. *B. occidentale* Underw.]—(LEATHERY GRAPE-FERN.) — Dry rocky glades, open woods, fields, and pastures, various provinces, rare and scattered in our range.—Spores mature, August and September.—The plant occurring in our range is the form known as *B. multifidum intermedium*.

BOTRYCHIUM MULTIFIDUM

The majority of our grape-ferns, both the endemic ones and those also occurring in the Old World, have a more extensive longitudinal than latitudinal distribution in North America. The present species is wholly North American, and ranges across southern Canada and the northern United States from the Atlantic to the Pacific. Although this fern was discovered in North America, it was first described in Europe in 1825. The original specimens were collected, according to the author of the species, at Nootka Sound on the western coast of North America. The leathery grape-fern, as this species is called, is one of the larger forms of the group with pubescent buds and late-summer- or fall-maturing spores. The foliage leaf has a long stalk, while the primary divisions of the blade are unusually long-stalked. The sporophyl is often very much compounded. The geographic range is decidedly boreal, extending from New Jersey to Oregon, British Columbia, Minnesota, and Maine. In the local-flora area this fern occurs only north of the glacial moraine, and has only been found at lower altitudes. The species is related to *Botrychium Matricariae* of Europe, of which some botanists have made it an American subspecies. It has also been described under the name *B. occidentale*, this name being founded on specimens from New Westminster, British Columbia. It is interesting to note that a fern growing in the Atlantic coastal region which was early settled, from New Jersey northward and in other parts of eastern North America, should have been described in two instances from specimens collected in the coastal regions of Pacific North America.

7. **B. virginianum** (L.) Sw. Leaf 8–80 cm. high, the common stalk stout or slender, comprising ½ to ⅔ the length of the plant and mostly aerial, with the bud for the following season exposed along one side: foliage-blade nearly or quite sessile, spreading, thin, deltoid, 1–4 dm. broad, nearly as long, ternate, the short-stalked primary divisions 1-pinnate or 2-pinnate, the segments 1- or 2-pinnatifid, the ultimate segments elliptic, lanceolate, or ovate, toothed at the apex: sporophyl erect, long-stalked,

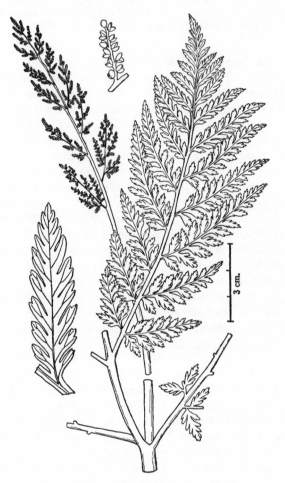

BOTRYCHIUM VIRGINIANUM

terminating in a panicle which is 2–3-pinnate, with slender branches: bud pubescent. [*Osmunda virginiana* L. *Botrychium virginicum* Willd. *B. gracile* Pursh.]— (RATTLESNAKE-FERN.) — Rich woods, thickets, and meadows, various provinces, throughout our range except the pine-barrens.—Spores mature, late May and June, rarely July.

The genus *Botrychium* naturally falls into two main groups. The rattlesnake-fern is the sole representative of the section or subgenus *Osmundopteris* in our area. The geographic distribution in North America is more extensive than that of any other species of *Botrychium*, as it includes almost the entire area within the extremes, reaching from Florida to Mexico, British Columbia and Labrador. It also occurs in Eurasia. It is found throughout the local flora area, except in the pine-barrens of the Coastal Plain, and it is more abundant northward where its maximum altitude is 2000 feet in the Pocono region. The exposed bud in the base of the stalk, the flexuous epidermal cells, and the thin texture of the blade of the foliage-leaf are outstanding characteristics for identification. The rattlesnake-fern is so common that it usually is the first species of *Botrychium* that the beginner meets with in collecting specimens of plants. Although this fern grows in latitudes of long summers or long winters, it is at its best in a climate of more balanced seasons. In and about the Linnaean period of botany the names of several political divisions of North America occurred frequently in botanical nomenclature. The Carolinas, Virginia, Pennsylvania, and Canada were the colonies most frequently commemorated by being used in specific names. These colonies had active botanists as residents, most of whom were in communication with the plant students of the Old World. The rattlesnake-fern was first found in the colony of Virginia in the early part of the eighteenth century and named and described in 1753.

Order 3. SALVINIALES

Aquatic or mud-inhabiting herbs, with horizontal or creeping stems, or floating plants. Leaves various, sometimes filiform, or blades dilated, entire, lobed, or 2–4-foliolate. Spores of two kinds, microspores and megaspores, contained in sporocarps, with both kinds of spores in one sporocarp or the different kinds in separate sporocarps. Megaspores germinating into simple prothallia which bear archegones. Microspores forming still simpler prothallia bearing antheridia, emitting antherozoids.—Consists of the following two families only.

KEY TO THE FAMILIES

Plants rooting in the mud: stems (rootstocks) creeping or horizontal: sporocarps uniform, containing both megaspores and microspores: leaves filiform or with 2- or 4-foliolate blades, the leaflets dilated. — Family 1. MARSILEACEAE.

Plants floating: stems pinnately branched: sporocarps of two kinds, small ones containing a megaspore, and larger ones containing pedicelled microsporangia: leaves with entire or 2-lobed blades. — Family 2. SALVINIACEAE.

Family 1. MARSILEACEAE

PEPPERWORT FAMILY

Perennial, herbaceous plants, rooting in mud and usually partly submerged, with slender often elongate branching rootstocks. Leaves erect, spreading, or floating, with 2-foliolate or 4-foliolate blades, or merely filiform. Asexual propagation carried out by sporocarps which are borne on peduncles arising from the rootstock near the leaf-stalk, or consolidated with the leaf-stalk. Each sporocarp contains both megaspores and microspores. Megaspores germinate into prothallia that bear mostly archegonia; microspores develop into prothallia that bear antheridia.—The family comprises three genera and more than sixty species of wide geographic distribution. Most of the species belong to the following genus:

MARSILEA QUADRIFOLIA

1. **MARSILEA** L.

Marsh or aquatic, anchored plants, either submersed or emersed. Leaves commonly floating on the surface of shallow water: blades slender-petioled, 4-foliolate. Leaflets broad, with many fine veins forming long and narrow areolae. Peduncles shorter than the petioles, arising from near their bases or more or less adnate to them. Sporocarps ovoid or ellipsoid, formed of two vertical valves each with several transverse compartments (sori), 2-valved at maturity and emitting a band of elastic tissue, which bears the sporangia on a number of short lobes.—PEPPERWORTS.—Contains more than fifty species of wide distribution. Four native species occur in the south central states, while the following, a naturalized species, occurs in the northeastern United States.— The genus is based on *Marsilea quadrifolia* L.—The name is in honor of Giovanni Marsigli, an Italian botanist.

1. **M. quadrifolia** L. Rootstock slender, horizontal in or creeping on the muddy bottoms of ponds, lakes, or streams: leaves glabrous, at least when mature; petioles slender, 5–15 cm. long or greatly elongate in deep water; leaflets spreading, usually floating, the blades cuneate to cuneate-obovate, mostly 0.5–1.5 cm. long and nearly as wide, entire: sporocarps 2 or rarely 3 borne on a stalk which is partly adnate to the petiole, ellipsoid, oval, or ovate, pedicelled, yellowish-brown and hairy when young, glabrous and dark purple at maturity: sori 8 or 9 in each valve.—(EUROPEAN-PEPPERWORT.)—Still water in the eastern part of our range.—Spores mature, June to October.

The pepperworts (*Marsilea*) are not naturally represented in northeastern North America. However, two species, *Marsilea vestita* and *M. uncinata,* both natives of the southwest, and the present species, a native of Eurasia, are naturalized in the United States east of the Mississippi River. This European pepperwort was, in some way, introduced into Bantam Lake, Connecticut, many years ago, at least its presence there was reported in 1862. From Bantam Lake, it spread both northward and southward in the Atlantic seaboard. The original specimens came from Europe and Asia. The species was named in 1753. Its distribution in North America ranges from Maryland to Massachusetts.

FAMILY 2. SALVINIACEAE

SALVINIA FAMILY

Small floating plants, with a more or less elongate and sometimes pinnately branching stem bearing apparently 2-ranked leaves: blades entire or 2-lobed. Sporocarps soft, thin-walled, often borne 2 or more on a common stalk, 1-celled, with a central simple or branched receptacle, which bears one or more megasporangia containing a single megaspore, or stalked microsporanges, each containing numerous microspores; the sporocarps containing megaspores often larger than those containing microspores. Megaspores develop into prothallia bearing archegonia, while microspores grow into prothallia that bear antheridia.—The family comprises the two following genera:

KEY TO THE GENERA

Leaves minute, imbricate on pinnately branching stems.
                                                    1. AZOLLA.
Leaves large (1–1.5 cm. long), 2-ranked and
    spreading on mostly simple stems.   2. SALVINIA.

1. AZOLLA Lam.

Minute, moss-like, reddish or green, floating plants, commonly resembling Hepaticae, often densely matted. Stems pinnately branched, covered with minute imbricate 2-lobed leaves, and emitting long rootlets beneath. Sporocarps of two kinds borne in the axils of the leaves, the smaller ovoid or acorn-shaped, containing a single megaspore at the base and a few minute bodies above it, the larger globose or globose-ovoid, containing many stalked sporangia borne in a cluster, each comprising several masses of microspores.—FLOATING-FERNS.—Comprises few, about five, species of wide geographic distribution.—The genus is based on *Azolla filiculoides* Lam.— The name is Greek and signifies killed by drought.

AZOLLA CAROLINIANA

1. A. caroliniana Willd. Plants greenish brown, or red, 7–25 mm. wide or sometimes smaller, deltoid or triangular-ovate, sometimes irregular, the stems pinnately branching: leaves with ovate lobes, their color varying with the amount of sunlight, the lower usually reddish, the upper green with a reddish border: megasporangia 1.5–2 mm. long: megaspores minutely granulate, with three accessory bodies: microsporangia about 0.5 mm. long, relatively narrower than the megasporangia: masses of microspores armed with rigid septate processes.— (MOSQUITO-FERN.)—Still water, ponds, and shores of streams, Coastal Plain and adj. provinces, eastern part of our range.—Spores mature, July and August.

Free-floating fern-plants are not numerous in our range, those of the present genus and of the following one constituting the sum. *Azolla* grows, mainly, on still bodies of water where it propagates rapidly and promptly forms a carpet dense enough wholly to conceal the water. As a result of varying light and nutriment the carpet may be green, red, or brown. It is sometimes called mosquito-fern because it is grown to check the natural breeding of mosquitos in pools where these pests generally breed. This fern-ally was discovered in the Carolinas about the beginning of the past century and was named in 1810. Its natural geographic range is extensive, reaching from Florida to Arizona, British Columbia, Ontario, and Massachusetts; also in Mexico. Although our area may be within the natural range of this species, it seems to occur there only as naturalized colonies. These establishments may represent the remains of plantings connected with mosquito-control activities, introductions having been found on Staten Island and Long Island, New York, and in Essex County, New Jersey.

2. **SALVINIA** Adans.

Plants much larger than those of *Azolla*, the leaves often resembling those of very large plants of *Lemna*. Stems simple or nearly so, bearing apparently 2-ranked leaves and a series of root-like fibers. Sporocarps borne in clusters, subglobose, 1 or 2 in each cluster containing many (10 or more) sessile megasporangia, each of which contains a single megaspore; the others containing numerous stalked, smaller microsporangia, each with very numerous microspores. — FLOATING-MOSSES. — Comprises about a dozen species of wide geographic distribution.— The genus is based on *Salvinia natans* L.—The name is in honor of Antonio Maria Salvini, an Italian scientist.

1. S. auriculata Aubl. Plant deep-green, more or less elongate: leaves horizontally spreading on the stem, mostly 1–2.5 cm. long; blades elliptic, obtuse or emarginate at the apex, entire, green and papillose above, brown-hairy beneath, rounded or cordate at the base: sporocarps clustered in 4's to 8's, the upper ones each containing about 10 megasporangia, each of which usually contains a single megaspore, the other sporocarps each containing numerous microsporangia, each of which in turn contains numerous microspores.—(FLOATING-MOSS.) —Still or stagnant water, often in ponds and along the shores of slow-floating streams, formerly in Silver Lake, Staten Island, New York, where introduced.—Spores mature, July and August. — Our plant represents the variety *Olfersiana*.

The plants of *Salvinia* float on the surface of the water and, if undisturbed, cover it with an unbroken, coarse, green carpet. It grows especially well in ponds and in coves of flowing streams. The genus *Salvinia* long known abroad was first reported as occurring in North America in 1814. The specimens were recorded as *Salvinia natans* L., which originally came from Italy. Rather recently plants occurring in Missouri and Minnesota have been definitely determined as that species. In 1898 specimens of a *Salvinia* were collected in Silver Lake and vicinity, Staten Island, New York. The specimens are imperfectly developed. They were erroneously recorded as *Salvinia natans* L. The specimens from the North American localities were carefully studied and the results recorded as follows: "The claim of *Salvinia natans* to a place in our flora rests, then, on one ancient and very doubtful report [Western New York], two misidentifications [Minnesota and Staten Island, New York], and a single authentic collection [Missouri], never re-

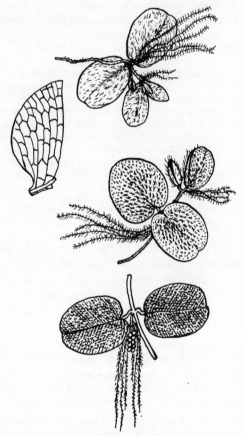

SALVINIA AURICULATA

peated, at a station which has not been re-discovered in
35 years."[1] The specimens from our area represent
a variety of *Salvinia auriculata,* a popular aquatic now
very widely cultivated. The species was discovered in
Guiana about the middle of the eighteenth century
and named in 1775. It has become a popular
subject for aquaria and ponds, both as a matter
of interest and for smothering mosquito larvae. It forms
a complete carpet on the surface of the water. The
Staten Island locality is probably non-existent, but
Salvinia, being an elusive and an evanescent plant, may
well appear in ponds and pools as a transient member of
our flora.

Order 4. EQUISETALES

Terrestrial, sometimes uliginous, rush-like plants,
with horizontal rootstocks and jointed, grooved stems,
the internodes provided with a double series of cavities and usually with a large central one (centrum),
the nodes provided with diaphragms. Leaves represented by toothed sheaths at the nodes of the stem.
Sporanges 1-celled, clustered underneath the scales of
terminal spike-like cones. Spores uniform, furnished
with 2 narrow paired appendages (elaters) attached
at the middle, coiling around the spores when moist,
and spreading when dry, in diverse ways.

Family 1. EQUISETACEAE

Horsetail Family

Perennial slender or stout herbs, with simple or
branched, sometimes bushy, cylindric but usually
fluted stems, with the branches, when present,
whorled at the stem-nodes, which are closed. Leaves
(scales) with their edges joined, thus making a cylindric or funnelform sheath. Sporophyls verticillate,
peltate, stalked, with 6 or 7 sporangia under each
cone-scale. Spores numerous, the elaters clavate.—

[1] C. A. Weatherby, Am. Fern Jour. 11: 52. 1921.

Consists of the following genus.—The species, owing frequently to the vacillating water-table, are variable and often difficult to determine.

1. **EQUISETUM** L.

Rigid plants with perennial, widely branching, often tuber-bearing rootstocks, the roots annual, felted. Stems jointed, with a coating of silex disposed in various patterns, the large central cavity (centrum) surrounded by a series of small cavities (vallecular holes) situated under each groove. Sporangia opening along the inner side where they discharge the green spores.—HORSETAILS. SCOURING-RUSHES.—Represented by about twenty-five species, of very wide geographic distribution.—The genus is based on *Equisetum fluviatile* L.—The name is Latin signifying horsetail, in allusion to the copious branching of the stems of some of the species.—Our species fall into two natural groups: the one with horizontal rootstocks which annually send up a series of branches simple at the base (the first group of 6 species); the other in which the branching rootstock merges into the branching bases of the perennial stems (of the second group of 3 species).

Stems annual, appearing in spring, dying down in fall, the sterile ones, at least, branched: spikes (cones) rounded at the apex.—**Equisetum.**   I. ARVENSES.

Stems perennial, evergreen, simple or with few irregular branches: spikes (cones) apiculate.—**Hippochaete.**   II. HYEMALES.

I. ARVENSES

Cone-bearing stems appearing before the sterile ones, succulent and early withering, sometimes only at the apex.

Cone-bearing stems simple, early withering.   1. *E. arvense.*

Cone-bearing stems branched, at least when old, withering only at the apex.

Branches of the stem simple, their sheaths with 3 erect lobes.   2. *E. pratense.*

Branches of the stem more or less forked, their sheaths with 3 acuminate more or less spreading lobes.   3. *E. sylvaticum.*

Cone-bearing and sterile stems, similar and contemporary, branched or individually simple.

Centrum small, about one-sixth the diameter of the stem: vallecular holes nearly as large as the centrum.   4. *E. palustre.*

Centrum large, one-half the diameter of the stem or more: vallecular holes relatively small or wanting.

Sheaths loose around the stem: centrum two-thirds the diameter of the stem or less: vallecular holes present.   5. *E. litorale.*

Sheaths tight around the stem: centrum about four-fifths the diameter of the stem: vallecular holes absent.   6. *E. fluviatile.*

II. HYEMALES

Plant small, the stem 1.5–3 dm. tall, 5–10-grooved: sheaths loose, with setaceous lobes.   7. *E. variegatum.*

Plant large, the stem 3–31 dm. tall, 8–34-grooved: sheaths cylindric or funnelform with acute or acuminate lobes.

Stem smooth or nearly so, rather frail: stem-sheaths funnelform.   8. *E. laevigatum.*

Stem tuberculate-roughened, very firm: stem-sheaths cylindric or nearly so.   9. *E. praealtum.*

1. E. arvense L. Stems annual, with scattered stomata, dimorphic, the fertile appearing in early spring before the sterile: cone-bearing stems 1–2.5 dm. high, not branched, soon withering, light-brown, their loose scarious sheaths mostly distant, whitish, ending in about 12 brown acuminate teeth: cone ovoid to cylindric, 1.5–3 cm. long, obtuse: sterile stems green, rather slender, 0.5–6 dm. high, 6–19-furrowed, with numerous long mostly simple whorled 4-angled or rarely 3-angled solid branches which stand erect or are strongly ascending, their sheaths 4-toothed, the stomata in two rows in the furrows.—*E. arvense serotinum* is an occasional form with a cone terminating the normally sterile plant.—(HORSETAIL. FIELD-HORSETAIL.)—Sandy or clayey soil, meadows, wet woods, stream-banks, lake shores, cultivated grounds, and railroad embankments, various provinces, general throughout our range, frequent as a weed in cultivated grounds.—Spores mature, April and May.

The common horsetail is the most widely distributed species of *Equisetum*, at least in North America. It is also known to a greater number of people than the other species. This wide acquaintance is due to the fact that the plant grows in cultivated sandy grounds, dumps, roadsides, and cinder piles, as well as in its natural

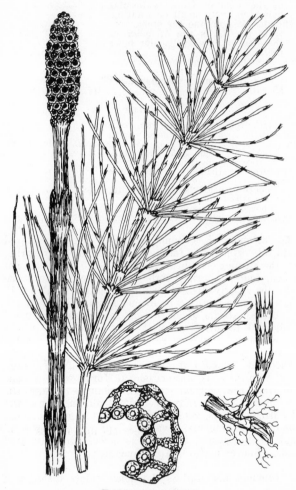

EQUISETUM ARVENSE

haunts, and appears early in the spring. The plants seem not only to thrive in soil almost devoid of nourishment, but to grow more luxuriantly there. The original specimens came from Europe and were named in 1753. There it was said to grow *ad ripas lacuum, fluviorum.* It inhabits similar localities in North America where it ranges from North Carolina to California, Alaska, Labrador, and Greenland; also found in Asia.

2. E. pratense Ehrh. Stems annual, dimorphic, the fertile appearing in early spring before the sterile: cone-bearing stems 2–4 dm. high, persistent, withering only at the apex, branching in age and becoming similar to the sterile stems, thus both kinds rough, 8–20-furrowed, the rather loose nearly cylindric or somewhat funnel-form sheaths ending in about 11 ovate-lanceolate or lanceolate teeth; branches usually numerous, often densely whorled and crowded, mostly slenderly elongate and whip-like, solid, 3-angled or rarely 4- or 5-angled, simple, their sheaths mostly 3-toothed: cone ellipsoid or slightly narrowed upward, 1–2.5 cm. long, obtuse.—(MEADOW-HORSE-TAIL.)—Wet soil and low sandy woods, various provinces, apparently very rare and local, in the more northern part of our range.—Spores mature, April and May.

The meadow-horsetail is not generally distributed in our range like *Equisetum arvense.* The habit is different, too; instead of the stiff erect or ascending branches of the common-horsetail, the meadow-horsetail has pliable, elongate, whip-like, more or less straggling branches that spread and even partly recurve. The original specimens were European and were named in 1753. In Europe it was said to grow in *pratis sylvaticis.* In North America it occurs in the same kind of habitats and ranges from New Jersey to Iowa, Colorado, Alaska, and Nova Scotia; also found in Asia.

3. E. sylvaticum L. Stems annual, dimorphic, the cone-bearing appearing in early spring before the sterile, at first simple, but becoming branched and resembling the sterile, which appear later, only the tip withering, usually 12-furrowed, the rather loose cylindric or campanulate sheaths ending in 8–14 rather broad teeth; branches numerous, often copious and crowded, forked,

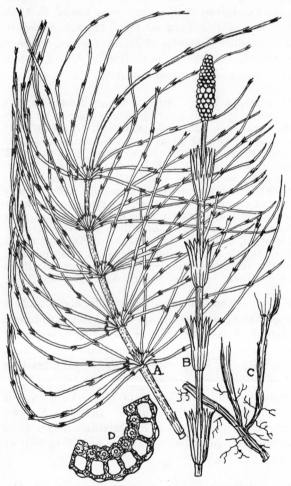

EQUISETUM PRATENSE

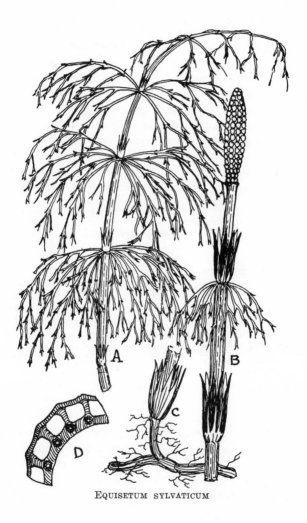

EQUISETUM SYLVATICUM

their sheaths with 4 or 5 teeth; branchlets like the branches curved downward and solid, their sheaths with 3 teeth: cone cylindric or slightly conic, 1.5–4 cm. long, obtuse.—(BOTTLE-BRUSH. WOOD-HORSETAIL.)—Bogs, swamp-margins, damp shaded slopes, rich sandy or clayey woods, and meadows, various provinces, generally scattered in most parts of our range.—Spores mature, May and June.

The bottle-brush has the same general habit as the branching plants of the two preceding species, but the branching is distinctive. The branches are compound, and are spreading and gracefully curved downward. The usually great number of branches on the sterile stem give it a more plumose appearance than in any other species. The original specimens came from Europe where the plants were said to grow on roadsides. The species was named in 1753. The bottle-brush is widely distributed in North America, ranging from North Carolina to Iowa, Alaska, Newfoundland and Greenland. It also occurs in Asia.

4. E. palustre L. Stems annual, all alike and contemporary, 2–5 dm. tall, slender, 5–9-furrowed, branched or individually simple, the rather loose, somewhat funnel-form sheaths ending in about 8 slender teeth; branches simple, few, but more numerous in the lower whorls, hollow, their sheaths mostly 5-toothed: cone cylindric or ellipsoid, 1–2 cm. long, obtuse.—(MARSH-HORSETAIL. SNAKE-PIPES. CAT-WHISTLES.)—Muddy or sandy river banks and lake shores, rare in our range, apparently only in the valley of the Connecticut River.—Spores mature, July and August.

The marsh-horsetail stands well by itself. The stems are usually uniformly branched, with the branches ascending or spreading; they too are often relatively stout. The original specimens came from Europe where the species was named in 1753. It was said to grow *aquosis*, a habitat that also holds in America. In North America the plant ranges from Connecticut to Illinois, Arizona, Alaska, and Nova Scotia. It also occurs in Asia.

5. E. litorale Kuehl. Stems annual, all alike and contemporary, 2–5 dm. tall, very slender, 6–10-furrowed,

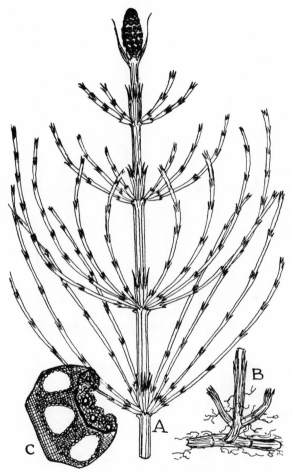

EQUISETUM PALUSTRE

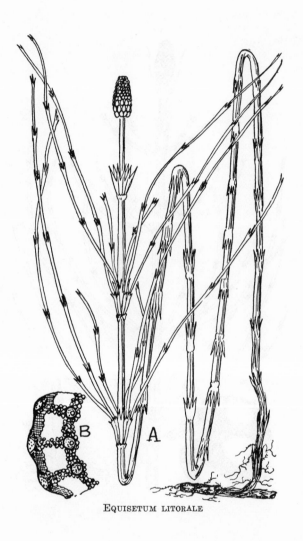

EQUISETUM LITORALE

branched, the rather loose somewhat funnelform or campanulate sheaths ending in about 8 slender teeth;
branches simple, with the first joint shorter or slightly
longer than the sheath, of two kinds, some 4-angled and
hollow, others 3-angled and solid: cone ellipsoid or
slightly narrowed upward, about 1 cm. long, obtuse.—
(SHORE-HORSETAIL.)—Sandy, muddy, or gravelly stream-
banks and shores of lakes, rare in our range, apparently
known mainly from the valley of the Delaware River.—
Spores mature, August and September.

The shore-horsetail has a somewhat wider distribution
than the preceding species, to which it is rather closely
related. The plants are not so symmetrically branched,
the branches often being unequal and straggling. The
plant is, by some, supposed to be a hybrid between two
other species of *Equisetum*. The original specimens came
from Russia where they were named in 1845.—It was
said to grow in *litore arenoso marino*. In North America it occurs from New Jersey to British Columbia, Ontario, and New Brunswick.—This species is sometimes
included in *E. palustre* L.

6. **E. fluviatile** L. Stems annual, all alike and con-
temporaneous, 5–12 dm. tall, smooth, 10–30-furrowed,
branching after the cone is formed, the short, appressed
or slightly loose sheath ending in about 18 short, dark
rigid teeth; branches variable in length, usually simple
(occasionally bearing cones), hollow, slender, sometimes
wanting: cones ovoid to slightly conic, 1.5–2.5 cm. long,
obtuse. [*E. limosum* L.]—(WATER-HORSETAIL. SWAMP-
HORSETAIL.)—Meadows, shores of ponds, lakes and
streams, various provinces, scattered throughout our
range, except, apparently, the pine-barrens and contiguous territory.—Spores mature, May and June.

The swamp-horsetail is usually a larger plant than the
next preceding species. The stem is usually much-
branched; the branches may be short and stout or elongate and slender, but they are usually quite uniformly
disposed. The original specimens came from Europe
where they were named in 1753. The habitat recorded is
ad ripas lacuum, fluviorum. In North America the range

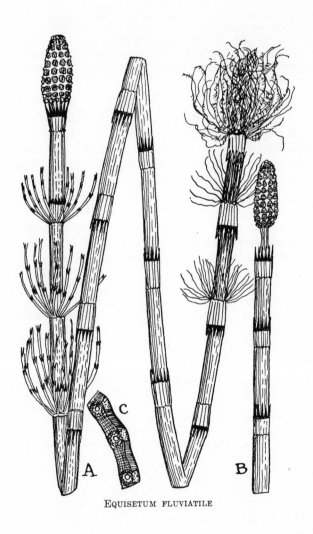

EQUISETUM FLUVIATILE

extends from Virginia to Nebraska, Washington, Alaska, and Nova Scotia; it also grows in Asia.

7. E. variegatum Schleich. Stems perennial, all alike, rather stiff, evergreen, 2–5 dm. tall, slender, 5–10-furrowed, often branched at the base and more or less tufted, often blackish and merging into the black root-stock, the campanulate or funnelform sheaths variegated green and black, with 5–10 broad teeth, each of which is tipped by a deciduous bristle; branches few or numerous, mostly simple above, very uneven in length: cone ellipsoid, about 1 cm. long, acute. (VARIEGATED-HORSE-TAIL. VARIEGATED SCOURING-RUSH.)—Sandy, muddy, gravelly, or rocky shores of streams, lakes, and ponds, and wet woods, rare in our range, definitely known in northern New Jersey and Connecticut.—Spores mature, May and June.

The variegated-horsetail, like the following species, differs from all the preceding ones in the peculiar basal branching habit. The original specimens came from Europe and were named in 1807. The species is widely distributed in North America, ranging from Connecticut to Nebraska, Nevada, Alaska, Labrador, and Greenland, and also in Asia.

8. E. laevigatum A. Br. Stems perennial, all alike, 3–15 dm. high, simple or little branched, evergreen, pale-green, rather frail, 14–30-furrowed, the ridges almost smooth; sheaths elongate, funnelform, with a black girdle at the base of the mostly deciduous, white-margined teeth and rarely also at their bases, their ridges with a faint central keel and sometimes with faint, lateral ones: cones ellipsoid, 1.5–2 cm. long, apiculate. [*Equisetum hyemale intermedium* A. A. Eaton.]—(SMOOTH SCOURING-RUSH.)—Along streams, especially in clay soil, various provinces, throughout our range.—Spores mature, May and June.

The great majority of our North American species of *Equisetum* also occur in Europe or Asia or in both of these regions. The present species however, is peculiarly American. It is widely distributed in the United States and southern Canada, except the northeastern parts. The original specimens came from the central States. The

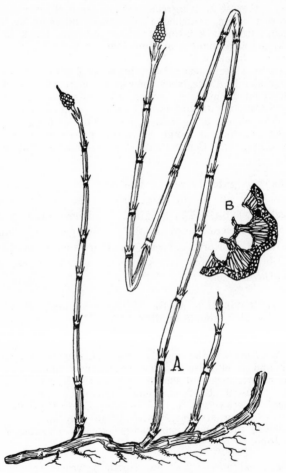

EQUISETUM VARIEGATUM

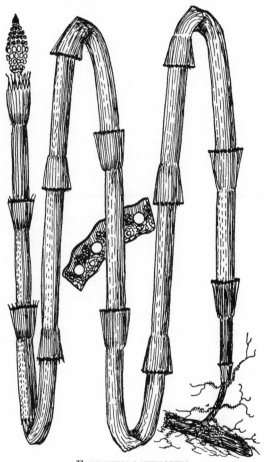

EQUISETUM LAEVIGATUM

locality cited with the original description is ''On poor
clayey soil, with *Andropogon* and other coarse grasses, at
the foot of the rocky Mississippi hills, on the banks of
the river, below St. Louis.'' The species was named in
1844.

9. E. praealtum Raf. Stems perennial, all alike,
rather stiff, evergreen, 6–31 dm. tall, stout or slender,
rough, 8–34-furrowed, the ridges with two indistinct lines
of tubercles, with the central cavity large, from one half
to two thirds the diameter, simple or rarely producing
branches which are usually short and occasionally
fertile; sheaths rather long-cylindric, marked with one or
two black girdles, their ridges obscurely 4-keeled, ending in brown membranous teeth, which are soon deciduous: cone ovoid, ellipsoid, or cylindric, 1.5–2.5 cm. long,
acute or abruptly pointed. [*Equisetum hyemale* Pursh,
not L. *E. robustum* A. Br. *E. hyemale affine* A. A.
Eaton.] —(SCOURING-RUSH. HORSE-PIPE. MARE'S-TAIL.
SHAVE-GRASS. DUTCH-RUSH. ROUGH-HORSETAIL. GUN-
BRIGHT.]—In wet places especially on river banks, wet
woods, and shaded slopes, general throughout our range,
except the pine-barrens and contiguous territory.—Spores
mature, May and June.

There is no lack of silex in the tissues of the scouring-
rush, as there is in those of the preceding species. This
mineral is so abundant that the stems of it were formerly used in rural districts in this country to scour tinware and other household and mechanical utensils. This
practice was also in vogue in the Old World. In describing this plant the author records that, ''A large
species akin to *E. hyemale,* grows on the banks of the
Mississippi [in Louisiana], in large bushes rising about
six feet; the stems are as thick as the finger: the cattle
are fond of it in winter, and the joiners employ it to
polish wood.'' The European *Equisetum hyemale* with
which this species is sometimes confused, occurs in
western North America, as well as in Asia. The typical
scouring-rush grows naturally from Florida to New
Mexico, British Columbia, Quebec, Massachusetts, and
North Carolina.

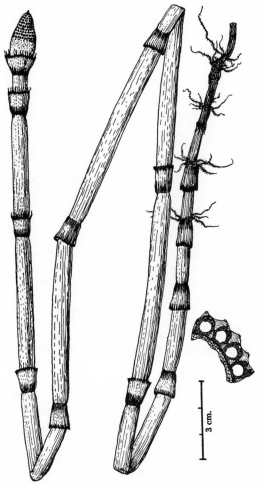

EQUISETUM PRAEALTUM

ORDER 5. **LYCOPODIALES**

Terrestrial or epiphytic, erect, creeping, or reclining plants. Sporangia borne in the axils of scale-like or elongate leaves (sporophyls), 1-celled or 2- or 3-celled. Spores all of one sort and size or of two kinds and sizes.—Embraces the following families:

KEY TO THE FAMILIES

Sporangia of one kind: spores minute, of one sort and size.
                      Family 1. LYCOPODIACEAE.

Sporangia of two kinds, some with many minute spores (microspores), others with few large spores (mega-spores).   Family 2. SELAGINELLACEAE.

FAMILY 1. **LYCOPODIACEAE**

CLUBMOSS FAMILY

Terrestrial or epiphytic plants, often resembling large mosses, with erect, trailing, or creeping stems. Leaves often numerous, in 2–several series, persistent: blades narrow or rarely broad. Sporangia 1-celled, solitary and hidden in the axils of leaf-like bracts (sporophyls), which sometimes form compact cones (strobiles, spikes). Spores uniform, minute. Prothallia (as far as known) monoecious, mostly subterranean.—Comprises three genera, the following and two others native of Australia.

1. **LYCOPODIUM** L.

Perennial, evergreen plants, various in habit. Leaves in 4–16 series, crowded or imbricate, radially spreading or twisted and lying in one plane: blades 1-veined. Sporangia usually reniform or subglobose, 1-celled, in the axils of more or less distinct leaf-like bracts or collected into terminal compact bracted cones, transversely 2-valved. Spores of one kind, sulphur-yellow, copious, readily inflammable.—CLUBMOSSES.—Contains about one hundred species of wide geographic distribution. Besides the following three other species occur in the southeastern states.—The genus is based on *Lycopodium clavatum* L.—The name is Greek, meaning wolf's-foot, used perhaps in some fancied allusion to some part of the plant.

Sporophyls not closely associated in terminal cones : plants gemmiparous in the upper leaf-axils.

    Stems and branches erect or stiffly up-curved from a short rootstock, tufted or densely matted : leaves entire or with an occasional minute tooth-like process on the side, not broadened above the middle.   I. SELAGONES.

    Stems and branches diffusely assurgent or widely spreading from an elongate rootstock or creeping bases : leaves toothed, broadened above the middle.   II. LUCIDULA.

Sporophyls closely associated in terminal cones : plants not gemmiparous.

    Sporophyls nearly or quite similar to the foliage leaves : sporangia subglobose.   III. PROSTRATA.

    Sporophyls specialized, unlike the foliage leaves, usually much broader and shorter : sporangia reniform.

        Stem prostrate or creeping, without leafy aerial branches, the erect, elongate scaly, cone-peduncles arising directly from the prostrate stem.   IV. CAROLINIANA.

        Stem subterranean or aerial, with numerous erect or assurgent leafy branches.

            Leaves of the ultimate branches in 6 or more rows, spreading, not scale-like : cones sessile at the end of the peduncle.

            Main stem (rootstock) spreading deep in the ground : aerial branches few, tree-like.   V. OBSCURA.

            Main stem merely prostrate : branches numerous, not tree-like.

                Cone solitary, sessile : leaves spine-tipped.   VI. ANNOTINA.

                Cones several, or individually solitary, long-peduncled : leaves hair-tipped.   VII. CLAVATA.

            Leaves of the ultimate branches in 4 rows, appressed, scale-like : cones stalked at the end of the peduncle.   VIII. COMPLANATA.

I. SELAGONES

Leaves ascending or appressed, acuminate. — 1. *L. Selago.*

Leaves spreading or partially reflexed, attenuate. — 2. *L. porophilum.*

II. LUCIDULA

Plant with diffusely assurgent or widely spreading stems and branches which are copiously clothed with spreading or reflexed shining leaves borne in irregular zones. — 3. *L. lucidulum.*

III. PROSTRATA

Sporophyls less than 6 mm. long, incurved, the base entire or nearly so : stems prostrate : leaves in several rows but more or less distichous.

Sporophyls lanceolate above the somewhat dilated base, which is entire or with a tooth on each side. — 4. *L. inundatum.*

Sporophyls subulate above a slightly dilated, sharply toothed base. — 5. *L. adpressum.*

Sporophyls over 8 mm. long, not incurved, attenuate-subulate, the base jagged-toothed : stems recurved or arching : leaves in many ranks, spreading radially. — 6. *L. alopecuroides.*

IV. CAROLINIANA

Creeping plant with the main stem leafless on the under side, but there rooting freely, the lateral leaves widely spreading. — 7. *L. carolinianum.*

V. OBSCURA

Subterranean rootstock giving off, irregularly, erect tree-like branches which are copiously leafy. — 8. *L. obscurum.*

VI. ANNOTINA

Branches from the main stem numerous, simple or forking, with very numerous spreading or reflexed leaves : cones sessile. — 9. *L. annotinum.*

VII. CLAVATA

Branches from the main stem irregular, mostly forked, copiously leafy, some of the branchlets terminating in a long peduncle which is topped by a cone or a cluster of cones. — 10. *L. clavatum.*

VIII. COMPLANATA

Ultimate branches conspicuously flattened : leaves of the under row greatly reduced, minute, triangular-cuspidate. — 11. *L. flabelliforme.*

Ultimate branches narrower and less
flattened : leaves of the under row
scarcely smaller, acicular.   12. *L. tristachyum.*

1. L. Selago L. Stem and branches rigidly erect
from a short slender curved base, several times dichotomous, the vertical branches forming compact, even tufts
or mats, 5–15 cm. long: leaves uniform, crowded, ascending (or appressed in *L. Selago adpressum*); blades narrowly deltoid-lanceolate or somewhat acicular from a
broader base, shining, pale-green or yellowish, 4–8 mm.
long, usually entire, acute: sporophyls (below the summit) a little shorter than the foliage leaves: plant often
gemmiparous. — (Fir-clubmoss.) — Rocks and shaded
cliffs, Appalachian Valley, Mount Minsi, Delaware Water
Gap, Pennsylvania.—Spores mature, September and
October.

The genus *Lycopodium* is represented in eastern North
America by about sixteen species. The great majority
of them are common to both north and the south. Two
species are confined to the southeastern states, while four
in the northeastern states do not reach the North Caro-
lina-Virginia state line. The original specimens of
Lycopodium Selago were of European origin and the
species was named in 1753. The plant is also Asiatic.
In the New World the geographic range extends from
Arctic America southward, gradually gaining altitude
until it reaches the high mountain summits over 6000
feet in the southern Blue Ridge. A subspecies occurs in
Quebec and Vermont. In addition to the common name
fir-clubmoss, the plant is known as fir-moss, tree-moss,
dwarf staghorn-moss, fox-feet. Cold cliffs and rocks
are the usual habitats, and apparently the plant is confined to the older geologic formations.

2. L. porophilum Lloyd & Underw. Stem and
branches rising 5–10 cm. from a curved or short-decum-
bent base, 1–3-times dichotomous, the branches densely
leafy, vertical, close: leaves bright-green, spreading or
somewhat deflexed, 4–7 mm. long; blades entire or
minutely denticulate, arranged in alternating zones of
longer and shorter, the former linear, not broad above
the middle, attenuate, the latter distinctly broadest at
the base, tapering thence to an acuminate apex: sporo-

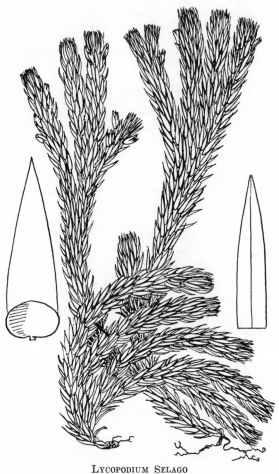

LYCOPODIUM SELAGO

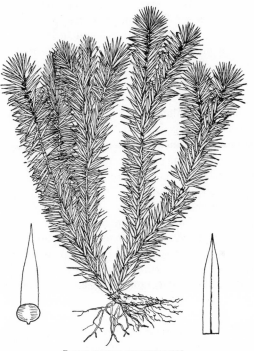

LYCOPODIUM POROPHILUM

phyls tapering from a broad base to the apex: plant
often gemmiparous. [*Lycopodium lucidulum porophilum*
Clute.]—(ROCK-CLUBMOSS.)—Partially shaded rocks,
usually sandstone, known in our range only in the Appalachian plateau province, Pike County, Pennsylvania.—
Spores mature, August to October.

The usual habitats of our lycopods range from rocks
and dry woods to marshes and swamps. As the specific
name indicates, the plants of the present species are
rock-lovers. In this character and in its habit the plants
resemble those of the more northern *Lycopodium Selago,*
and in the minute characters they are also related to that
species. The geographic distribution is unique in North
America, being chiefly in the central United States between the highlands and the Mississippi River. The
other rock-loving lycopod, *L. Selago,* ranges southward
only on the summits of the Blue Ridge. Curiously
enough, this plant eluded not only botanists, but also
collectors, in a region where there was much plant activity for nearly a century. Then within seven years after
it was discovered in Indiana, in 1891, it was successively
found in Wisconsin, Kentucky, Alabama, and Pennsylvania. The petrographic range of the plant, like the geologic range, is also limited, for as far as known it occurs
only on weathered sedimentary outcrops. It has not been
found on the older igneous rocks to which the related
species, *Lycopodium Selago,* is largely confined. A few
hundred feet represent its maximum altitude in our
range.—The American name *Lycopodium porophilum* is
still retained for this plant although it may be found
that it is identical with the European plant described as
Lycopodium recurvum Willd. or *Plananthus patens* Beauv.

3. L. lucidulum Michx. Stem and branches rising
1.5–2.5 dm. from a decumbent base, 1–3 times dichotomous, the few leafy vertical branches often loosely clustered: leaves dark-green, shining, wide-spreading or finally
deflexed; blades acute and firm-tipped, broadened upward, oblanceolate, broadest above the middle and there
erose-serrulate, tapering to a narrower base, 8–11 mm.
long, arranged in alternating zones of longer and shorter

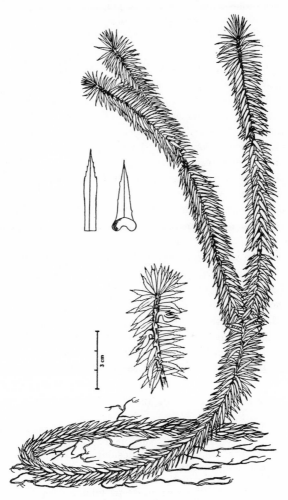

Lycopodium lucidulum

leaves: sporophyls shorter than the foliage leaves and less denticulate, or entire: plant often gemmiparous.— (STAGHORN-MOSS.   TRAILING-EVERGREEN.) — Low cool, often damp, woods, general in our range, except in the pine-barrens of New Jersey.—Spores mature, July to September.

The preceding species is a cliff or rock dweller, so to speak. The present species, its most closely related one in habit, is a wood-plant. It is also larger, and of quite different aspect. The author of the species, in naming and describing it, recorded (1803) that the plant ranged from Canada to the Carolina mountains. Since this original record was made the geographic range has been extended so that it includes boreal North America south to South Carolina, Tennessee, and Iowa. The species is represented nearly as high as 4000 feet in our area, and plants grow luxuriantly at an altitude of about 6000 feet in the southern highlands. Besides the popular name trailing-evergreen, the plant is also known as shining-clubmoss and moon-fruit pine. The development of the foliage of the trailing-evergreen is almost unique among our lycopods. The leaves are extremely hardy and long-persistent, even when buried in acid humus in which the plants often grow. On the aerial branches they are developed in zones of seasonal growths, long and short, often to such an extent that the branches have a ragged appearance. This character is shown to a less degree in the growth of the preceding species.

4. L. inundatum L. Stem and branches prostrate, creeping, 1–2 dm. long, very leafy: cauline leaves more or less spreading; blades lanceolate to linear-lanceolate, 3–6 mm. long, entire: cone-bearing branches (peduncles) slender, arising directly from the prostrate stem, 0.5 dm. tall, with erect linear-subulate to subulate leaves, passing abruptly into the cone: cones cylindric or nearly so, stout, 1–2 cm. long; sporophyls lanceolate, lax but somewhat incurved, sometimes toothed at the base: sporangia about as wide as the dilated base of the sporophyl.— (BOG-CLUBMOSS.)—Sandy shores and sphagnum bogs, various provinces, in our range in northern Pennsylvania,

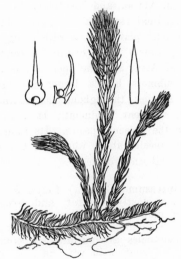

LYCOPODIUM INUNDATUM

northern New Jersey, and Connecticut.—Spores mature, August to October.

The geographic distribution of the lycopods is interesting from several different angles. In the present case, as in that of *Lycopodium annotinum*, both northern types, the southern limit closely follows the east-west line of the terminal moraine of the Ice Ages. Its general range is through various plant provinces, from northern New Jersey to southern Pennsylvania, Illinois, Idaho, Washington, Alaska, and Newfoundland, with but rather slight altitudinal range in our area. The bog-clubmoss is not a robust plant, but is rather suggestive of weakness and puniness. The original specimens came from Europe and Asia, and the species was named in 1753. The bog-clubmoss has a larger counterpart the next following species, throughout the southeastern Coastal Plain and adjacent Piedmont. It is a more abundant plant than the present species. Its range meets that of the present species about where the Coastal Plain meets the more northern provinces.

5. L. adpressum (Chapm.) Lloyd & Underw. Stem and branches mostly prostrate and creeping, 1.5–4 dm. long, often simple, very leafy: cauline-leaves lanceolate-acuminate, 6–7 mm. long, curved upward, irregularly toothed: peduncles arising directly from the creeping stem, 1–3 dm. long, with very narrow, incurved, mostly appressed, yellowish-green leaves, those near the base toothed, those above nearly or quite entire: cone elongate, slender-cylindric, 2–12 cm. long: sporophyls mostly incurved and subappressed, subulate above a slightly broader more or less toothed base. [*L. inundatum Bigelovii* Tuckerm. *L. Chapmanii* Underw.]—(CHAPMAN'S CLUBMOSS.) — Moist banks, bogs, and borders of swamps, usually in acid soil, Coastal Plain and adjacent Piedmont, New Jersey and eastern Pennsylvania to Connecticut.—Spores mature, August to October.

This lycopod is intermediate in habit, as well as technical characters, between *Lycopodium carolinianum* and the following species. It is less stiff than the former and more stiff than the following. The leaves of the

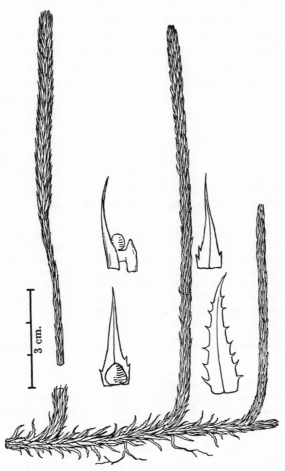

3 cm.

LYCOPODIUM ADPRESSUM

peduncle are placed close together and rather loosely imbricate. The leaves of the prostrate-creeping stem and
branches are very numerous and are not distinctly distichous as they are in *L. carolinianum*. It was discovered in Florida about the middle of the last century and
named in 1883. It occurs in the Coastal Plain, and
locally in the adjacent Piedmont, and consequently does
not reach any great altitude, ranging from Florida to
Louisiana and Massachusetts. This species has a smaller
counterpart, *Lycopodium inundatum*, in the region northward. The ranges of the two meet about where the
Coastal Plain meets the more northern provinces. Like
Lycopodium carolinianum this is typically a southern
species. However, if it migrated from the southern
Coastal Plain it adapted itself more readily than did the
Carolina-lycopod, both in the extent of its range as indicated above, and the abundance of growth.

 6. L. alopecuroides L. Stem and branches stout,
mostly recurved and more or less arching, 3–6 dm. long,
densely leafy throughout: cauline leaves very numerous,
spreading in all directions; blades narrowly lanceolate
or linear-lanceolate, mostly 6–8 mm. long, irregularly
saliently toothed: peduncles stout, 2–3 dm. tall, arising
usually from the arches of the stem, copiously leafy, the
leaves nearly similar to those of the stem, but narrower,
lax or ascending: cones stout-cylindric, 2.5–10 cm. long:
sporophyls similar to the leaves of the peduncle, but
much longer, broader and few-toothed at the base, ascending, spreading, or finally reflexed: sporangia globose.
—(Fox-tail clubmoss.)—Wet pinelands, bogs, and borders of swamps, Coastal Plain, New Jersey to Long
Island, New York.—Spores mature, September and
October.

The fox-tail lycopod, while plants of the next preceding species sometimes equal it in size, is, in general, the
most conspicuous member of the genus in our flora. If
plants of the preceding species have more feathery stems
and branches, those of the present one have more showy
plume-like cones. It was first found in Virginia and
"Canada" early in the eighteenth century, Canada having

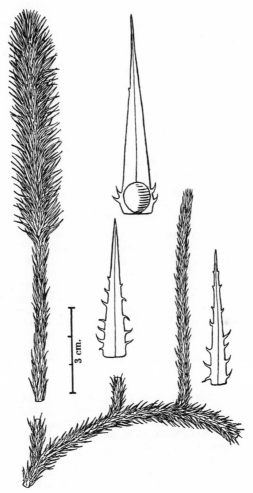

3 cm.

LYCOPODIUM ALOPECUROIDES

been used by Linnaeus in a very broad sense, for this is
a southern type which reaches its northern limit on Nan-
tucket, Massachusetts. It is the most outstanding lycopod in our range, the peculiar growth of the stems and
the large bushy cones, whence its popular name, individ-
ualizing it. It ranges in the Coastal Plain with but little
elevation above sea-level, from Florida to Mississippi and
Massachusetts. After a great interruption in its range
southward, it appears again in northern South America.
Although this showy clubmoss is in a group with the
two preceding species, it stands well isolated by habit
and by technical characters, and has no counterpart in
the north. It may be interesting to note that it has a
counterpart within its own range, namely *Lycopodium
prostratum*, but this plant does not reach our area, being
known only from Florida, Alabama, and Georgia.

7. **L. carolinianum** L. Stem and branches prostrate
and creeping, usually closely appressed to the ground,
1–15 cm. long, pinnately branching: cauline leaves of 2
kinds, blades of the apparently lateral ones ovate-lanceolate, 5–6 mm. long, somewhat falcate, recurved, acute or
short-acuminate, entire, with the midrib asymmetrically
placed: leaves of the upper side of the stem 3–4 mm.
long; blades subulate above the dilated base: peduncle
slender, 5–22 cm. tall, with few whorled or scattered,
narrow, entire leaves: cones slender-cylindric, 1–5 cm.
long, decidedly thicker than the supporting peduncle:
sporophyls triangular-ovate in outline, acuminate, usually
shallowly toothed all around: sporangia compressed,
reniform, narrower than the dilated bases of the sporophyls. — (CAROLINA CLUB-MOSS.) — Sandy bogs, swamps,
and damp pinelands, Coastal Plain, pine-barrens of New
Jersey and New York, and contiguous area.—Spores mature, August to November.

The plants of this species are more slender than those
of any of its relatives with the same habit of growth.
It differs from the other kinds in the relatively few and
separate rigid leaves of the peduncle and the rigid short-
tipped sporophyls which are closely imbricate at their
bases. It prefers to grow in open sandy places where
the main stem and its branches lie closely appressed to

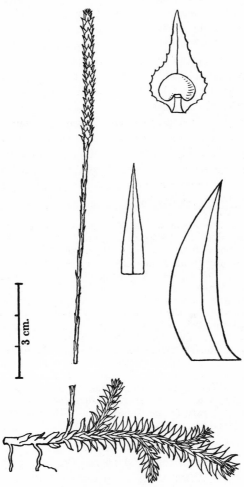

3 cm.

LYCOPODIUM CAROLINIANUM

the ground with the leaves of the lower plane stiffly
spreading as if two-ranked. It was first found in the
Carolinas in the earlier part of the eighteenth century,
and was named in 1753. Its geographical range extends
from Florida westward to Mississippi and northward in
the Coastal Plain to New Jersey and Long Island, New
York. Being an inhabitant of the coastal region in our
range, its altitudinal range is therefore slight. This
southern lycopod has been known from the New Jersey
coastal regions since the earlier days of local botanical
activities. Curiously enough, it was not found on Long
Island, New York, until 1921. It occurs there in typical
form in Suffolk County. This fact carries with it a definite suggestion that the curly-grass (*Schizaea pusilla*)
may grow there too since these two plants are almost in-
separable associates in the pine-barrens of New Jersey.

8. L. obscurum L. Main stem creeping horizontally,
usually deep in the ground, giving off a few distant up-
right aerial branches 1–2.5 dm. high, these tree-like with
few or numerous bushy branches: leaves 8-ranked on the
lower branches, 6-ranked on the terminal ultimate ones,
those of the upper and lower series smaller than the
others and appressed, (or equal and erect or incurved in
L. obscurum dendroideum); blades linear-lanceolate,
curved upward, twisted (especially above), the branches
thus more or less dorsiventral: cones slender, conic-cylindric or almost cylindric, 1.5–5.5 cm. long: sporophyls
broadly ovate, subulate, the margins scarious and erose.
[Including *Lycopodium dendroideum* Michx.]—(GROUND-
PINE.)—Woods, often coniferous, in dry or moist usually
strongly acid soil, various provinces, throughout our
range, but rare in the pine-barrens.—Spores mature, July
to September.

The genus *Lycopodium* has, through the ages, developed different lines of descent. On the morphological
characters shown along these lines the genus may definitely be divided into groups or subgenera. In the case
of *Lycopodium*, at least in our region, these groups are
mostly clear-cut. Some of them consist of but one species,
while others comprise several. The present species
varies little in size and habit even at the extremes of its

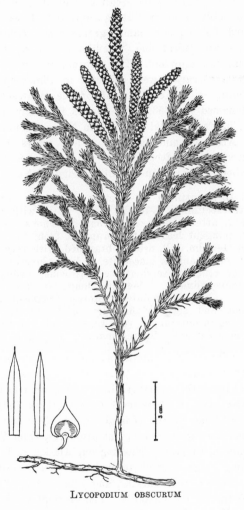

LYCOPODIUM OBSCURUM

geographic range. It is rather constant in the morphological characters and in its habit. It is a very outstanding plant and its peculiar habit of growth, creating
a resemblance to miniature coniferous trees early suggested its popular name, ground-pine. Other popular
names are spiral-pine, tree-like club-moss, bunch-ever-
green, and crowfoot. The original specimens of *Lycopodium obscurum* were collected at Philadelphia, Pennsylvania, in the earlier half of the eighteenth century
and named in 1753. The species is widely distributed,
ranging from boreal America to North Carolina, Tennessee, Alabama, and Indiana; it also grows in Asia. It
occurs at 2500 feet altitude in the Pocono region and
at about the same in the Blue Ridge of North Carolina.

9. L. annotinum L. Stem and branches creeping or
partly reclining, 3–10 dm. long, wiry, with irregularly
placed, often spaced, somewhat distichous, firm, lanceolate, pungent leaves; the branches from the main stem
erect, 1–3 dm. tall, usually branched, with very numerous,
close-set, 8-ranked, lanceolate or linear-lanceolate, spreading or reflexed, serrulate leaves: cone sessile, cylindric
or conic-cylindric, 1.5–4 cm. long: sporophyls broadly
ovate, abruptly pointed, erose.—(STIFF-CLUBMOSS.)—
Woods and scrubby hillsides, north of the terminal
moraine in our range; very rare outside the Catskill and
Pocono plateaus.—Spores mature, August to November.

A mixture of southern and northern types of lycopods
constitutes our representation of the genus *Lycopodium.*
Some reach their northern limit in our area (*Lycopodium
carolinianum*); others reach their southern limit in about
our latitude, in the coastal region. The stiff-clubmoss
ranges through various plant provinces, from Virginia to
Michigan, Colorado, Washington, Alaska, and Labrador,
making its greatest altitudinal record in the Adirondacks
and the White Mountains, and attaining nearly or quite
4000 feet in the Catskills. The original specimens came
from Europe where the species was named in 1753. It
also occurs in Asia. Like the following species and the
Christmas-greens, this is a dry woods or sometimes a bog
plant. Its usual dry soil habitat seems to be reflected

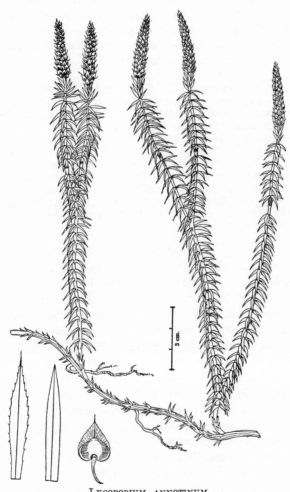

LYCOPODIUM ANNOTINUM

in the plant itself, for the tissues usually are hard and the stems rigid and wiry, as is also the case in the running-pine. Although the cones are solitary on a branch, they are often conspicuous on account of numbers, for the cone-bearing branches may be many together and the cones themselves bright-yellow. The plant is also known as interrupted-clubmoss.

10. L. clavatum L. Stem and branches creeping, 3–9 dm. long, stiff, with close-set or imbricate, appressed, linear-lanceolate, denticulate, pungent leaves; the branches from the main stem erect or ascending, 1–2 dm. long, branched, with very numerous, crowded, many-ranked, hair-tipped, linear-lanceolate leaves: cones narrowly cylindric, usually 2–4 together, (solitary in *L. clavatum monostachyon*), 2–7 cm. long: sporophyls deltoid or ovate-deltoid, bristle-tipped, with erose, scarious margins.—(RUNNING-PINE.) — Dry or moist woods, various provinces, north of the pine-barrens.—Spores mature, August to October.

Like many plants of ancient types this lycopod is circumboreal in its distribution. The original specimens came from Europe and were named in 1753. The species was found in North America during the early years of botanical activity and later its geographic range was shown to be very wide, extending from the highlands of North Carolina and Virginia to Michigan, Washington, Alaska, and Labrador. It is represented in tropical America and Asia. Like the Christmas-greens this plant thrives in dry woods, and produces remarkably long stems, when the sterile soil and scanty supply of moisture are considered. Besides the wide geographic distribution extending through many plant provinces, the altitudinal range is great. The maximum in our area is in the Catskills, while fully 6000 feet in the Blue Ridge, North Carolina overtops all other records. As a result of its wide distribution many popular names have become associated with the plant: running-moss, buck's-grass, fox-tail, staghorn-moss, snake-moss, ground-pine, creeping-jennie, buck's-horn, wolf's-claws, toad's-tail.

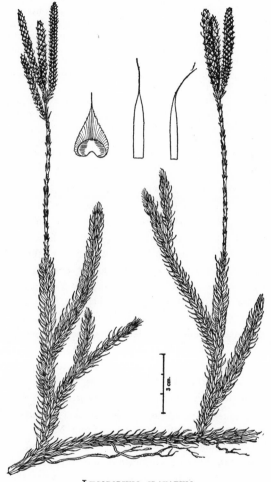

LYCOPODIUM CLAVATUM

11. L. flabelliforme (Fernald) Blanchard. Stem and branches horizontal, wide-creeping along the ground, flattish above, with many erect, irregularly forked, aerial branches or branchlets, the branches broadly flattened, 2- or 3-forked, the divisions few, or often numerous and fan-like, leafy throughout: leaves 4-ranked, minute and (excepting those of the under row) imbricate and decurrent, those of the upper row narrow and incurved, of the lateral rows broad, with spreading tips, and of the under row triangular-cuspidate, spreading: cone-bearing branches slender, 2–13 cm. (usually 6–10 cm.) long, bracteate, simple to twice-dichotomous: cones slender, cylindric, 1.5–2.5 cm. long: sporophyls broadly ovate, acuminate. [*Lycopodium complanatum flabelliforme* Fernald.]—(GROUND-CEDAR. RUNNING-CEDAR.)—Dry, deciduous or coniferous woods, various provinces, general except the pine-barrens.—Spores mature, August.

This and the following species constitute a natural group, with a characteristic growth habit as well as morphological characters. Contrary to the choice of many of our species of *Lycopodium*, these two plants prefer dry, often coniferous woods for their habitat. Curiously enough, in spite of the dryness of their habitats and often sterility of the soil, the stem and branches of these two plants frequently become very long. They trail over the ground under herbs and shrubs. In the autumn the plants are usually buried in leaves, being visible only through the long-peduncled yellow cones that protrude above the forest carpet. Accompanying the original description of this species, when it was named in 1753, the geographic range was given as Europe and America. As known in North America the area extends through various plant provinces, from North Carolina to Indiana, Idaho, Alaska, and Newfoundland. With a wide geographic and altitudinal distribution, at 2500 feet in the Pocono region and up to nearly 4000 feet in the Blue Ridge of North Carolina and Tennessee, this plant has received many popular names, such as: trailing Christmas-green, festoon-pine, crowfoot, hag-bed, and creeping-jennie.

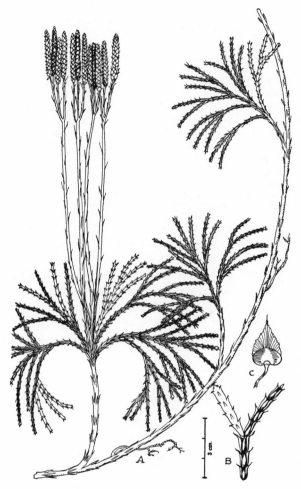

LYCOPODIUM FLABELLIFORME

12. L. tristachyum Pursh.   Stem and branches horizontal, widely creeping, often 2–10 cm. below the surface
of the ground, terete, with numerous erect or assurgent,
much-forked aerial branches or branchlets, the branches
narrow, flattish, with very numerous, crowded, erect
divisions, the ultimate ones leafy throughout: leaves
4-ranked, minute, imbricate, appressed, strongly decurrent, nearly equal and alike, those of the lateral rows a
little thicker, with the tips usually incurved downward:
cone-bearing branches 7–13 cm. long, bracteate, usually
twice-dichotomous at the summit: spike and sporophyls
nearly similar to those of the preceding.   [*L. Chamaecyparissus* A. Br.]—(GROUND-CEDAR.)—Dryish open woods
or clearings, usually in sandy soil, various provinces,
throughout our range, but very rare in the pine-barrens.
—Spores mature, July and August.

The earlier discovered and described related species of
this group in our range, *L. flabelliforme,* has a wide geographic distribution at the north, ranging up into Arctic
North America.   The present species is also mainly
boreal, though its range falls short of the Arctic regions,
and while it extends slightly further south than the
ground-cedar, it covers considerably less territory.   The
original specimens were American, having been collected
on high mountains in Virginia near the Sweet Springs.
The species was named in 1814, independently in America and Europe.   The plants of this species have somewhat the same habit of growth as those of *Lycopodium
flabelliforme,* but the rootstock is subterranean and all
the parts usually slightly smaller.   It ranges through
various plant provinces from the highlands of Georgia to
Minnesota and Maine, reaching 2500 feet in the Pocono
region.

FAMILY 2.   SELAGINELLACEAE

SPIKE-MOSS FAMILY

Annual or perennial, often moss-like, very leafy
plants, with usually much-branched stems.   Leaves
scale-like, uniform and several-ranked, or of 2 kinds
and in 2 planes.   Sporangia 1-celled, of two kinds,
disposed in 4-sided cones, solitary in the axils of

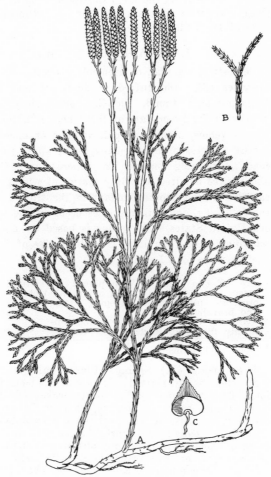

LYCOPODIUM TRISTACHYUM

bracts, some (megasporangia) containing 4 megaspores, others (microsporangia) containing numerous microspores; the spores develop into small prothallia, those from the megaspores bearing archegones,
those from the microspores bearing antherids.—Consists of the following genus:

1. SELAGINELLA Beauv.

Terrestrial, paludal, or arenicolous plants. Stems and
branches erect and tufted or depressed and creeping.
Megasporangia tumid, globular or slightly elongate,
usually in the lower part of the cone, containing mostly
3 or 4 yellow, orange, or red, angular or uneven megaspores. Microsporangia usually in the upper part of the
cone, containing powder-like microspores.—Comprises
about three hundred and fifty species of wide geographical distribution, most abundant in the tropics. Besides
the following, four other species occur in the southeastern United States.—The genus is based on *Lycopodium
selaginoides* L.—The name is a diminutive of *Selago*, an
ancient name of a Lycopod.

Leaves of two kinds, in two planes, the lateral ones the
　larger and 2-ranked; blades not bristle-tipped: diffuse or
　prostrate plants with creeping stems
　and branches.　　　　　　　　　　　　　　1. *S. apoda.*
Leaves all alike, several-ranked and uni-
　formly disposed; blades bristle-tipped:
　tufted plants with erect or ascending
　stems and branches.　　　　　　　　　　2. *S. rupestris.*

1. S. apoda (L.) Spring. Plants pale-green, creeping, often loosely matted: stems and branches 5–15 cm.
long, flaccid, pinnately branched: leaves of the lower
plane ovate, acute or acutish, sharply fine-toothed on
the margins, those of the upper plane lanceolate or ovate-
lanceolate, acuminate, shortly spine-pointed, minutely
toothed: cones 6–15 mm. long, obscurely 4-angled: sporophyls ovate or ovate-lanceolate, acuminate, minutely
toothed above the base, acutely keeled above: megasporangia 0.5–0.6 mm. in diameter. [*Lycopodium apodum*
L.]—(Creeping-selaginella. Meadow Spike-moss.)—
Wet woods, meadows, muddy, mossy, or grassy places in
and about swamps, along streams, and ditches, various
provinces, throughout our range.—Spores mature, June to
September.

SELAGINELLA APODA

The majority of selaginellas prefer to grow in dry soil or even on dry rocks. However, the present species and its relatives are more at home in moist places. This creeping-selaginella was first recorded from Carolina, Virginia, and Pennsylvania in the earlier half of the eighteenth century. It is widely distributed and ranges through various plant provinces, from Florida to Texas, British Columbia, and Maine, reaching an altitude of at least 1000 feet in our area and still higher in the southern highlands. Besides growing in its natural situations, this plant has a habit of suddenly appearing in moist lawns and well-watered flower-beds. The creeping pellucid plants of this species so much resemble a hepatic that the novice often does not realize that a selaginella is involved, especially in the stage before the cones of sporangia are formed. Sometimes, because of elongate branches, the growth is open and lace-like, but at other times a copious growth of many short branches give it the form of a mat. However, the plants are never densely tufted as in the case of the following spike-moss, *Selaginella rupestris*.

2. **S. rupestris** (L.) Spring. Plants dark-green or gray-green, more or less creeping, but often tufted: stems and branches 5–10 cm. long, zigzag, ascending at the tips; primary branches short: leaves closely imbricate, about 8-ranked, 0.3–0.38 mm. wide, deeply channeled dorsally, with 6–9 cilia on each side, tipped with a white spinulose awn about 1 mm. long: cones 1–1.5 cm. long, sharply 4-angled: sporophyls similar to the leaves but broader and with short awns and more cilia. [*Lycopodium rupestre* L.]—(DWARF-LYCOPOD. ROCK-SELAGINELLA. ROCK SPIKE-MOSS.)—Dry rocks, throughout our range except the Coastal Plain, but in scattered localities.— Spores mature, June to September.

Our dwarf-lycopods made a rather scant specific showing up to about the end of the past century, because of the neglect of students of this group. Nearly every plant resembling the present species in habit was referred to *Selaginella rupestris*. Two species were found to be generally distributed in eastern North America.

SELAGINELLA RUPESTRIS

Another was restricted to the northeast, while the fourth
one was confined to the lowlands of the southeast, and
a fifth to the highlands. The five species fell into two
groups, which are both represented by one of the two
species in our range. Three of the five species, *Selaginella apoda, S. selaginoides,* and *S. rupestris,* were known
to Linnaeus. The fourth and fifth species, *S. ludo-
viciana* and *S. tortipila,* were described much later than
the Linnaean period. After a half-century of inactivity,
studies resulted in a considerable increase in the number
of our species, particularly in Florida and contiguous
territory. When originally named, in 1753, the dwarf-
lycopod treated here was said to occur in Virginia, Canada, and Siberia. At present the known geographical
range of this plant extends from Georgia to Missouri,
Ontario and Maine. In our area it occurs from near
sea-level to almost 4000 feet in the Catskills, and to
nearly 6000 feet in the southern Blue Ridge. Contrary
to the evident creeping and hepatic-like habit of *Selaginella apoda,* this plant has a tufted growth resembling
that of the apocarpous mosses. The stems and branches,
repeatedly divided, usually have short internodes and
slow growth, probably due to the lack of moisture and
poor soil. Through generous multiplication, rigid, copiously leafy branches accumulate *in situ* and make dense
tufts, the real creeping habit being thus hidden.

ORDER 6. **ISOETALES**[1]

Aquatic, amphibious, or uliginous plants. Leaves
in a crown, elongate-subulate rising from a more or
less 2–3-lobed, or rarely 5-lobed, fleshy short stem,

[1] This treatment of *Isoetales* is in accordance with the
"Monograph of Isoetaceae" by Norma E. Pfeiffer. A
simple figure, drawn by Dr. Pfeiffer, is given to illustrate the quillworts. The plants of the several species
are rather uniform in habit, except that the amphibious
or submerged aquatic forms often have loosely or widely
spreading leaves. The diagnostic characters lie largely
in the size and marking of the megaspores.

each bearing a small membranous member (ligule) within above the base. Sporangia sessile, solitary, each in a basal cavity of a leaf, more or less covered with a fold of tissue on the inner side of the leaf-blades (velum); sporangia of two sorts, variously distributed; one sort containing few large (tetrahedral) mostly sculptured megaspores, the other containing minute powdery oval microspores; the former germinate into prothallia bearing only archegones, the latter into prothallia bearing a single antherid.—Contains only the following family:

FAMILY 1. ISOETACEAE

QUILLWORT FAMILY

Aquatic to terrestrial herbs with a short unbranched, lobed, subterranean axis producing many dichotomous roots and grass-like leaves, the enlarged bases of which contain solitary, sessile, adaxial sporangia, more or less covered by a thin extension of tissue or velum. Sporangia of two sorts, producing large tetrahedral megaspores and minute powdery microspores, respectively.—Owing to their elusive habit and more or less aquatic habitats, the species are popularly little known.

1. ISOETES L.

Perennials, submerged, amphibious, or terrestrial, with a 2- or 3-lobed, short fleshy axis or corm giving rise to numerous branched roots and to a rosette of elongate, somewhat triangular or quadrangular leaves. Leaves with 4 transversely septate, longitudinal air-channels, with central fibro-vascular bundle; peripheral groups of supporting cells present or absent; stomata present or absent. Ligule a small, delicate triangular extension of tissue on the inner face of a leaf above the sporangium. Sporangium solitary, sessile, on adaxial side of a leaf, contained in a basal cavity, and more or less covered by a membranous tissue, the velum, on the inner leaf-face.

Sporangia of two types, microsporangia and megasporangia, bearing respectively microspores and megaspores, which on germination develop gametophytes, the former with a single antherid, the latter with an archegone. Megaspores hemispherical at base, with an equatorial ridge, and three other crests joined at the apex, with variously sculptured walls. Microspores minute, powdery, usually oval.—QUILLWORTS.—About sixty-five species, of wide geographic distribution.—The genus is based on *Isoetes lacustris* L.—The name is ancient Greek, apparently applied to some succulent plant.

Megaspores with chiefly spiny surfaces.   I. ECHINATAE.
Megaspores with irregularly crested or
   reticulate surfaces.
   Megaspores irregularly crested.   II. CRISTATAE.
   Megaspores reticulate, at least on the
     basal face.   III. RETICULATAE.

I. ECHINATAE

Submersed plant with usually numerous
   leaves up to 25 cm. long and bearing
   stomata: megaspores with sharp
   spines.   1. *I. Braunii.*

II. CRISTATAE

Megaspores marked with very densely
   crowded prominences.   2. *I. Eatoni.*
Megaspores marked with less densely
   crowded prominences.   3. *I. riparia.*

III. RETICULATAE

Submersed plants: leaves with very few
   or no stomata.
   Megaspores chiefly 600–800 μ in di-
    ameter.   4. *I. macrospora.*
   Megaspores chiefly 460–600 μ in di-
    ameter.   5. *I. Tuckermani.*
Amphibious plants: leaves with stomata,
   at least near the tip.   6. *I. Engelmanni.*

1. I. Braunii Durieu. Corm 2-lobed: leaves usually 10–35, in robust forms 27–55, 8–25 cm. long, or rarely longer, straight or recurved, firm, tapering to apex, with rather wide base with membranaceous borders; stomata present, usually few; peripheral strands none; ligule deltoid; sporangia oblong, spotted, 4–7 mm. long, with the velum ½ to completely covering it; megaspores white, 420–580 μ in diameter, marked with numerous spines ranging from simple slender spines to those toothed or even confluent in short ridges; microspores fawn-colored, 23–33 μ long, smooth to slightly roughened on the sur-

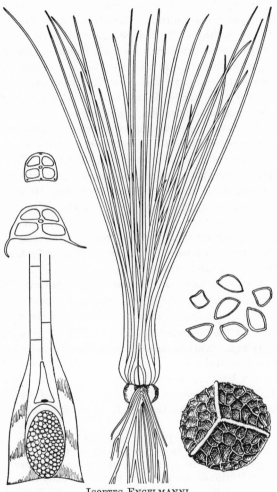

ISOETES ENGELMANNI

face.—Ponds, lakes, and slow streams, various provinces throughout our range.

Among North American quillworts, this species has the widest distribution, extending across the continent in the northern United States and southern Canada, with only one region for which stations have not been reported to date. It also represents the quillwort most frequently seen in the New England and New York territory, in ponds, lakes, or slow streams, with wide variation in substratum, including soft mud, sandy bottom, gravel, or even rocky crevices. Related to the submersed habit is the relative scarcity of stomata. The species is readily identified by means of the white spiny megaspores which mature in the latter part of the summer. Many varieties have been described. The original specimens came from Lake Winnepesaukee, New Hampshire. The species was named in 1864. The general distribution ranges from New Jersey to Ohio, California, British Columbia, Ontario, Quebec, Newfoundland, and Greenland.

A stouter form, *I. Braunii* f. *robusta*, with leaves as numerous as 75, 12–15 cm. long and usually with more stomata than the species, resembles it in the spiny character of the megaspores, although they are less regular in markings. This is one of the quillworts which deserves experimental work in order to clarify its relationships. It has been considered worthy of specific rank by A. A. Eaton who called it *I. Gravesii*, and of varietal rank by Clute, who considered it *I. valida Gravesii*.

2. **I. Eatoni** R. Dodge. Corm 2-lobed; leaves 25–200, 10–60 cm. in length, much shorter in summer (10–15 cm. long), coarser in spring forms; stomata numerous; peripheral strands variable in number, sometimes wanting: sporangia oblong, 6–11 mm. long, brown-spotted, $\frac{1}{6}$–$\frac{1}{4}$ covered by the velum; megaspores white, 396–520 μ, rarely more, in diameter, with irregular commissural ridges and with faces marked very irregularly by crowded short meandriform elevations, sometimes with rounded teeth; microspores 25–33 μ long, smooth to slightly

papillose.—River-shores and about ponds, various provinces, in more eastern part of our range.

This amphibious quillwort is much more restricted in distribution than the preceding species, and is variable in appearance, inasmuch as the spring form is apt to have coarser and longer leaves than the summer form. Stomata are found on the leaves throughout the season. The plant occurs along the shores of ponds or rivers, the original specimens coming from Kingston, New Hampshire. The species was named in 1896. In North America the species ranges from New Jersey to New Hampshire and Massachusetts.

3. I. riparia Engelm. Corm 2-lobed; leaves 10–30, 9–30 cm. long, rather rigid, more slender than *I. lacustris*, deep-green in color, with the membranaceous margins but briefly extended; stomata numerous; peripheral strands lacking; ligule elongate, with a narrow tip, ovate at base; sporangia spotted with brown cells, oblong, 4–7 mm. long, with a narrow velum (covering the sporangia ¼–⅓); megaspores white, 440–660 μ in diameter, marked with conspicuous jagged crests, often with isolated peaks standing out sharply, sometimes anastomosing slightly: microspores cream-colored in mass, 25–33 μ long, tuberculate.—River-shores and pond-margins, various provinces, eastern part of our range.

This historic species from the shores of the Delaware River was among the first to be collected in America. It was described in 1846 from specimens collected near Philadelphia. It is amphibious, growing where it is subject to direct wave action, according to one collector who found the plants growing along a stony stretch of the beach, almost as thick as grass on a lawn.

A larger quillwort, *I. riparia canadensis* Engelm., about which there has been disagreement as to its systematic position, seems from spore characters to be related to *I riparia* Engelm. As a result of field experience and study of dried material, A. A. Eaton placed it in different positions from time to time, but eventually considered it a distinct species, *I. Dodgei*, and then

restricted *I. riparia* to the Delaware River stations. It
is highly desirable that there be more observations of
this quillwort, both in the field and in culture if possible. Ecological variations can thus be evaluated, a
point quite necessary in plants that respond to depth of
water in the habitat.

4. I. macrospora Durieu. Corm 2-lobed: leaves usually
13–40, occasionally more numerous, 5–22 cm. in length,
rigid, slightly coarse to decidedly so, abruptly tapering
to the apex; peripheral strands lacking; stomata absent
or very rare: ligule short-triangular: sporangia 3–5
mm. long, with a narrow velum: megaspores white, 600
(550) –800 μ, or more in rare cases, with sculpture of
irregular ridges more or less parallel, with little conflu-
ence on upper faces, anastomosing, sometimes with clear
reticulations on the lower face: microspores 33–45 (50)
μ long, short-spinulose.—Shallow or deep water, near the
shores of rivers, ponds, and lakes, various provinces,
eastern part of our range.

Among the more widely distributed species, *Isoetes
macrospora* is found in approximately the eastern half
of the range of *I. Braunii*, although fewer recorded stations make the distribution seem less continuous. It is
similar to the latter species in its submersed habit, often
growing in two or more feet of water. The corms, rich
in reserve food, evidently are consumed by water animals,
with the result that large numbers of the leaves, being
freed, float on the water, buoyed up by the gas in the air-
channels. It has been reported that the corms of the
European counterpart, *I. lacustris* L., are sometimes uprooted by fish which feed on the tender leaves. It is
likely that the stems of any of the species may represent
desirable food for some animal, but that the use of
only the common ones has been observed and recorded.
The original specimens came from the Catskill Mountains,
New York. The species was named in 1864. In North
America the range extends from New York and Pennsylvania to Minnesota, Quebec, Newfoundland, and Nova
Scotia.

5. I. Tuckermani A. Br. Corm 2-lobed, rarely 3: leaves 5–38, 3–18 cm. long, very slender, tapering, olive-green, outer leaves frequently recurved; stomata lacking or few in number; peripheral strands none: sporangia orbicular to oblong, 2–5 mm. long, often brown-spotted: velum incomplete, covering about ⅓ of sporangium: megaspores white, 460–600, rarely 650 μ, in diameter, with upper segments marked with somewhat parallel and branching thin ridges, chiefly irregular at margins, lower segment with reticulate ridges: microspores 26–34 μ, rarely more (40) in length, smooth to minutely papillose.—Streams, ponds, and lakes, often deeply submerged, various provinces, extreme eastern part of our range.

Of common occurrence in large ponds, this stout dark-green quillwort is of a gregarious habit, often forming a turf-like growth. The colonies may be found under water at a depth of one to four feet. Like *Isoetes macrospora*, it has few or no stomata, and no peripheral strands of mechanical tissue, both features related to the submersed habit. The megaspores and microspores are smaller than those of the large-spored *I. macrospora*. The species was named in 1867 from specimens coming from Mystic Pond near Boston, Massachusetts. The range in North America extends from Connecticut to Quebec, Labrador, Newfoundland, and Nova Scotia.

6. I. Engelmanni A. Br. Corm 2-lobed: leaves 15–60 (100), 13–50 cm. long, light-green; stomata numerous; peripheral strands variable in number or none: sporangia oblong, unspotted, with a narrow velum: megaspores white, 400–570 (615) μ in diameter, distinctly marked with a honeycomb network of narrow ridges: microspores 21–30 μ, seldom 33 μ, in length, smooth to minutely roughened.—Brooks, ponds, and swamps, various provinces, general in our range.—Figure of *Isoetes Engelmanni* A. Br. showing mature plant; base of sporophyll, with megasporangium, narrow velum, ligule; cross section of leaf in lower and upper regions; microspores; megaspore with commissural ridges and reticulate surface markings.

This fine quillwort was named in 1846 for the American student of the genus by his friend, Alexander Braun, an outstanding European contributor to our knowledge of the same field. It is fairly abundant in a range extending as far west as that of *Isoetes macrospora,* but it also is of a decidedly more southerly occurrence; it may be found in brooks or ponds, often entirely under water in spring and completely exposed in the later and drier season. The plants are among the largest of the genus, both in the length and the number of leaves. In contrast to the submersed *Isoetes macrospora* and *I. Tuckermani,* the leaves are light-green in color. The original specimens came from near St. Louis, Missouri. In North America the species ranges from North Carolina and Virginia to Missouri, New Hampshire, and Massachusetts.

———

Specimens of an *Isoetes* from the Cape May region of New Jersey have been determined by some botanists as *Isoetes melanopoda* (Gay & Durieu; Durieu, Bull. Soc. Bot. France **11**: 102. 1864). This species was described in 1864 from specimens collected at Athens, Illinois, and is now known to range from Texas to Iowa and Illinois. The Cape May material needs further study.— J. K. S.

TAXONOMIC LIST, WITH CITATIONS[1]

FILICALES

POLYPODIACEAE

POLYPODIUM [Tourn.] L. Sp. Pl. 1082. 1753.
Polypodium virginianum L. Sp. Pl. 1085. 1753.
Polypodium vulgare Michx. Fl. Bor. Am. 2:271. 1803.
Not *P. vulgare* L. 1753.
Polypodium vulgare acuminatum Gilbert, Fern Bull.
10:13. 1902.
Polypodium vulgare f. *deltoideum* Gilbert, Fern Bull.
14:37. 1906.
Polypodium virginianum f. *acuminatum* Fernald,
Rhodora 24:141. 1922.
Polypodium virginianum f. *deltoideum* Fernald, Rhodora
24:141. 1922.
Polypodium virginianum f. *cambricoides* F. W. Gray,
Am. Fern Jour. 14:5. 1924.

PTERIS L. Sp. Pl. 1073. 1753.
Pteris latiuscula Desv. Mém. Soc. Linn. Paris 6:303.
1827.
Pteris aquilina Michx. Fl. Bor. Am. 2:262, in part.
1803. Not *P. aquilina* L. 1753.
Pteris aquilina lanuginosa Bong. Mém. Acad. St.-
Pétersb. VI. 2:176. 1832. Not *P. lanuginosa* Bory,
1810.
Pteridium aquilinum Kuhn, in Decken, Reisen Ost-
Afrika 3³: Bot. 11, in part. 1879.
Pteris aquilina pseudocaudata Clute, Fern Bull. 8:39.
1900.
Pteridium latiusculum Hieron.; R. E. Fries, Wiss.
Ergebn. Schwed. Rhod.-Kongo-Exp. 1:7. 1914.
Pteris latiuscula pseudocaudata St. John fr. Am. Fern
Jour. 25:40. 1935.
Pteris latiuscula lanuginosa Small, Ferns N. Y. 36.
1935.

ADIANTUM [Tourn.] L. Sp. Pl. 1094. 1753.
Adiantum pedatum L. Sp. Pl. 1095. 1753.

CHEILANTHES Sw. Syn. Fil. 126. 1806.
Cheilanthes lanosa (Michx.) Watt, Jour. Bot. 12:48.
1874.

[1] Contributed by JOHN HENDLEY BARNHART.

Nephrodium lanosum Michx. Fl. Bor. Am. 2:270. 1803.
Adiantum vestitum Spreng. Anl. 3:122. 1804.
Cheilanthes vestita Sw. Syn. Fil. 128. 1806.

PELLAEA Link, Fil. Sp. 59. 1841.
Pellaea atropurpurea (L.) Link, Fil. Sp. 59. 1841.
Pteris atropurpurea L. Sp. Pl. 1076. 1753.
Pellaea glabella Mett.; Kuhn, Linnaea 36:87. 1869.
Pellaea atropurpurea Bushii Mackenzie; Mackenzie &
Bush, Man. Fl. Jackson Co. 5. 1902.

CRYPTOGRAMMA R. Br. in Frankl. Journey 767.
1823.
Cryptogramma Stelleri (S. G. Gmel.) Prantl, Bot. Jahrb.
3:413. 1882.
Pteris Stelleri S. G. Gmel. Novi Comm. Acad. Petrop.
12:519. 1768.
Pteris gracilis Michx. Fl. Bor. Am. 2:262. 1803.
Pellaea gracilis Hook. Sp. Fil. 2:138. 1858.

ANCHISTEA Presl, Epim. Bot. 71. 1851.
Anchistea virginica (L.) Presl, Epim. Bot. 71. 1851.
Blechnum virginicum L. Mant. 307. 1771.
Woodwardia virginica Smith, Mém. Acad. Turin 5:412.
1793.

LORINSERIA Presl, Epim. Bot. 72. 1851.
Lorinseria areolata (L.) Presl, Epim. Bot. 72. 1851.
Acrostichum areolatum L. Sp. Pl. 1069. 1753.
Woodwardia angustifolia Smith, Mém. Acad. Turin
5:411. 1793.
Woodwardia areolata Moore, Index Fil. xlv. 1857.

ASPLENIUM L. Sp. Pl. 1078. 1753.
Asplenium pinnatifidum Nutt. Gen. 2:251. 1818.
Antigramma pinnatifida Wood, Class-Book ed. 1861.
822. 1861.
Camptosorus pinnatifidus Wood, Bot. & Fl. 373. 1870.
Asplenium Trudelli Wherry, Am. Fern Jour. 15:47.
1925.
Asplenium montanum Willd. Sp. Pl. 5:342. 1810.
Asplenium cryptolepis Fernald, Rhodora 30:41. 1928.
Asplenium Ruta-muraria Michx. Fl. Bor. Am. 2:266.
1803. Not *A. Ruta-muraria* L. 1753.
Asplenium ebenoides R. R. Scott, Gard. Mo. 7:267.
1865.
Asplenium Bradleyi D. C. Eaton, Bull. Torrey Club
4:11. 1873.

Asplenium Trichomanes L. Sp. Pl. 1080. 1753.
Asplenium platyneuron (L.) Oakes; D. C. Eaton, Ferns
N. Am. 1:24. 1878.
Acrostichum platyneuros L. Sp. Pl. 1069. 1753.
Asplenium ebeneum Ait. Hort. Kew. 3:462. 1789.
Asplenium ebeneum incisum E. C. Howe; Peck, Ann.
Rep. N. Y. State Cab. 22:104. 1869.
Asplenium ebeneum serratum E. S. Miller, Bull. Tor-
rey Club 4:41. 1873.
Asplenium platyneuron serratum B. S. P. Prel. Cat. N.
Y. 73. 1888.
Asplenium platyneuron incisum B. L. Robinson,
Rhodora 10:29. 1908.

ATHYRIUM Roth, Fl. Germ. 3^1:58. 1799.
Athyrium asplenioides (Michx.) Eaton, Man. 122.
1817.
Nephrodium asplenioides Michx. Fl. Bor. Am. 2:268.
1803.
Asplenium Athyrium Spreng. Anl. 3:113. 1804.
Aspidium asplenioides Sw. Syn. Fil. 60. 1806.
Athyrium angustum (Willd.) Presl, Rel. Haenk. 1:39.
1825.
Polypodium Filix-foemina Michx. Fl. Bor. Am. 2:268.
1803. Not *P. Filix-foemina* L. 1753.
Aspidium angustum Willd. Sp. Pl. 5:277. 1810.
Aspidium Filix-foemina Pursh, Fl. Am. Sept. 664.
1814. Not *A. Filix-foemina* Sw. 1801.
Asplenium elatius Link, Fil Sp. 94. 1841.
Asplenium Filix-foemina Wood, Class-Book 161. 1845.
Not *A. Filix-foemina* Bernh. 1806.
Athyrium Filix-foemina rubellum Gilbert, List 35.
1901.
Athyrium angustum elatius Butters, Rhodora 19:191.
1917.
Athyrium angustum rubellum Butters, Rhodora 19:193.
1917.

DIPLAZIUM Sw. Jour. Bot. Schrad. 1800^2:61. 1801.
Diplazium acrostichoides (Sw.) Butters, Rhodora 19:178.
1917.
Asplenium acrostichoides. Sw. Jour. Bot. Schrad.
1800^2:54. 1801.
Asplenium thelypteroides Michx. Fl. Bor. Am. 2:265.
1803.
Athyrium thelypteroides Desv. Mém. Soc. Linn. Paris
6:266. 1827.
Diplazium thelypteroides Presl, Tent. Pterid. 114. 1836.
Athyrium acrostichoides Diels, in E. & P. Nat. Pfl. 1^2:
223. 1899.

HOMALOSORUS Small, Ferns N. Y. 80. 1935.
Homalosorus pycnocarpus (Spreng.) Small, Ferns N. Y.
80. 1935.
Asplenium angustifolium Michx. Fl. Bor. Am. 2:265.
1803. Not *A. angustifolium* Jacq. 1786.
Asplenium pycnocarpum Spreng. Anl. 3:112. 1804.
Athyrium angustifolium Milde, Bot. Zeit. 24:376.
1866.
Athyrium pycnocarpum Tidestrom, Elys. Marianum
Ferns 36. 1906.
Diplazium angustifolium Butters, Rhodora 19:178.
1917.

CAMPTOSORUS Link, Hort. Berol. 2:69. 1833.
Camptosorus rhizophyllus (L.) Link, Hort. Berol. 2:69.
1833.
Asplenium rhizophylla L. Sp. Pl. 1078. 1753.
Antigramma rhizophylla J. Smith, Jour. Bot. Hook.
4:176. 1841.

THELYPTERIS Schmidel, Ic. Pl. 45. 1762.
Thelypteris noveboracensis (L.) Nieuwl. Am. Midl. Nat.
1:226. 1910.
Polypodium noveboracense L. Sp. Pl. 1091. 1753.
Aspidium noveboracense Sw. Jour. Bot. Schrad.
1800²:38. 1801.
Dryopteris noveboracensis A. Gray, Man. 630. 1848.
Thelypteris Thelypteris (L.) Nieuwl. Am. Midl. Nat.
1:226. 1910.
Acrostichum Thelypteris L. Sp. Pl. 1071. 1753.
Polypodium palustre Salisb. Prodr. 403. 1796.
Aspidium Thelypteris Sw. Jour. Bot. Schrad. 1800²:33.
1801.
Aspidium palustre S. F. Gray, Nat. Arr. Brit. Pl.
2:9. 1821.
Lastraea Thelypteris Bory, Dict. Class. 9:233. 1826.
Thelypteris palustris Schott, Gen. Fil. [under *pl. 10*].
1834.
Dryopteris Thelypteris A. Gray, Man. 630. 1848.
Lastraea Thelypteris pubescens Lawson, Edinb. New
Phil. Jour. II. 19:277. 1864.
Thelypteris palustris pubescens Fernald, Rhodora 31:34.
1929.
Thelypteris simulata (Davenp.) Nieuwl. Am. Midl. Nat.
1:226. 1910.
Aspidium simulatum Davenp. Bot. Gaz. 19:495. 1894.
Dryopteris simulata Davenp. Bot. Gaz. 19:497. 1894.
Nephrodium simulatum Davenp. Bot. Gaz. 19:497. 1894.
Lastraea simulata Davenp. Bot. Gaz. 19:497. 1894.

DRYOPTERIS Adans. Fam. Pl. 2:20, 551. 1763.
Dryopteris marginalis (L.) A. Gray, Man. 632. 1848.
Polypodium marginale L. Sp. Pl. 1091. 1753.
Aspidium marginale Sw. Jour. Bot. Schrad. 1800²:35.
1801.
Nephrodium marginale Michx. Fl. Bor. Am. 2:267.
1803.
Thelypteris marginalis Nieuwl. Am. Midl. Nat. 1:226.
1910.
Dryopteris cristata (L.) A. Gray, Man. 631. 1848.
Polypodium cristatum L. Sp. Pl. 1090. 1753.
Aspidium cristatum Sw. Jour. Bot. Schrad. 1800²:37.
1801.
Nephrodium cristatum Michx. Fl. Bor. Am. 2:269.
1803.
Thelypteris cristata Nieuwl. Am. Midl. Nat. 1:226.
1910.
Dryopteris Boottii (Tuckerm.) Underw. Our Nat. Ferns
ed. 4. 117. 1893.
Aspidium Boottii Tuckerm. Mag. Hort. 9:145. 1843.
Aspidium spinulosum Boottii A. Gray, Man. ed. 2.
598. 1856.
Thelypteris Boottii Nieuwl. Am. Midl. Nat. 1:226.
1910.
Dryopteris Clintoniana (D. C. Eaton) Dowell, Proc.
Staten Id. Assoc. 1:64. 1906.
Aspidium cristatum Clintonianum D. C. Eaton, in A.
Gray, Man. ed. 5. 665. 1867.
Dryopteris cristata Clintoniana Underw. Our Nat.
Ferns ed. 4. 115. 1893.
Thelypteris cristata Clintoniana Weatherby, Rhodora
21:177. 1919.
Thelypteris Clintoniana House, N. Y. State Mus. Bull.
233–234; 69. 1922.
Dryopteris Goldiana (Hook.) A. Gray, Man. 631. 1848.
Aspidium Goldianum Hook. Edinb. Phil. Jour. 6:333.
1822.
Nephrodium Goldianum Hook. & Grev. Ic. Fil. *pl. 102.*
1829.
Lastraea Goldiana Presl, Tent. Pterid. 76. 1836.
Thelypteris Goldiana Nieuwl. Am. Midl. Nat. 1:226.
1910.
Dryopteris intermedia (Muhl.) A. Gray, Man. 630. 1848.
Aspidium intermedium Muhl.; Willd. Sp. Pl. 5:262.
1810.
Polypodium intermedium Muhl.; Willd. Sp. Pl. 5:262,
as syn. 1810.

Nephrodium intermedium Presl, Rel. Haenk. 1:38.
1825.
Lastraea intermedia Presl, Tent. Pterid. 77. 1836.
Aspidium spinulosum intermedium D. C. Eaton, in A.
Gray, Man. ed. 5. 665. 1867.
Dryopteris spinulosa intermedia Underw. Our Nat.
Ferns ed. 4. 116. 1893.
Thelypteris spinulosa intermedia Weatherby, Rhodora
21:178. 1919.
Thelypteris intermedia House, N. Y. State Mus. Bull.
233–234:69. 1922.
Dryopteris spinulosa (Muell.) Kuntze, Rev. Gen. 813.
1891.
Polypodium spinulosum Muell. Fl. Dan. 12:5. 1777.
Aspidium spinulosum Sw. Jour. Bot. Schrad. 1800²:38.
1801.
Thelypteris spinulosa Nieuwl. Am. Midl. Nat. 1:226.
1910.
Dryopteris campyloptera (Kunze) Clarkson, Am. Fern
Jour. 20:118. 1930.
Aspidium spinulosum dilatatum Link, Fil. Sp. 106.
1841.
Aspidium spinulosum americanum Fischer; Kunze, Am.
Jour. Sci. II. 6:84. 1848.
Aspidium campylopterum Kunze, Am. Jour. Sci. II.
6:84. 1848.
Dryopteris dilatata A. Gray, Man. 631, in part. 1848.
Dryopteris spinulosa dilatata Underw. Our Nat. Ferns
ed. 4. 116. 1893.
Dryopteris spinulosa americana Fernald, Rhodora 17:48.
1915.
Dryopteris dilatata americana Benedict, Am. Fern
Jour. 6:34. 1916.
Thelypteris spinulosa americana Weatherby, Rhodora
21:178. 1919.
Thelypteris dilatata americana House, N. Y. State Mus.
Bull. 233–234:69. 1922.

POLYSTICHUM Roth, Fl. Germ. 3¹:69. 1799.
Polystichum acrostichoides (Michx.) Schott, Gen. Fil.
[under *pl. 9*]. 1834.
Nephrodium acrostichoides Michx. Fl. Bor. Am. 2:267.
1803.
Aspidium acrostichoides Sw. Syn. Fil. 44. 1806.
Aspidium Schweinitzii Beck, Bot. U. S. 449. 1833.
Polystichum acrostichoides incisum A. Gray, Man. 632.
1848.

Aspidium acrostichoides incisum A. Gray, Man. ed. 2. 599. 1856.

Dryopteris acrostichoides Kuntze, Rev. Gen. 812. 1891.

Dryopteris acrostichoides incisum Underw. Our Nat. Ferns ed. 4. 111. 1893.

Polystichum acrostichoides Schweinitzii Small, Bull. Torrey Club 20:464. 1893.

Polystichum Braunii (Spenner) Fée, Gen. Fil. 278. 1853.

Aspidium Braunii Spenner, Fl. Frib. 1:9. 1825.

Aspidium aculeatum Braunii Döll, Rhein. Fl. 21. 1843.

Dryopteris aculeata Braunii Underw. Our Nat. Ferns ed. 4. 112. 1893.

Dryopteris Braunii Underw. in Britt. & Brown, Ill. Fl. 1:15. 1896.

Polystichum Braunii Purshii Fernald, Rhodora 30:30. 1928.

PHEGOPTERIS Fée, Gen. Fil. 242. 1853.

Phegopteris hexagonoptera (Michx.) Fée, Gen. Fil. 243. 1853.

Polypodium hexagonoptervm Michx. Fl. Bor. Am. 2:271. 1803.

Nephrodium hexagonopterum Diels, in E. & P. Nat. Pfl. 1⁴:169. 1899.

Dryopteris hexagonoptera C. Chr. Index Fil. 270. 1905.

Thelypteris hexagonoptera Weatherby, Rhodora 21:179. 1919.

Phegopteris Phegopteris (L.) Keyserl. Polyp. Cyath. Herb. Bung. 50. 1873.

Polypodium Phegopteris L. Sp. Pl. 1089. 1753.

Gymnocarpium Phegopteris Newman, Phytologist 4: App. xxiii. 1851.

Phegopteris polypodioides Fée, Gen. Fil. 243. 1853.

Nephrodium Phegopteris Prantl, Exc.-fl. Baiern 23. 1884.

Dryopteris Phegopteris C. Chr. Index Fil. 284. 1905.

Thelypteris Phegopteris Slosson, in Rydb. Fl. Rocky Mts. 1043. 1917.

Phegopteris Dryopteris (L.) Fée, Gen. Fil. 243. 1853.

Polypodium Dryopteris L. Sp. Pl. 1093. 1753.

Nephrodium Dryopteris Michx. Fl. Bor. Am. 2:270. 1803.

Gymnocarpium Dryopteris Newman, Phytologist 4: App. xxiv. 1851.

Dryopteris Linneana C. Chr. Index Fil. 275. 1905.

Dryopteris Dryopteris Britton; Britt. & Brown, Ill. Fl. ed. 2. 1:23. 1913.

Thelypteris Dryopteris Slosson, in Rydb. Fl. Rocky
Mts. 1044. 1917.

CYSTOPTERIS Bernh. Neues Jour. Bot. Schrad.
1²:26. 1806.
Cystopteris fragilis (L.) Bernh. Neues Jour. Bot. Schrad.
1²:27. 1806.
Polypodium fragile L. Sp. Pl. 1091. 1753.
Filix fragilis Underw. Our Nat. Ferns ed. 6. 119.
1900.
Cystopteris bulbifera (L.) Bernh. Neues Jour. Bot.
Schrad. 1²:10. 1806.
Polypodium bulbiferum L. Sp. Pl. 1091. 1753.
Filix bulbifera Underw. Our Nat. Ferns ed. 6. 119.
1900.

WOODSIA R. Br. Prodr. 1:158. 1810 (*"Woodia"*);
Trans. Linn. Soc. 11:170. 1813.
Woodsia ilvensis (L.) R. Br. Trans. Linn. Soc. 11:173.
1813.
Acrostichum ilvense L. Sp. Pl. 1071. 1753.
Woodsia glabella R. Br. in Frankl. Journey 754.
1823.
Woodsia obtusa (Spreng.) Torr. Cat. Pl. Geol. Rep.
N. Y. 195. 1840.
Polypodium obtusum Spreng. Anl. 3:92. 1804.

DENNSTAEDTIA Bernh. Jour. Bot. Schrad. 1800²:124.
1801.
Dennstaedtia punctilobula (Michx.) Moore, Index Fil.
xcvii. 1857.
Nephrodium punctilobulum Michx. Fl. Bor. Am. 2:268.
1803.
Dicksonia pilosiuscula Willd. Enum. 1076. 1809.
Dicksonia punctilobula A. Gray, Man. 628. 1848.

ONOCLEA L. Sp. Pl. 1062. 1753.
Onoclea sensibilis L. Sp. Pl. 1062. 1753.
Onoclea obtusilobata Schkuhr, Krypt. Gew. 1:95.
1809.
Onoclea sensibilis obtusilobata Torr. Fl. N. Y. 2:499.
1843.

PTERETIS Raf. Am. Mo. Mag. 2:268. 1818.
Pteretis nodulosa (Michx.) Nieuwl. Am. Midl. Nat.
4:334. 1916.
Onoclea nodulosa Michx. Fl. Bor. Am. 2:272. 1803.
Struthiopteris pensylvanica Willd. Sp. Pl. 5:289. 1810.

Struthiopteris nodulosa Desv. Mém. Soc. Linn. Paris
6:287. 1827.
Struthiopteris germanica Beck, Bot. U. S. 456. 1833.
Not *S. germanica* Willd. 1809.
Struthiopteris germanica pennsylvanica Lowe, Ferns
2:138. 1858.
Onoclea Struthiopteris D. C. Eaton, Ferns N. Am.
2:201. 1880. Not *O. Struthiopteris* Hoffm. 1795.
Matteuccia Struthiopteris Underw. Our Nat. Ferns
ed. 6. 120. 1900. Not *M. Struthiopteris* Todaro,
1866.
Matteuccia nodulosa Fernald, Rhodora 17:164. 1915.

SCHIZAEACEAE

SCHIZAEA Smith, Mém. Acad. Turin 5:419. *pl. 19, f. 9.*
1793.
Schizaea pusilla Pursh, Fl. Am. Sept. 657. 1814.

LYGODIUM Sw. Jour. Bot. Schrad. 1800^2:106. 1801.
Lygodium palmatum (Bernh.) Sw. Syn. Fil. 154. 1806.
Gisopteris palmata Bernh. Jour. Bot. Schrad. 1800^2:129.
1801.
Hydroglossum palmatum Willd. Schr. Akad. Erfurt
1802:25. 1802.
Cteisium paniculatum Michx. Fl. Bor. Am. 2:275.
1803.

OSMUNDACEAE

OSMUNDA [Tourn.] L. Sp. Pl. 1063. 1753.
Osmunda regalis L. Sp. Pl. 1065. 1753.
Osmunda spectabilis Willd. Sp. Pl. 5:98. 1810.
Osmunda regalis spectabilis A. Gray, Man. ed. 2.
600. 1856.
Osmunda cinnamomea L. Sp. Pl. 1066. 1753.
Osmunda cinnamomea frondosa A. Gray, Man. 635.
1848.
Osmunda cinnamomea incisa Huntington, Fern. Bull.
7:12. 1899.
Osmunda cinnamomea glandulosa Waters, Fern Bull.
10:21. 1902.
Osmunda Claytoniana L. Sp. Pl. 1066. 1753.
Osmunda interrupta Michx. Fl. Bor. Am. 2:273. 1803.

OPHIOGLOSSALES

OPHIOGLOSSACEAE

OPHIOGLOSSUM [Tourn.] L. Sp. Pl. 1062. 1753.

Ophioglossum vulgatum L. Sp. Pl. 1062. 1753.

Ophioglossum Grayi Beck, Bot. U. S. 458. 1833.

Ophioglossum vulgatum minus Moore, Ferns Gr. Brit. under *pl. 51 B.* 1856.

Ophioglossum arenarium E. G. Britton, Bull. Torrey Club 24:555. 1897.

BOTRYCHIUM Sw. Jour. Bot. Schrad. 1800²:8, 110. 1801.

Botrychium lanceolatum (S. G. Gmel.) Ångstr. Bot. Notiser 1854:68. 1854.

Osmunda lanceolata S. G. Gmel. Novi Comm. Acad. Petrop. 12:516. 1768.

Botrychium lanceolatum angustisegmentum Pease & Moore, Rhodora 8:229. 1906.

Botrychium angustisegmentum Fernald, Rhodora 17:87. 1915.

Botrychium matricariaefolium A. Br.; Döll, Rhein. Fl. 24, as synonym. 1843; Koch, Syn. Fl. Germ. ed. 2. 972. 1845.

Botrychium Lunaria matricariaefolium Döll, Rhein. Fl. 24. 1843.

Botrychium neglectum Wood, Class-Book ed. 2. 635. 1847.

Botrychium ramosum Rob. & Fern. Man. 48. 1908. Not *B. ramosum* Asch. 1864.

Botrychium simplex E. Hitchc. Am. Jour. Sci. 6:103. 1823.

Botrychium virginicum simplex A. Gray, Man. ed. 2. 602. 1856.

Botrychium tenebrosum A. A. Eaton, Fern Bull. 7:8. 1899.

Botrychium obliquum Muhl.; Willd. Sp. Pl. 5:63. 1810.

Botrychium lunarioides obliquum A. Gray, Man. 635. 1848.

Botrychium ternatum Hook. & Baker, Syn. Fil. 448, in part. 1868. Not *B. ternatum* Sw. 1801.

Botrychium ternatum obliquum D. C. Eaton, Ferns N. Am. 1:149. 1878.

Botrychium ternatum oneidense Gilbert, Fern Bull. 9: 27. 1901.

Botrychium dissectum obliquum Clute, Fern Bull. 10:76. 1902.

Botrychium dissectum oneidense Clute, Fern Bull. 10: 76. 1902.

Botrychium tenuifolium Underw. Bull. Torrey Club 30:52. 1903.

Botrychium obliquum oneidense Waters, Ferns 334.
1903.
Sceptridium obliquum Lyon, Bot. Gaz. 40:458. 1905.
Sceptridium obliquum oneidense Lyon, Bot. Gaz. 40:
458. 1905.
Botrychium dissectum Spreng. Anl. 3:172. 1804.
Botrychium fumarioides dissectum Oakes, in Z. Thompson, Hist. Vermont 207. 1842.
Botrychium lunarioides dissectum A. Gray, Man. 635.
1848.
Botrychium ternatum dissectum D. C. Eaton, Ferns N.
Am. 1:150. 1878.
Botrychium obliquum dissectum Prantl, Jahrb. Bot.
Gart. Berlin 3:342. 1884.
Sceptridium dissectum Lyon, Bot. Gaz. 40:457. 1905.
Sceptridium ternatum dissectum Clute, Fern Bull. 14:
48. 1906.
Botrychium multifidum (S. G. Gmel.) Rupr. Beitr. Pfl.
Russ. Reich. 11:40. 1859.
Osmunda multifida S. G. Gmel. Novi Comm. Acad.
Petrop. 12:517. 1768.
Botrychium silaifolium Presl, Rel. Haenk. 1:76. 1825.
Botrychium ternatum intermedium D. C. Eaton, Ferns
N. Am. 1:149. 1878.
Botrychium occidentale Underw. Bull. Torrey Club
25:538. 1898.
Sceptridium silaifolium Lyon, Bot. Gaz. 40:458. 1905.
Botrychium multifidum intermedium Farwell, Rep.
Mich. Acad. 18:87. 1916.
Botrychium virginianum (L.) Sw. Jour. Bot. Schrad.
1800[2]:111. 1801.
Osmunda virginiana L. Sp. Pl. 1064. 1753.
Osmunda virginica L. Syst. Nat. ed. 12. 2:685. 1767.
Botrychium virginicum Willd. Sp. Pl. 5:64. 1810.
Botrychium gracile Pursh, Fl. Am. Sept. 656. 1814.

SALVINIALES
MARSILEACEAE

MARSILEA L. Sp. Pl. 1099. 1753.
Marsilea quadrifolia L. Sp. Pl. 1099. 1753.

SALVINIACEAE

AZOLLA Lam. Encyc. 1:343. 1783.
Azolla caroliniana Willd. Sp. Pl. 5:541. 1810.

SALVINIA Adans. Fam. Pl. 2:15. 1763.
Salvinia auriculata Aubl. Pl. Guian. 969. 1775.
Salvinia natans Pursh, Fl. Am. Sept. 672. 1814. Not
    S. natans All. 1785.
Salvinia auriculata Olfersiana Klotzsch; Baker, Handb.
    Fern-All. 136. 1887.

EQUISETALES

EQUISETACEAE

EQUISETUM [Tourn.] L. Sp. Pl. 1061. 1753.
Equisetum arvense L. Sp. Pl. 1061. 1753.
Equisetum arvense serotinum G. Meyer, Chlor. Hanov.
    666. 1836.
Equisetum pratense Ehrh. Hannov. Mag. 22:138. 1784.
Equisetum sylvaticum L. Sp. Pl. 1061. 1753.
Equisetum palustre L. Sp. Pl. 1061. 1753.
Equisetum palustre americanum Victorin, Contr. Bot.
    Univ. Montréal 9:51. 1927.
Equisetum litorale Kühl.; Rupr. Beitr. Pfl. Russ. Reichs.
    4:91. 1845.
Equisetum fluviatile L. Sp. Pl. 1062. 1753.
Equisetum limosum L. Sp. Pl. 1062. 1753.
Equisetum variegatum Schleich. Cat. Pl. Helvet. 27.
    1807.
Equisetum variegatum Nelsoni A. A. Eaton, Fern Bull.
    12:41. 1904.
Hippochaete variegata Farwell, Mem. N. Y. Bot. Gard.
    6:466. 1916.
Hippochaete Nelsoni Farwell, Mem. N. Y. Bot. Gard. 6:
    472. 1916.
Equisetum Nelsoni J. H. Schaffn. Am. Fern Jour.
    16:46. 1926.
Equisetum laevigatum A. Br. Am. Jour. Sci. 46:87.
    1844.
Equisetum hyemale intermedium A. A. Eaton, Fern
    Bull. 11:108. 1903.
Equisetum praealtum Raf. Fl. Ludov. 13. 1817.
Equisetum hyemale Pursh, Fl. Am. Sept. 652. 1814.
    Not *E. hyemale* L. 1753.
Equisetum robustum A. Br. Am. Jour. Sci. 46:88. 1844.
Equisetum robustum affine Engelm.; A. Br. Am. Jour.
    Sci. 46:88. 1844.
Equisetum variegatum Jesupi A. A. Eaton; Gilbert,
    List 9, 27. 1901.
Equisetum hyemale affine A. A. Eaton, Fern Bull. 11:
    75, 111. 1903.

Equisetum hyemale robustum A. A. Eaton, Fern Bull.
11:75, 112. 1903.
Hippochaete hyemalis Jesupi Farwell, Mem. N. Y. Bot.
Gard. 6:465. 1916.
Hippochaete praealta Farwell, Mem. N. Y. Bot. Gard.
6:467. 1916.
Equisetum hyemale Jesupi Victorin, Contr. Bot. Univ.
Montréal 9:90. 1927.

LYCOPODIALES
LYCOPODIACEAE

LYCOPODIUM [Dill.] L. Sp. Pl. 1100. 1753.
Lycopodium Selago L. Sp. Pl. 1102. 1753.
Lycopodium Selago appressum Desv. Mém. Soc. Linn.
Paris 6:180. 1827.
Lycopodium appressum Petrov, Fl. Iakut. 37. 1930.
Not *L. adpressum* Lloyd & Underw. 1900.
Lycopodium porophilum Lloyd & Underw. Bull. Torrey
Club 27:150. 1900.
Lycopodium lucidulum porophilum Clute, Fern Allies
262. 1905.
Lycopodium lucidulum Michx. Fl. Bor. Am. 2:284. 1803.
Lycopodium inundatum L. Sp. Pl. 1102. 1753.
Lycopodium inundatum alopecuroides Tuckerm. Am.
Jour. Sci. 45:47. 1843.
Lycopodium adpressum (Chapm.) Lloyd & Underw.
Bull. Torrey Club 27:153. 1900.
Lycopodium inundatum Bigelovii Tuckerm. Am. Jour.
Sci. 45:47. 1843.
Lycopodium inundatum adpressum Chapm. Fl. S. U. S.
ed. 2. 671. 1883.
Lycopodium alopecuroides adpressum Chapm. Fl. S.
U. S. ed. 3. 638. 1897.
Lycopodium Chapmani Underw.; Maxon, Proc. U. S.
Nat. Mus. 23:646. 1901.
Lycopodium alopecuroides L. Sp. Pl. 1102. 1753.
Lycopodium carolinianum L. Sp. Pl. 1104. 1753.
Lycopodium obscurum L. Sp. Pl. 1102. 1753.
Lycopodium dendroideum Michx. Fl. Bor. Am. 2:282.
1803.
Lycopodium obscurum dendroideum D. C. Eaton, in A.
Gray, Man. ed. 6. 696. 1890.
Lycopodium annotinum L. Sp. Pl. 1103. 1753.
Lycopodium clavatum L. Sp. Pl. 1101. 1753.
Lycopodium clavatum monostachyon B. L. Robinson,
Rhodora 3:237. 1901. Not *L. clavatum monostach-
yon* Hook. & Grev. 1831.

Lycopodium clavatum megastachyum Fernald & Bissell, Rhodora 12:53. 1910.

Lycopodium flabelliforme (Fernald) Blanchard, Rhodora 13:168. 1911.

Lycopodium complanatum L. Sp. Pl. 1104, in part. 1753.

Lycopodium complanatum flabelliforme Fernald, Rhodora 3:280. 1901.

Lycopodium tristachyum Pursh, Fl. Am. Sept. 653. 1814.

Lycopodium Chamaecyparissus A. Br.; Döll, Rhein. Fl. 36. 1843.

Lycopodium complanatum Chamaecyparissus D. C. Eaton, in A. Gray, Man. ed. 6. 697. 1890.

SELAGINELLACEAE

SELAGINELLA Beauv. Prodr. Aetheog. 101. 1805.

Selaginella apoda (L.) Spring, in Mart. Fl. Bras. 1²:119. 1840. (*S. "apus."*)

Lycopodium apodum L. Sp. Pl. 1105. 1753.

Selaginella rupestris (L.) Spring, Flora 21:149, 182. 1838.

Lycopodium rupestre L. Sp. Pl. 1101. 1753.

ISOETALES

ISOETACEAE

ISOETES L. Sp. Pl. 1100. 1753.

Isoetes Braunii Durieu, Bull. Soc. Bot. France 11:101. 1864.

Isoetes echinospora Braunii Engelm. in A. Gray, Man. ed. 5. 676. 1867.

Isoetes echinospora robusta Engelm. Trans. Acad. St. Louis 4:380. 1882.

Isoetes Gravesii A. A. Eaton, Fernw. Pap. 14. 1900.

Isoetes valida Gravesii Clute, Fern Allies. 243. 1905.

Isoetes Braunii f. *robusta* N. Pfeiffer, Ann. Mo. Bot. Gard. 9:173. 1922.

Isoetes Eatoni R. Dodge, Ferns New Engl. 39. 1896.

Isoetes riparia Engelm.; A. Br. Flora 29:178. 1846.

Isoetes saccharata Engelm. in A. Gray, Man. ed. 5. 676. 1867.

Isoetes riparia canadensis Engelm. Trans. Acad. St. Louis 4:383. 1882.

Isoetes Dodgei A. A. Eaton, Fern Bull. 6:6. 1898.

Isoetes canadensis A. A. Eaton; Maxon, Proc. U. S. Nat. Mus. 23:650. 1901.

Isoetes macrospora Durieu, Bull. Soc. Bot. France
11:101. 1864.

Isoetes lacustris Pursh, Fl. Am. Sept. 671. 1814. Not
I. lacustris L. 1753.

Isoetes heterospora A. A. Eaton, Fernw. Pap. 8. 1900.

Isoetes Harveyi A. A. Eaton, Fernw. Pap. 10. 1900.

Isoetes Tuckermani A. Br.; Engelm. in A. Gray, Man.
ed. 5. 676. 1867.

Isoetes Engelmanni A. Br. Flora 29:178. 1846.

Isoetes Engelmanni gracilis Engelm. in A. Gray, Man.
ed. 5. 677. 1867.

Isoetes Engelmanni valida Engelm. in A. Gray, Man.
ed. 5. 677. 1867.

Isoetes valida Clute, Fern Allies. 236. 1905.

COMPARATIVE LIST

Showing the generic and specific names used in this work, in Gray's Manual of Botany, and in Britton and Brown's Illustrated Flora.[1]

FERNS OF NEW YORK 1935	GRAY'S NEW MANUAL SEVENTH EDITION, 1908	B. & B. ILL. FLORA SECOND EDITION, 1913
Polypodium virginianum	Polypodium vulgare	Polypodium vulgare
Pteris latiuscula	Pteris aquilina	Pteridium aquilinum
Adiantum pedatum	Adiantum pedatum	Adiantum pedatum
Cheilanthes lanosa	Cheilanthes lanosa	Cheilanthes lanosa
Pellaea atropurpurea glabella	Pellaea atropurpurea	Pellaea atropurpurea
Cryptogramma Stelleri	Cryptogramma Stelleri	Cryptogramma Stelleri
Anchistea virginica	Woodwardia virginica	Anchistea virginica
Lorinseria areolata	Woodwardia areolata	Lorinseria areolata
Asplenium pinnatifidum ebenoides Trichomanes platyneuron montanum cryptolepis Bradleyi	Asplenium pinnatifidum ebenoides Trichomanes platyneuron montanum Ruta-Muraria Bradleyi	Asplenium pinnatifidum* ebenoides Trichomanes platyneuron montanum Ruta-Muraria Bradleyi
Athyrium asplenioides angustum	Asplenium Filix-femina	Athyrium Filix-foemina
Diplazium acrostichoides	Asplenium acrostichoides	Athyrium thelypteroides
Homalosorus pycnocarpus	Asplenium angustifolium	Asplenium** pycnocarpon
Camptosorus rhizophyllus	Camptosorus rhizophyllus	Camptosorus rhizophyllus
Thelypteris noveboracensis simulata Thelypteris	Aspidium noveboracense simulatum Thelypteris	Dryopteris*** noveboracensis simulata Thelypteris

[1] Contributed by JAMES L. EDWARDS.

* Termed *Camptosorus pinnatifidus* in House, Ann. List Ferns and Fl. Plants N. Y. State 26. 1924. (Not new with House.)

** Also known as *Athyrium pycnocarpon*.

*** Another generic synonym occasionally used is *Nephrodium*.

FERNS OF NEW YORK 1935	GRAY'S NEW MANUAL SEVENTH EDITION, 1908	B. & B. ILL. FLORA SECOND EDITION, 1913
Dryopteris marginalis cristata Clintoniana	*Aspidium marginale cristatum cristatum Clintonianum*	*Dryopteris* * *marginalis cristata Clintoniana*
Goldiana Boottii intermedia	*Goldianum Boottii spinulosum intermedium*	*Goldiana Boottii intermedia*
spinulosa campyloptera	*spinulosum spinulosum dilatatum*	*spinulosa dilatata*
Polystichum acrostichoides Braunii	*Polystichum acrostichoides Braunii*	*Polystichum acrostichoides Braunii*
Phegopteris hexagonoptera Phegopteris Dryopteris	*Phegopteris hexagonoptera polypodioides Dryopteris*	*Dryopteris hexagonoptera polypodioides Dryopteris*
Cystopteris fragilis bulbifera	*Cystopteris fragilis bulbifera*	*Filix fragilis bulbifera*
Woodsia ilvensis glabella obtusa	*Woodsia ilvensis glabella obtusa*	*Woodsia ilvensis glabella obtusa*
Dennstaedtia punctilobula	*Dicksonia punctilobula*	*Dennstaedtia punctilobula*
Onoclea sensibilis	*Onoclea sensibilis*	*Onoclea sensibilis*
Pteretis nodulosa	*Onoclea Struthiopteris*	*Matteuccia* ** *Struthiopteris*
Schizaea pusilla	*Schizaea pusilla*	*Schizaea pusilla*
Lygodium palmatum	*Lygodium palmatum*	*Lygodium palmatum*
Osmunda regalis cinnamomea Claytoniana	*Osmunda regalis cinnamomea Claytoniana*	*Osmunda regalis cinnamomea Claytoniana*

* Also sometimes assigned to the generic names *Nephrodium* and *Thelypteris*.

** *Struthiopteris* has also been suggested as a generic name.

FERNS OF NEW YORK 1935	GRAY'S NEW MANUAL SEVENTH EDITION, 1908	B. & B. ILL. FLORA SECOND EDITION, 1913
Ophioglossum vulgatum	*Ophioglossum vulgatum*	*Ophioglossum vulgatum arenarium*
Botrychium lanceolatum	*Botrychium lanceolatum var. angustisegmentum*	*Botrychium lanceolatum* *
matricariaefolium	*ramosum*	*neglectum*
simplex	*simplex*	*simplex tenebrosum*
obliquum	*obliquum*	*obliquum*
dissectum	*obliquum dissectum*	*dissectum*
multifidum	*ternatum intermedium*	*silaifolium*
virginianum	*virginianum*	*virginianum*
Marsilea quadrifolia	*Marsilea quadrifolia*	*Marsilea quadrifolia*
Azolla caroliniana	*Azolla caroliniana*	*Azolla caroliniana*
Salvinia auriculata		*Salvinia natans*
Equisetum	*Equisetum*	*Equisetum*
arvense	*arvense*	*arvense*
pratense	*pratense*	*pratense*
sylvaticum	*sylvaticum*	*sylvaticum* **
palustre	*palustre*	*palustre*
littorale	*littorale*	*littorale*
fluviatile	*fluviatile*	*fluviatile*
variegatum	*variegatum*	*variegatum*
laevigatum	*hyemale intermedium*	*hyemale* ***
praealtum	*hyemale*	*robustum*
Lycopodium	*Lycopodium*	*Lycopodium*
Selago	*Selago*	*Selago*
porophilum	*lucidulum porophilum*	*porophilum*
lucidulum	*lucidulum*	*lucidulum*
inundatum	*inundatum*	*inundatum*
adpressum	*inundatum Bigelovii*	*adpressum*
alopecuroides	*alopecuroides*	*alopecuroides*
carolinianum	*carolinianum*	*carolinianum*
obscurum	*obscurum*	*obscurum*

* Termed *Botrychium angustisegmentum* in House, Ann. List Ferns and Fl. Plants N. Y. State 14. 1924. (Not new with House.)
** Sometimes spelled *silvaticum*.
*** Sometimes spelled *hiemale*.

FERNS OF NEW YORK 1935	GRAY'S NEW MANUAL SEVENTH EDITION, 1908	B. & B. ILL. FLORA SECOND EDITION, 1913
annotinum	*annotinum*	*annotinum*
clavatum	*clavatum*	*clavatum*
flabelliforme	*complanatum*	*complanatum*
	flabelliforme	
tristachyum	*tristachyum*	*tristachyum*
Selaginella	*Selaginella*	*Selaginella*
apoda	*apus*	*apus*
rupestris	*rupestris*	*rupestris*
Isoetes	*Isoetes*	*Isoetes*
Braunii	*echinospora*	*Braunii*
	Braunii	
Eatoni	*Eatoni*	*Eatoni*
riparia	*riparia*	*riparia*
	saccharata	*saccharata*
macrospora	*macrospora*	*macrospora*
Tuckermani	*Tuckermani*	*Tuckermani*
Engelmanni	*Engelmanni*	*Engelmanni*

AUTHORITIES CITED IN THE WORK[1]

ADANSON, MICHEL, 1727–1806.—(Adans.)
AITON, WILLIAM, 1731–1793.—(Ait.)
ALLIONI, CARLO, 1728–1804.—(All.)
ÅNGSTRÖM, JOHAN, 1813–1879.—(Ångstr.)
ASCHERSON, PAUL FRIEDRICH AUGUST, 1834–1913.—
    (Asch.)
AUBLET, JEAN BAPTISTE CHRISTOPHE FUSÉE, 1720–1778.—
    (Aubl.)

BAKER, JOHN GILBERT, 1834–1920.—(Baker)
BEAUVOIS, see PALISOT DE BEAUVOIS
BECK, LEWIS CALEB, 1798–1853.—(Beck)
BENEDICT, RALPH CURTISS, 1883–   .—(Benedict)
BERNHARDI, JOHANN JACOB, 1774–1850.—(Bernh.)
BLANCHARD, WILLIAM HENRY, 1850–1922.—(Blanchard)
BONGARD, AUGUST GUSTAV HEINRICH, 1786–1839.—
    (Bong.)
BORY DE SAINT-VINCENT, JEAN BAPTISTE GEORGES MAR-
    CELLIN, 1778–1846.—(Bory)
BRAUN, ALEXANDER CARL HEINRICH, 1805–1877.—(A. Br.)
BRITTON, ELIZABETH GERTRUDE (KNIGHT), 1858–1934.—
    (E. G. Britton)
BRITTON, NATHANIEL LORD, 1859–1934.   (Britton)
BRITTON, NATHANIEL LORD, 1859–1934; BROWN, ADDISON,
    1830–1913.—(Britt. & Brown)
BRITTON, NATHANIEL LORD, 1859–1934; STERNS, EMERSON
    ELLICK, 1846–1926; POGGENBURG, JUSTUS FERDINAND,
    1840–1893.—(B. S. P.)
BROWN, ROBERT, 1773–1858.—(R. Br.)
BUTTERS, FREDERIC KING, 1878–   .—(Butters)

CHAPMAN, ALVAN WENTWORTH, 1809–1899.—(Chapm.)
CHRISTENSEN, CARL FREDERIK ALBERT, 1872–   .—(C.
    Chr.)
CLARKSON, EDWARD HALE, 1866–1934.—(Clarkson)
CLUTE, WILLARD NELSON, 1869–   .—(Clute)

[1] Contributed by JOHN HENDLEY BARNHART.

DAVENPORT, GEORGE EDWARD, 1833–1907.—(Davenp.)

DESVAUX, NIÇAISE AUGUSTE, 1784–1856.—(Desv.)

DIELS, FRIEDRICH LUDWIG EMIL, 1874– .—(Diels)

DILLENIUS, JOHANN JACOB, 1684–1747.—(Dill.)

DODGE, RAYNAL, 1844–1918.—(R. Dodge)

DÖLL, JOHANN CHRISTOPH, 1808–1885.—(Döll)

DOWELL, PHILIP, 1864– .—(Dowell)

DURIEU DE MAISONNEUVE, MICHEL CHARLES, 1797–1878.—
(Durieu)

EATON, ALVAH AUGUSTUS, 1865–1908.—(A. A. Eaton)

EATON, AMOS, 1776–1842.—(Eaton)

EATON, DANIEL CADY, 1834–1895.—(D. C. Eaton)

EHRHART, FRIEDRICH, 1742–1795.—(Ehrh.)

ENGELMANN, GEORGE, 1809–1884.—(Engelm.)

FARWELL, OLIVER ATKINS, 1867– .—(Farwell)

FÉE, ANTOINE LAURENT APOLLINAIRE, 1789–1874.—(Fée)

FERNALD, MERRITT LYNDON, 1873– .—(Fernald)

FERNALD, MERRITT LYNDON, 1873– ; BISSELL, CHARLES
HUMPHREY, 1857–1925.—(Fernald & Bissell)

FISCHER, FRIEDRICH ERNST LUDWIG VON, 1782–1854.—
(Fischer)

FRIES, KLAS ROBERT ELIAS, 1876– .—(R. E. Fries)

GILBERT, BENJAMIN DAVIS, 1835–1907.—(Gilbert)

GMELIN, SAMUEL GOTTLIEB, 1745–1774.—(S. G. Gmel.)

GRAY, ASA, 1819–1888.—(A. Gray)

GRAY, FREDERICK WILLIAM, 1878– .—(F. W. Gray)

GRAY, SAMUEL FREDERICK, 1766–1836.—(S. F. Gray)

HIERONYMUS, HANS GEORG EMMO WOLFGANG, 1846–1921.
—(Hieron.)

HITCHCOCK, EDWARD, 1793–1864.—(E. Hitchc.)

HOFFMAN, GEORG FRANZ, 1761–1826.—(Hoffm.)

HOOKER, WILLIAM JACKSON, 1785–1865.—(Hook.)

HOOKER, WILLIAM JACKSON, 1785–1865; BAKER, JOHN
GILBERT, 1834–1920.—(Hook. & Baker)

HOOKER, WILLIAM JACKSON, 1785–1865; GREVILLE, ROB-
ERT KAYE, 1794–1866.—(Hook. & Grev.)

HOUSE, HOMER DOLIVER, 1878-   .—(House)
HOWE, ELLIOT CALVIN, 1828–1899.—(E. C. Howe)
HUNTINGTON, JOHN WARREN, 1853-   .—(Huntington)

JACQUIN, NIKOLAUS JOSEPH VON, 1727–1817.—(Jacq.)

KEYSERLING, ALEXANDER FRIEDRICH MICHEL LEBERECHT
   ARTHUR VON, 1815–1891.—(Keyserl.)
KOCH, WILHELM DANIEL JOSEPH, 1771–1849.—(Koch)
KÜHLEWEIN, PAUL EDUARD, 1798–1870.—(Kühl.)
KUHN, MAXIMILIAN FRIEDRICH ADALBERT, 1842–1894.—
   (Kuhn)
KUNTZE, CARL ERNST OTTO, 1843–1907.—(Kuntze)
KUNZE, GUSTAV, 1793–1851.—(Kunze)

LAMARCK, JEAN BAPTISTE ANTOINE PIERRE MONNET DE,
   1744–1829.—(Lam.)
LAWSON, GEORGE, 1827–1895.—(Lawson)
LINK, JOHANN HEINRICH FRIEDRICH, 1767–1851.—(Link)
LINNAEUS, CARL, 1707–1778.—(L.)
LLOYD, FRANCIS ERNEST, 1868-   ; UNDERWOOD,
   LUCIEN MARCUS, 1853–1907.—(Lloyd & Underw.)
LOWE, EDWARD JOSEPH, 1825–1900.—(Lowe)
LYON, HAROLD LLOYD, 1879-   .—(Lyon)

MACKENZIE, KENNETH KENT, 1877–1934.—(Mackenzie)
MAXON, WILLIAM RALPH, 1877-   .—(Maxon)
METTENIUS, GEORG HEINRICH, 1823–1866.—(Mett.)
MEYER, GEORG FRIEDRICH WILHELM, 1782–1856.—(G.
   Meyer)
MICHAUX, ANDRÉ, 1746–1802.—(Michx.)
MILDE, CARL AUGUST JULIUS, 1824–1871.—(Milde)
MILLER, ELIHU SANFORD, 1848-   .—(E. S. Miller)
MOORE, THOMAS, 1821–1887.—(Moore)
MUELLER, OTTO FRIDRICH, 1730–1784.—(Muell.)
MUHLENBERG, GOTTHILF HENRY ERNEST, 1753–1815.—
   (Muhl.)

NEWMAN, EDWARD, 1801–1876.—(Newman)

NIEUWLAND, JULIUS ALOYSIUS ARTHUR, 1878–   .—
(Nieuwl.)
NUTTALL, THOMAS, 1786–1859.—(Nutt.)

OAKES, WILLIAM, 1799–1848.—(Oakes)

PALISOT DE BEAUVOIS, AMBROISE MARIE FRANÇOIS
JOSEPH, 1752–1820.—(Beauv.)
PEASE, ARTHUR STANLEY, 1881–   ; MOORE, ALBERT
HANFORD, 1883–   .—(Pease & Moore)
PETROV, VSEVOLOD ALEXEEVICH, 1896–   .—(Petrov)
PFEIFFER, NORMA ETTA, 1889–   .—(N. Pfeiffer)
PRANTL, KARL ANTON EUGEN, 1849–1893.—(Prantl)
PRESL, KAREL BOŘIWOG, 1794–1852.—(Presl)
PURSH, FREDERICK TRAUGOTT, 1774–1820.—(Pursh)

RAFINESQUE, CONSTANTINE SAMUEL, 1783–1840.—(Raf.)
ROBINSON, BENJAMIN LINCOLN, 1864–1935.—(B. L.
Robinson)
ROBINSON, BENJAMIN LINCOLN, 1864–1935; FERNALD,
MERRITT LYNDON, 1873–   .—(Rob. & Fern.)
ROTH, ALBRECHT WILHELM, 1757–1834.—(Roth)
RUPRECHT, FRANZ JOSEF, 1814–1870.—(Rupr.)
RYDBERG, PER AXEL, 1860–1931.—(Rydb.)

ST. JOHN, EDWARD PORTER, 1866–   ; ST. JOHN, ROBERT
PORTER, 1869–   .—(St. John fr.)
SALISBURY, RICHARD ANTHONY, 1761–1829.—(Salisb.)
SCHAFFNER, JOHN HENRY, 1866–   .—(J. H. Schaffn.)
SCHKUHR, CHRISTIAN, 1741–1811.—(Schkuhr)
SCHLEICHER, JOHANN CHRISTOPH, 1768–1834.—(Schleich.)
SCHMIDEL, CASIMIR CHRISTOPH, 1718–1792.—(Schmidel)
SCHOTT, HEINRICH WILHELM, 1794–1865.—(Schott)
SCOTT, ROBERT ROBINSON, 1827–1877.—(R. R. Scott)
SLOSSON, MARGARET, 1872?–   .—(Slosson)
SMALL, JOHN KUNKEL, 1869–   .—(Small)
SMITH, JAMES EDWARD, 1759–1828.—(Smith)
SMITH, JOHN, 1798–1888.—(J. Smith)
SPENNER, FRIDOLIN CARL LEOPOLD, 1798–1841. —
(Spenner)

SPRENGEL, CURT POLYCARP JOACHIM, 1766–1833.—
(Spreng.)
SPRING, ANTON FRIEDRICH, 1814–1872.—(Spring)
SWARTZ, OLOF PETER, 1760–1818.—(Sw.)

TIDESTROM, IVAR, 1865–   .—(Tidestrom)
TODARO, AGOSTINO, 1818–1892.—(Todaro)
TORREY, JOHN, 1796–1873.—(Torr.)
TOURNEFORT, JOSEPH PITTON DE, 1656–1708.—(Tourn.)
TUCKERMAN, EDWARD, 1817–1886.—(Tuckerm.)

UNDERWOOD, LUCIEN MARCUS, 1853–1907.—(Underw.)

VICTORIN, MARIE [KIROUAC, CONRAD], 1855– .—
(Victorin)

WATERS, CAMPBELL EASTER, 1872–   .—(Waters)
WATT, DAVID ALLAN POE, 1830–1917.—(Watt)
WEATHERBY, CHARLES ALFRED, 1875–   .—(Weatherby)
WHERRY, EDGAR THEODORE, 1885–   .—(Wherry)
WILLDENOW, CARL LUDWIG, 1765–1812.—(Willd.)
WOOD, ALPHONSO, 1810–1881.—(Wood)

GLOSSARY

ACICULAR. Needle-shaped.

ACUMINATE. Tapering to the end.

ACUTE. Ending in a sharp angle.

ADAXIAL. Opposite an axil.

ADNATE. United, used in reference to the union of parts of different organs.

AMPHIBIOUS. Living both on land and in water.

ANASTOMOSE. To run together or to unite.

ANNUAL. Having one season's duration.

ANNULUS. The elastic ring of cells in the sporangia.

ANTHERIDIUM. The organ in ferns, corresponding to an anther in flowering plants.

ANTHEROZOID. A minute organ developed in an antheridium.

APICULATE. Ending in a short pointed tip.

AQUATIC. Living in water.

ARCHEGONIUM. The organ in ferns, corresponding to the pistil in flowering plants.

ARCUATE. Bowed or arched.

ARENICOLOUS. Living in sand.

AREOLA. A space marked out by veins or veinlets.

ARTICULATE. Jointed.

ASSURGENT. Abruptly ascending.

ATTENUATE. Slenderly tapering.

AURICLE. An ear-shaped appendage.

AURICULATE. With ear-shaped appendages.

AWL-SHAPED. Tapering from a base to a slender tip.

AWN. A bristle-like appendage.

AXIL. The angle formed by a branch, or a leaf, with the stem from which it arises.

BIENNIAL. Having two seasons' duration.

BIPINNATIFID. Twice pinnately cleft.

BLADE. The dilated part of a leaf.

BRACT. A leaf, often much reduced, subtending an organ.

BULBLET. A small bulb.

CAMPANULATE. Bell-shaped.

CAUDATE. With a tail-like appendage.

CAUDEX. The persistent base of perennial herbaceous plants.

CAULINE. Belonging to the stem.

CELL. The smallest element in the structure of a living organism.

CENTRUM. The central air-space in a stem, as in *Equisetum*.

CHAFF. A scale, usually dry and membranous.

CHANNELED. Grooved longitudinally.

CHLOROPHYL. The green coloring matter in plants.

CILIA. Slender hairs in a row.

COALESCENT. United, used in reference to the union of parts or organs of the same kind.

COMPOUND. Having two or more similar parts.

CONCOLOROUS. Of similar color.

CONE. A structure with imbricated scales around an elongate axis.

CONFLUENT. Running into each other.

CONIFEROUS. Cone-bearing.

CORDATE. Having two obtuse lobes and a sinus at the base.

CORIACEOUS. Leathery in texture.

CORM. The swollen base of a stem; like a bulb, but solid.

CREEPING. Lying on the ground and rooting at the nodes.

CRENATE. Dentate with rounded teeth.

CRENULATE. Having small rounded teeth.

CUNEATE. Wedge-shaped.

CYLINDRIC. Roller-shaped.

DECIDUOUS. Not evergreen; not persistent.

DECOMPOUND. More than once compound.

DECUMBENT. Reclining or procumbent but with the tip ascending.

DECURRENT. Extending down below the point of insertion.

DEFLEXED. Bent or turned abruptly downward.

DEHISCENT. Opening regularly.

DELTOID. Shaped like the Greek letter Δ.

DENTATE. Toothed, with the teeth directed outward.

DENTICULATE. Finely dentate.

DIAPHRAGM. A partition.

DICHOTOMOUS. Forking regularly by pairs.

DIFFUSE. Loosely or widely spreading.

DIMORPHIC. Occuring in two forms.

DIOECIOUS. With the sexes on different plants.

DISSECTED. Lobed to the base.

DISTAL. Remote from the point of attachment.

DISTICHOUS. In two vertical ranks.

DORSAL. Relating to the back of an organ.

DORSIVENTRAL. With distinction of back and front.

ECOLOGICAL. Concerning the relation of plants to one another and to their surroundings.

ELATER. One of the four filamentous appendages of the spores in *Equisetum*.

ELLIPSOID. A solid body, elliptic in section.

ELLIPTIC. Having the outline of an ellipse; oval.

EMARGINATE. Having a shallow notch at the apex.

ENDOPHYTIC. Growing within a plant, usually parasitic.

ENTIRE. Without toothing or lobing.

EPIDERMAL. Pertaining to the superficial layer of cells.

EPIPHYTIC. Growing attached to other plants; but not parasitic.

EROSE. Uneven, as if gnawed.

EVANESCENT. Fleeting.

FALCATE. Scythe-shaped.

FIBROUS. Resembling or consisting of fibers.

FILAMENTOSE. Having thread-like structures.

FILIFORM. Thread-shaped.

FIMBRIATE. Fringed.

FLABELLATE. Fan-shaped.

FLACCID. Lax and weak.

FLEXUOUS. Zigzag.

FOLIAR. Leaf-like.

FOLIOLATE. Having leaflets.

FREE. Said of veins in a leaf that are simple or forked, but whose branches do not unite.

FRONDS. Leaves, of ferns.
FUGACIOUS. Falling away early.
FUSIFORM. Spindle-shaped.

GAMETOPHYTE. The phase of a fern that produces the
    sexual organs.
GEMMIPAROUS. Producing gemmae.
GLABROUS. Without hairs.
GLANDULAR. Bearing glands.
GLAUCOUS. Covered with a white or pale bloom.
GLOBOSE. Spherical.
GREGARIOUS. Growing in groups or colonies.

HASTATE. Shaped like an arrow-head with the basal lobes
    directed outward.
HIRSUTE. Bearing stiff or coarse hairs.
HYALINE. Transparent or translucent.
HYBRID. A cross between two species.

IMBRICATE. Overlapping.
INCISED. Sharply and deeply cut.
INDUSIUM. The covering of the sorus of a fern.
INFERIOR. Lower or below.
INSERTION. Attachment.
INTERNODE. Part of a stem between two nodes.

LABYRINTHIFORM. Having complicated curved lines.
LANCEOLATE. Shaped like a lance-head.
LEAFLET. A division of a compound leaf.
LIGULE. A projection at the top of a sheath.
LINEAR. Long and narrow, with parallel sides.
LIP-CELLS. The line of cells between which the sporangia
    dehisce.
LOBE. A segment, usually rounded.
LOBED. Having rounded segments.
LOBULE. A small lobe.
LUNATE. Crescent or halfmoon-shaped.

MEGASPORANGIUM. The envelopes in which megaspores
    are developed or contained.

MEGASPORE. The larger kind of a spore if there are two kinds.

MICROSPORANGIUM. The receptacle in which the microspores are developed.

MICROSPORE. The smaller kind of spore if there are two kinds.

MIDRIB. The main vein of a leaf or of a leaflet.

MIDVEIN. The central rib of a leaf or leaflet.

MONOECIOUS. With both sexes on the same plant.

MUCRONATE. Ending in a small abrupt tip.

MYCORRHIZA. A fungus mycelium which invests or inhabits the roots or root-hairs of a plant.

NERVE. A simple thread of fibrovo-vascular tissue.

NODE. Point on a stem which normally bears a leaf or a whorl of leaves.

OB-. In combination, meaning inversion.

OBLANCEOLATE. Inverted lance-shaped.

OBLIQUE. Slanting.

OBLONG. Longer than broad with nearly parallel sides.

OBOVOID. Inverted egg-shaped.

OBTUSE. Blunt or rounded.

ORBICULAR. Circular.

OVAL. Broadly elliptic.

OVATE. Egg-shaped in outline.

OVOID. Shaped like a hen's egg.

PALMATE. Radiately lobed or divided.

PALUDAL. Of or pertaining to a marsh or a swamp.

PANICLE. A loose compound sporophyl with pedicellate sporangia.

PAPILLOSE. Having minute nipple-shaped projections.

PEDATE. Radiately lobed or compound with the lateral lobes or parts cleft.

PEDUNCLE. A primary stalk.

PELTATE. Shield-shaped, with an attachment on the lower surface.

PENDULOUS. Hanging.

PENICILLATE. Tipped with fine hairs.

PENTAGONAL. Five-angled.

PERENNIAL. Having several or many years' duration.

PERSISTENT. Evergreen. Remaining attached.

PETIOLE. The stalk of a leaf.

PETIOLULE. A secondary petiole.

PILOSE. Hairy, with soft hairs.

PINNA. A leaflet.

PINNATE. Compound and with the leaflets arranged on each side of a common rachis.

PINNATIFID. Pinnately cleft.

PINNULE. A secondary pinna.

PROCUMBENT. Lying on the ground, but not rooting.

PROTHALLUS. A usually flat and thallus-like growth, resulting from the germination of a spore. Upon this are developed sexual organs or new plants.

PROXIMAL. Close to the point of attachment.

PUBESCENT. Bearing hairs.

PUNCTATE. Marked with depressions or internal glands.

PYRIFORM. Pear-shaped.

RACHIS. The axis of a compound leaf or of an inflorescence.

RECEPTACLE. An expanded structure that bears other organs.

REFLEXED. Bent abruptly downward.

RENIFORM. Kidney-shaped.

RETICULATE. Like a net-work.

REVOLUTE. Rolled backward from the margin or apex.

RHOMB. An equilateral parallelogram having oblique angles.

RING. Same as annulus.

ROOTSTOCK. A subterranean stem.

SCALE. A more or less flattened trichome borne on various parts of a fern.

SCANDENT. Climbing.

SCARIOUS. Thin, dry, and not green.

SEGMENT. A part of a cleft leaf-blade.

SEPTATE. Divided by partitions.

SERRATE. With sharp teeth pointing forward.

SERRULATE. Diminutive of serrate.

SESSILE. Without a stalk.

SETACEOUS. Bristle-like.

SHEATH. A tubular or funnelform envelope.

SILEX. A white or colorless, extremely hard crystalline mineral substance.

SIMPLE. Of one piece, as distinguished from compound.

SINUATE. With a strongly wavy margin.

SINUS. The recess between two lobes.

SORUS. A heap or cluster, as of spores.

SPATULATE. Gradually dilated upward to a rounded apex.

SPERMATOZOID. The motile male reproductive cell.

SPIKE. A form of sporophyl with the sporangia sessile on a common rachis.

SPINULOSE. Diminutive of spinose.

SPORANGIUM. A spore-case.

SPORE. An asexual reproductive cell.

SPORELING. A young plant developed from a spore.

SPOROCARP. A capsular organ containing spores or sporangia.

SPOROPHYL. A leaf bearing spores.

SPOROPHYTE. A phase of a plant that bears the asexual spores.

SPUR. A sac-like or tubular extension, usually hollow.

STELLATE. Star-shaped.

STERILE. Unproductive.

STOLON. A runner from the base of a plant.

STOMA. An orifice in the epidermis of a leaf or stem.

STRAMINEOUS. Straw-colored.

STROBILE. A structure with imbricate scales shaped like a cone.

SUB–. Latin prefix, signifying slightly or somewhat.

SUBULATE. Awl-shaped.

SUCCULENT. Fleshy.

TERETE. Circular in cross-section.

TERNATE. In threes.

TERRESTRIAL. Growing on the ground.

TETRAHEDRAL. Having the form of a tetrahedron, *i.e.*, a solid with four triangular faces.

THALLOID. Resembling a thallus.

THALLUS. In ferns, cellular expansion taking the place of the stem and leaves in higher plants.

TOMENTUM. Densely matted wool.

TRI–. Latin prefix, signifying three or thrice.

TRICHOME. An epidermal hair or hair-like structure, various in form.

TRIQUETROUS. Having three salient angles.

TRUNCATE. Abrupt, as if cut off transversely.

TUBERCLE. A small tuber or tuber-like body.

TUBEROUS. Tuber-like.

TUMID. Swollen.

TURGID. Swollen, as if by pressure from within.

ULIGINOUS. Living in mud.

UNDULATE. Having a wavy edge.

URCEOLATE. Urn-shaped.

VALLECULAR. Of or near a groove.

VALVE. One of the pieces into which a conceptacle or capsule splits.

VASCULAR. Having vessels or ducts.

VEIN. A thread of fibro-vascular tissue in a leaf, usually branching.

VEINLETS. Branches of veins.

VELUM. The membranous indusium in *Isoetes*.

VENATION. The arrangement of the veins.

VENTRAL. Relating to the front of an organ.

VERNATION. The arrangement of the leaves in a bud.

VERTICILLATE. Disposed in a whorl.

VILLOUS. Bearing long soft hairs.

WHORL. Arrangement of leaves or branches in a circle around a node.

INDEX

A CATALOGUE OF SELECTED DOVER BOOKS
IN ALL FIELDS OF INTEREST

A CATALOGUE OF SELECTED DOVER BOOKS
IN ALL FIELDS OF INTEREST

AMERICA'S OLD MASTERS, James T. Flexner. Four men emerged unexpectedly from provincial 18th century America to leadership in European art: Benjamin West, J. S. Copley, C. R. Peale, Gilbert Stuart. Brilliant coverage of lives and contributions. Revised, 1967 edition. 69 plates. 365pp. of text.

21806-6 Paperbound $3.00

FIRST FLOWERS OF OUR WILDERNESS: AMERICAN PAINTING, THE COLONIAL PERIOD, James T. Flexner. Painters, and regional painting traditions from earliest Colonial times up to the emergence of Copley, West and Peale Sr., Foster, Gustavus Hesselius, Feke, John Smibert and many anonymous painters in the primitive manner. Engaging presentation, with 162 illustrations. xxii + 368pp.

22180-6 Paperbound $3.50

THE LIGHT OF DISTANT SKIES: AMERICAN PAINTING, 1760-1835, James T. Flexner. The great generation of early American painters goes to Europe to learn and to teach: West, Copley, Gilbert Stuart and others. Allston, Trumbull, Morse; also contemporary American painters—primitives, derivatives, academics—who remained in America. 102 illustrations. xiii + 306pp.   22179-2 Paperbound $3.50

A HISTORY OF THE RISE AND PROGRESS OF THE ARTS OF DESIGN IN THE UNITED STATES, William Dunlap. Much the richest mine of information on early American painters, sculptors, architects, engravers, miniaturists, etc. The only source of information for scores of artists, the major primary source for many others. Unabridged reprint of rare original 1834 edition, with new introduction by James T. Flexner, and 394 new illustrations. Edited by Rita Weiss. 6⅝ x 9⅝.

21695-0, 21696-9, 21697-7 Three volumes, Paperbound $15.00

EPOCHS OF CHINESE AND JAPANESE ART, Ernest F. Fenollosa. From primitive Chinese art to the 20th century, thorough history, explanation of every important art period and form, including Japanese woodcuts; main stress on China and Japan, but Tibet, Korea also included. Still unexcelled for its detailed, rich coverage of cultural background, aesthetic elements, diffusion studies, particularly of the historical period. 2nd, 1913 edition. 242 illustrations. lii + 439pp. of text.

20364-6, 20365-4 Two volumes, Paperbound $6.00

THE GENTLE ART OF MAKING ENEMIES, James A. M. Whistler. Greatest wit of his day deflates Oscar Wilde, Ruskin, Swinburne; strikes back at inane critics, exhibitions, art journalism; aesthetics of impressionist revolution in most striking form. Highly readable classic by great painter. Reproduction of edition designed by Whistler. Introduction by Alfred Werner. xxxvi + 334pp.

21875-9 Paperbound $3.00

VISUAL ILLUSIONS: THEIR CAUSES, CHARACTERISTICS, AND APPLICATIONS, Matthew Luckiesh. Thorough description and discussion of optical illusion, geometric and perspective, particularly; size and shape distortions, illusions of color, of motion; natural illusions; use of illusion in art and magic, industry, etc. Most useful today with op art, also for classical art. Scores of effects illustrated. Introduction by William H. Ittleson. 100 illustrations. xxi + 252pp.

21530-X Paperbound $2.00

A HANDBOOK OF ANATOMY FOR ART STUDENTS, Arthur Thomson. Thorough, virtually exhaustive coverage of skeletal structure, musculature, etc. Full text, supplemented by anatomical diagrams and drawings and by photographs of undraped figures. Unique in its comparison of male and female forms, pointing out differences of contour, texture, form. 211 figures, 40 drawings, 86 photographs. xx + 459pp. 5⅜ x 8⅜.

21163-0 Paperbound $3.50

150 MASTERPIECES OF DRAWING, Selected by Anthony Toney. Full page reproductions of drawings from the early 16th to the end of the 18th century, all beautifully reproduced: Rembrandt, Michelangelo, Dürer, Fragonard, Urs, Graf, Wouwerman, many others. First-rate browsing book, model book for artists. xviii + 150pp. 8⅜ x 11¼.

21032-4 Paperbound $2.50

THE LATER WORK OF AUBREY BEARDSLEY, Aubrey Beardsley. Exotic, erotic, ironic masterpieces in full maturity: Comedy Ballet, Venus and Tannhauser, Pierrot, Lysistrata, Rape of the Lock, Savoy material, Ali Baba, Volpone, etc. This material revolutionized the art world, and is still powerful, fresh, brilliant. With *The Early Work,* all Beardsley's finest work. 174 plates, 2 in color. xiv + 176pp. 8⅛ x 11.

21817-1 Paperbound $3.00

DRAWINGS OF REMBRANDT, Rembrandt van Rijn. Complete reproduction of fabulously rare edition by Lippmann and Hofstede de Groot, completely reedited, updated, improved by Prof. Seymour Slive, Fogg Museum. Portraits, Biblical sketches, landscapes, Oriental types, nudes, episodes from classical mythology—All Rembrandt's fertile genius. Also selection of drawings by his pupils and followers. "Stunning volumes," *Saturday Review.* 550 illustrations. lxxviii + 552pp. 9⅛ x 12¼.

21485-0, 21486-9 Two volumes, Paperbound $10.00

THE DISASTERS OF WAR, Francisco Goya. One of the masterpieces of Western civilization—83 etchings that record Goya's shattering, bitter reaction to the Napoleonic war that swept through Spain after the insurrection of 1808 and to war in general. Reprint of the first edition, with three additional plates from Boston's Museum of Fine Arts. All plates facsimile size. Introduction by Philip Hofer, Fogg Museum. v + 97pp. 9⅜ x 8¼.

21872-4 Paperbound $2.00

GRAPHIC WORKS OF ODILON REDON. Largest collection of Redon's graphic works ever assembled: 172 lithographs, 28 etchings and engravings, 9 drawings. These include some of his most famous works. All the plates from *Odilon Redon: oeuvre graphique complet,* plus additional plates. New introduction and caption translations by Alfred Werner. 209 illustrations. xxvii + 209pp. 9⅛ x 12¼.

21966-8 Paperbound $4.50

DESIGN BY ACCIDENT; A BOOK OF "ACCIDENTAL EFFECTS" FOR ARTISTS AND DESIGNERS, James F. O'Brien. Create your own unique, striking, imaginative effects by "controlled accident" interaction of materials: paints and lacquers, oil and water based paints, splatter, crackling materials, shatter, similar items. Everything you do will be different; first book on this limitless art, so useful to both fine artist and commercial artist. Full instructions. 192 plates showing "accidents," 8 in color. viii + 215pp. 8⅜ x 11¼. 21942-9 Paperbound $3.75

THE BOOK OF SIGNS, Rudolf Koch. Famed German type designer draws 493 beautiful symbols: religious, mystical, alchemical, imperial, property marks, runes, etc. Remarkable fusion of traditional and modern. Good for suggestions of timelessness, smartness, modernity. Text. vi + 104pp. 6⅛ x 9¼.
20162-7 Paperbound $1.25

HISTORY OF INDIAN AND INDONESIAN ART, Ananda K. Coomaraswamy. An unabridged republication of one of the finest books by a great scholar in Eastern art. Rich in descriptive material, history, social backgrounds; Sunga reliefs, Rajput paintings, Gupta temples, Burmese frescoes, textiles, jewelry, sculpture, etc. 400 photos. viii + 423pp. 6⅜ x 9¾. 21436-2 Paperbound $5.00

PRIMITIVE ART, Franz Boas. America's foremost anthropologist surveys textiles, ceramics, woodcarving, basketry, metalwork, etc.; patterns, technology, creation of symbols, style origins. All areas of world, but very full on Northwest Coast Indians. More than 350 illustrations of baskets, boxes, totem poles, weapons, etc. 378 pp.
20025-6 Paperbound $3.00

THE GENTLEMAN AND CABINET MAKER'S DIRECTOR, Thomas Chippendale. Full reprint (third edition, 1762) of most influential furniture book of all time, by master cabinetmaker. 200 plates, illustrating chairs, sofas, mirrors, tables, cabinets, plus 24 photographs of surviving pieces. Biographical introduction by N. Bienenstock. vi + 249pp. 9⅞ x 12¾. 21601-2 Paperbound $4.00

AMERICAN ANTIQUE FURNITURE, Edgar G. Miller, Jr. The basic coverage of all American furniture before 1840. Individual chapters cover type of furniture—clocks, tables, sideboards, etc.—chronologically, with inexhaustible wealth of data. More than 2100 photographs, all identified, commented on. Essential to all early American collectors. Introduction by H. E. Keyes. vi + 1106pp. 7⅞ x 10¾.
21599-7, 21600-4 Two volumes, Paperbound $11.00

PENNSYLVANIA DUTCH AMERICAN FOLK ART, Henry J. Kauffman. 279 photos, 28 drawings of tulipware, Fraktur script, painted tinware, toys, flowered furniture, quilts, samplers, hex signs, house interiors, etc. Full descriptive text. Excellent for tourist, rewarding for designer, collector. Map. 146pp. 7⅞ x 10¾.
21205-X Paperbound $2.50

EARLY NEW ENGLAND GRAVESTONE RUBBINGS, Edmund V. Gillon, Jr. 43 photographs, 226 carefully reproduced rubbings show heavily symbolic, sometimes macabre early gravestones, up to early 19th century. Remarkable early American primitive art, occasionally strikingly beautiful; always powerful. Text. xxvi + 207pp. 8⅜ x 11¼. 21380-3 Paperbound $3.50

ALPHABETS AND ORNAMENTS, Ernst Lehner. Well-known pictorial source for decorative alphabets, script examples, cartouches, frames, decorative title pages, calligraphic initials, borders, similar material. 14th to 19th century, mostly European. Useful in almost any graphic arts designing, varied styles. 750 illustrations. 256pp. 7 x 10. 21905-4 Paperbound $4.00

PAINTING: A CREATIVE APPROACH, Norman Colquhoun. For the beginner simple guide provides an instructive approach to painting: major stumbling blocks for beginner; overcoming them, technical points; paints and pigments; oil painting; watercolor and other media and color. New section on "plastic" paints. Glossary. Formerly *Paint Your Own Pictures*. 221pp. 22000-1 Paperbound $1.75

THE ENJOYMENT AND USE OF COLOR, Walter Sargent. Explanation of the relations between colors themselves and between colors in nature and art, including hundreds of little-known facts about color values, intensities, effects of high and low illumination, complementary colors. Many practical hints for painters, references to great masters. 7 color plates, 29 illustrations. x + 274pp.
20944-X Paperbound $2.75

THE NOTEBOOKS OF LEONARDO DA VINCI, compiled and edited by Jean Paul Richter. 1566 extracts from original manuscripts reveal the full range of Leonardo's versatile genius: all his writings on painting, sculpture, architecture, anatomy, astronomy, geography, topography, physiology, mining, music, etc., in both Italian and English, with 186 plates of manuscript pages and more than 500 additional drawings. Includes studies for the Last Supper, the lost Sforza monument, and other works. Total of xlvii + 866pp. 7⅞ x 10¾.
22572-0, 22573-9 Two volumes, Paperbound $11.00

MONTGOMERY WARD CATALOGUE OF 1895. Tea gowns, yards of flannel and pillow-case lace, stereoscopes, books of gospel hymns, the New Improved Singer Sewing Machine, side saddles, milk skimmers, straight-edged razors, high-button shoes, spittoons, and on and on . . . listing some 25,000 items, practically all illustrated. Essential to the shoppers of the 1890's, it is our truest record of the spirit of the period. Unaltered reprint of Issue No. 57, Spring and Summer 1895. Introduction by Boris Emmet. Innumerable illustrations. xiii + 624pp. 8½ x 11⅝.
22377-9 Paperbound $6.95

THE CRYSTAL PALACE EXHIBITION ILLUSTRATED CATALOGUE (LONDON, 1851). One of the wonders of the modern world—the Crystal Palace Exhibition in which all the nations of the civilized world exhibited their achievements in the arts and sciences—presented in an equally important illustrated catalogue. More than 1700 items pictured with accompanying text—ceramics, textiles, cast-iron work, carpets, pianos, sleds, razors, wall-papers, billiard tables, beehives, silverware and hundreds of other artifacts—represent the focal point of Victorian culture in the Western World. Probably the largest collection of Victorian decorative art ever assembled—indispensable for antiquarians and designers. Unabridged republication of the Art-Journal Catalogue of the Great Exhibition of 1851, with all terminal essays. New introduction by John Gloag, F.S.A. xxxiv + 426pp. 9 x 12.
22503-8 Paperbound $5.00

A HISTORY OF COSTUME, Carl Köhler. Definitive history, based on surviving pieces of clothing primarily, and paintings, statues, etc. secondarily. Highly readable text, supplemented by 594 illustrations of costumes of the ancient Mediterranean peoples, Greece and Rome, the Teutonic prehistoric period; costumes of the Middle Ages, Renaissance, Baroque, 18th and 19th centuries. Clear, measured patterns are provided for many clothing articles. Approach is practical throughout. Enlarged by Emma von Sichart. 464pp. 21030-8 Paperbound $3.50.

ORIENTAL RUGS, ANTIQUE AND MODERN, Walter A. Hawley. A complete and authoritative treatise on the Oriental rug—where they are made, by whom and how, designs and symbols, characteristics in detail of the six major groups, how to distinguish them and how to buy them. Detailed technical data is provided on periods, weaves, warps, wefts, textures, sides, ends and knots, although no technical background is required for an understanding. 11 color plates, 80 halftones, 4 maps. vi + 320pp. 6⅛ x 9⅛. 22366-3 Paperbound $5.00

TEN BOOKS ON ARCHITECTURE, Vitruvius. By any standards the most important book on architecture ever written. Early Roman discussion of aesthetics of building, construction methods, orders, sites, and every other aspect of architecture has inspired, instructed architecture for about 2,000 years. Stands behind Palladio, Michelangelo, Bramante, Wren, countless others. Definitive Morris H. Morgan translation. 68 illustrations. xii + 331pp. 20645-9 Paperbound $3.00

THE FOUR BOOKS OF ARCHITECTURE, Andrea Palladio. Translated into every major Western European language in the two centuries following its publication in 1570, this has been one of the most influential books in the history of architecture. Complete reprint of the 1738 Isaac Ware edition. New introduction by Adolf Placzek, Columbia Univ. 216 plates. xxii + 110pp. of text. 9½ x 12¾. 21308-0 Clothbound $12.50

STICKS AND STONES: A STUDY OF AMERICAN ARCHITECTURE AND CIVILIZATION, Lewis Mumford.One of the great classics of American cultural history. American architecture from the medieval-inspired earliest forms to the early 20th century; evolution of structure and style, and reciprocal influences on environment. 21 photographic illustrations. 238pp. 20202-X Paperbound $2.00

THE AMERICAN BUILDER'S COMPANION, Asher Benjamin. The most widely used early 19th century architectural style and source book, for colonial up into Greek Revival periods. Extensive development of geometry of carpentering, construction of sashes, frames, doors, stairs; plans and elevations of domestic and other buildings. Hundreds of thousands of houses were built according to this book, now invaluable to historians, architects, restorers, etc. 1827 edition. 59 plates. 114pp. 7⅞ x 10¾. 22236-5 Paperbound $3.50

DUTCH HOUSES IN THE HUDSON VALLEY BEFORE 1776, Helen Wilkinson Reynolds. The standard survey of the Dutch colonial house and outbuildings, with constructional features, decoration, and local history associated with individual homesteads. Introduction by Franklin D. Roosevelt. Map. 150 illustrations. 469pp. 6⅝ x 9¼. 21469-9 Paperbound $5.00

THE ARCHITECTURE OF COUNTRY HOUSES, Andrew J. Downing. Together with Vaux's *Villas and Cottages* this is the basic book for Hudson River Gothic architecture of the middle Victorian period. Full, sound discussions of general aspects of housing, architecture, style, decoration, furnishing, together with scores of detailed house plans, illustrations of specific buildings, accompanied by full text. Perhaps the most influential single American architectural book. 1850 edition. Introduction by J. Stewart Johnson. 321 figures, 34 architectural designs. xvi + 560pp.
22003-6 Paperbound $4.00

LOST EXAMPLES OF COLONIAL ARCHITECTURE, John Mead Howells. Full-page photographs of buildings that have disappeared or been so altered as to be denatured, including many designed by major early American architects. 245 plates. xvii + 248pp. 7⅞ x 10¾.
21143-6 Paperbound $3.50

DOMESTIC ARCHITECTURE OF THE AMERICAN COLONIES AND OF THE EARLY REPUBLIC, Fiske Kimball. Foremost architect and restorer of Williamsburg and Monticello covers nearly 200 homes between 1620-1825. Architectural details, construction, style features, special fixtures, floor plans, etc. Generally considered finest work in its area. 219 illustrations of houses, doorways, windows, capital mantels. xx + 314pp. 7⅞ x 10¾.
21743-4 Paperbound $4.00

EARLY AMERICAN ROOMS: 1650-1858, edited by Russell Hawes Kettell. Tour of 12 rooms, each representative of a different era in American history and each furnished, decorated, designed and occupied in the style of the era. 72 plans and elevations, 8-page color section, etc., show fabrics, wall papers, arrangements, etc. Full descriptive text. xvii + 200pp. of text. 8⅜ x 11¼.
21633-0 Paperbound $5.00

THE FITZWILLIAM VIRGINAL BOOK, edited by J. Fuller Maitland and W. B. Squire. Full modern printing of famous early 17th-century ms. volume of 300 works by Morley, Byrd, Bull, Gibbons, etc. For piano or other modern keyboard instrument; easy to read format. xxxvi + 938pp. 8⅜ x 11.
21068-5, 21069-3 Two volumes, Paperbound $10.00

KEYBOARD MUSIC, Johann Sebastian Bach. Bach Gesellschaft edition. A rich selection of Bach's masterpieces for the harpsichord: the six English Suites, six French Suites, the six Partitas (Clavierübung part I), the Goldberg Variations (Clavierübung part IV), the fifteen Two-Part Inventions and the fifteen Three-Part Sinfonias. Clearly reproduced on large sheets with ample margins; eminently playable. vi + 312pp. 8⅛ x 11.
22360-4 Paperbound $5.00

THE MUSIC OF BACH: AN INTRODUCTION, Charles Sanford Terry. A fine, nontechnical introduction to Bach's music, both instrumental and vocal. Covers organ music, chamber music, passion music, other types. Analyzes themes, developments, innovations. x + 114pp.
21075-8 Paperbound $1.50

BEETHOVEN AND HIS NINE SYMPHONIES, Sir George Grove. Noted British musicologist provides best history, analysis, commentary on symphonies. Very thorough, rigorously accurate; necessary to both advanced student and amateur music lover. 436 musical passages. vii + 407 pp.
20334-4 Paperbound $2.75

JOHANN SEBASTIAN BACH, Philipp Spitta. One of the great classics of musicology, this definitive analysis of Bach's music (and life) has never been surpassed. Lucid, nontechnical analyses of hundreds of pieces (30 pages devoted to St. Matthew Passion, 26 to B Minor Mass). Also includes major analysis of 18th-century music. 450 musical examples. 40-page musical supplement. Total of xx + 1799pp.
(EUK) 22278-0, 22279-9 Two volumes, Clothbound $17.50

MOZART AND HIS PIANO CONCERTOS, Cuthbert Girdlestone. The only full-length study of an important area of Mozart's creativity. Provides detailed analyses of all 23 concertos, traces inspirational sources. 417 musical examples. Second edition. 509pp. 21271-8 Paperbound $3.50

THE PERFECT WAGNERITE: A COMMENTARY ON THE NIBLUNG'S RING, George Bernard Shaw. Brilliant and still relevant criticism in remarkable essays on Wagner's Ring cycle, Shaw's ideas on political and social ideology behind the plots, role of Leitmotifs, vocal requisites, etc. Prefaces. xxi + 136pp.
(USO) 21707-8 Paperbound $1.75

DON GIOVANNI, W. A. Mozart. Complete libretto, modern English translation; biographies of composer and librettist; accounts of early performances and critical reaction. Lavishly illustrated. All the material you need to understand and appreciate this great work. Dover Opera Guide and Libretto Series; translated and introduced by Ellen Bleiler. 92 illustrations. 209pp.
21134-7 Paperbound $2.00

BASIC ELECTRICITY, U. S. Bureau of Naval Personel. Originally a training course, best non-technical coverage of basic theory of electricity and its applications. Fundamental concepts, batteries, circuits, conductors and wiring techniques, AC and DC, inductance and capacitance, generators, motors, transformers, magnetic amplifiers, synchros, servomechanisms, etc. Also covers blue-prints, electrical diagrams, etc. Many questions, with answers. 349 illustrations. x + 448pp. 6½ x 9¼.
20973-3 Paperbound $3.50

REPRODUCTION OF SOUND, Edgar Villchur. Thorough coverage for laymen of high fidelity systems, reproducing systems in general, needles, amplifiers, preamps, loudspeakers, feedback, explaining physical background. "A rare talent for making technicalities vividly comprehensible," R. Darrell, High Fidelity. 69 figures. iv + 92pp. 21515-6 Paperbound $1.35

HEAR ME TALKIN' TO YA: THE STORY OF JAZZ AS TOLD BY THE MEN WHO MADE IT, Nat Shapiro and Nat Hentoff. Louis Armstrong, Fats Waller, Jo Jones, Clarence Williams, Billy Holiday, Duke Ellington, Jelly Roll Morton and dozens of other jazz greats tell how it was in Chicago's South Side, New Orleans, depression Harlem and the modern West Coast as jazz was born and grew. xvi + 429pp.
21726-4 Paperbound $3.00

FABLES OF AESOP, translated by Sir Roger L'Estrange. A reproduction of the very rare 1931 Paris edition; a selection of the most interesting fables, together with 50 imaginative drawings by Alexander Calder. v + 128pp. 6½x9¼.
21780-9 Paperbound $1.50

AGAINST THE GRAIN (A REBOURS), Joris K. Huysmans. Filled with weird images, evidences of a bizarre imagination, exotic experiments with hallucinatory drugs, rich tastes and smells and the diversions of its sybarite hero Duc Jean des Esseintes, this classic novel pushed 19th-century literary decadence to its limits. Full unabridged edition. Do not confuse this with abridged editions generally sold. Introduction by Havelock Ellis. xlix + 206pp. 22190-3 Paperbound $2.50

VARIORUM SHAKESPEARE: HAMLET. Edited by Horace H. Furness; a landmark of American scholarship. Exhaustive footnotes and appendices treat all doubtful words and phrases, as well as suggested critical emendations throughout the play's history. First volume contains editor's own text, collated with all Quartos and Folios. Second volume contains full first Quarto, translations of Shakespeare's sources (Belleforest, and Saxo Grammaticus), Der Bestrafte Brudermord, and many essays on critical and historical points of interest by major authorities of past and present. Includes details of staging and costuming over the years. By far the best edition available for serious students of Shakespeare. Total of xx + 905pp. 21004-9, 21005-7, 2 volumes, Paperbound $7.00

A LIFE OF WILLIAM SHAKESPEARE, Sir Sidney Lee. This is the standard life of Shakespeare, summarizing everything known about Shakespeare and his plays. Incredibly rich in material, broad in coverage, clear and judicious, it has served thousands as the best introduction to Shakespeare. 1931 edition. 9 plates. xxix + 792pp. 21967-4 Paperbound $3.75

MASTERS OF THE DRAMA, John Gassner. Most comprehensive history of the drama in print, covering every tradition from Greeks to modern Europe and America, including India, Far East, etc. Covers more than 800 dramatists, 2000 plays, with biographical material, plot summaries, theatre history, criticism, etc. "Best of its kind in English," *New Republic*. 77 illustrations. xxii + 890pp. 20100-7 Clothbound $10.00

THE EVOLUTION OF THE ENGLISH LANGUAGE, George McKnight. The growth of English, from the 14th century to the present. Unusual, non-technical account presents basic information in very interesting form: sound shifts, change in grammar and syntax, vocabulary growth, similar topics. Abundantly illustrated with quotations. Formerly *Modern English in the Making*. xii + 590pp. 21932-1 Paperbound $3.50

AN ETYMOLOGICAL DICTIONARY OF MODERN ENGLISH, Ernest Weekley. Fullest, richest work of its sort, by foremost British lexicographer. Detailed word histories, including many colloquial and archaic words; extensive quotations. Do not confuse this with the Concise Etymological Dictionary, which is much abridged. Total of xxvii + 830pp. 6½ x 9¼. 21873-2, 21874-0 Two volumes, Paperbound $7.90

FLATLAND: A ROMANCE OF MANY DIMENSIONS, E. A. Abbott. Classic of science-fiction explores ramifications of life in a two-dimensional world, and what happens when a three-dimensional being intrudes. Amusing reading, but also useful as introduction to thought about hyperspace. Introduction by Banesh Hoffmann. 16 illustrations. xx + 103pp. 20001-9 Paperbound $1.00

POEMS OF ANNE BRADSTREET, edited with an introduction by Robert Hutchinson. A new selection of poems by America's first poet and perhaps the first significant woman poet in the English language. 48 poems display her development in works of considerable variety—love poems, domestic poems, religious meditations, formal elegies, "quaternions," etc. Notes, bibliography. viii + 222pp.

22160-1 Paperbound $2.50

THREE GOTHIC NOVELS: THE CASTLE OF OTRANTO BY HORACE WALPOLE; VATHEK BY WILLIAM BECKFORD; THE VAMPYRE BY JOHN POLIDORI, WITH FRAGMENT OF A NOVEL BY LORD BYRON, edited by E. F. Bleiler. The first Gothic novel, by Walpole; the finest Oriental tale in English, by Beckford; powerful Romantic supernatural story in versions by Polidori and Byron. All extremely important in history of literature; all still exciting, packed with supernatural thrills, ghosts, haunted castles, magic, etc. xl + 291pp.

21232-7 Paperbound $2.50

THE BEST TALES OF HOFFMANN, E. T. A. Hoffmann. 10 of Hoffmann's most important stories, in modern re-editings of standard translations: Nutcracker and the King of Mice, Signor Formica, Automata, The Sandman, Rath Krespel, The Golden Flowerpot, Master Martin the Cooper, The Mines of Falun, The King's Betrothed, A New Year's Eve Adventure. 7 illustrations by Hoffmann. Edited by E. F. Bleiler. xxxix + 419pp.

21793-0 Paperbound $3.00

GHOST AND HORROR STORIES OF AMBROSE BIERCE, Ambrose Bierce. 23 strikingly modern stories of the horrors latent in the human mind: The Eyes of the Panther, The Damned Thing, An Occurrence at Owl Creek Bridge, An Inhabitant of Carcosa, etc., plus the dream-essay, Visions of the Night. Edited by E. F. Bleiler. xxii + 199pp.

20767-6 Paperbound $1.50

BEST GHOST STORIES OF J. S. LEFANU, J. Sheridan LeFanu. Finest stories by Victorian master often considered greatest supernatural writer of all. Carmilla, Green Tea, The Haunted Baronet, The Familiar, and 12 others. Most never before available in the U. S. A. Edited by E. F. Bleiler. 8 illustrations from Victorian publications. xvii + 467pp.

20415-4 Paperbound $3.00

MATHEMATICAL FOUNDATIONS OF INFORMATION THEORY, A. I. Khinchin. Comprehensive introduction to work of Shannon, McMillan, Feinstein and Khinchin, placing these investigations on a rigorous mathematical basis. Covers entropy concept in probability theory, uniqueness theorem, Shannon's inequality, ergodic sources, the E property, martingale concept, noise, Feinstein's fundamental lemma, Shanon's first and second theorems. Translated by R. A. Silverman and M. D. Friedman. iii + 120pp.

60434-9 Paperbound $2.00

SEVEN SCIENCE FICTION NOVELS, H. G. Wells. The standard collection of the great novels. Complete, unabridged. *First Men in the Moon, Island of Dr. Moreau, War of the Worlds, Food of the Gods, Invisible Man, Time Machine, In the Days of the Comet.* Not only science fiction fans, but every educated person owes it to himself to read these novels. 1015pp.

(USO) 20264-X Clothbound $6.00

LAST AND FIRST MEN AND STAR MAKER, TWO SCIENCE FICTION NOVELS, Olaf Stapledon. Greatest future histories in science fiction. In the first, human intelligence is the "hero," through strange paths of evolution, interplanetary invasions, incredible technologies, near extinctions and reemergences. Star Maker describes the quest of a band of star rovers for intelligence itself, through time and space: weird inhuman civilizations, crustacean minds, symbiotic worlds, etc. Complete, unabridged. v + 438pp. (USO) 21962-3 Paperbound $2.50

THREE PROPHETIC NOVELS, H. G. WELLS. Stages of a consistently planned future for mankind. *When the Sleeper Wakes,* and *A Story of the Days to Come,* anticipate *Brave New World* and *1984,* in the 21st Century; *The Time Machine,* only complete version in print, shows farther future and the end of mankind. All show Wells's greatest gifts as storyteller and novelist. Edited by E. F. Bleiler. x + 335pp. (USO) 20605-X Paperbound $2.50

THE DEVIL'S DICTIONARY, Ambrose Bierce. America's own Oscar Wilde—Ambrose Bierce—offers his barbed iconoclastic wisdom in over 1,000 definitions hailed by H. L. Mencken as "some of the most gorgeous witticisms in the English language." 145pp. 20487-1 Paperbound $1.25

MAX AND MORITZ, Wilhelm Busch. Great children's classic, father of comic strip, of two bad boys, Max and Moritz. Also Ker and Plunk (Plisch und Plumm), Cat and Mouse, Deceitful Henry, Ice-Peter, The Boy and the Pipe, and five other pieces. Original German, with English translation. Edited by H. Arthur Klein; translations by various hands and H. Arthur Klein. vi + 216pp.
20181-3 Paperbound $2.00

PIGS IS PIGS AND OTHER FAVORITES, Ellis Parker Butler. The title story is one of the best humor short stories, as Mike Flannery obfuscates biology and English. Also included, That Pup of Murchison's, The Great American Pie Company, and Perkins of Portland. 14 illustrations. v + 109pp. 21532-6 Paperbound $1.25

THE PETERKIN PAPERS, Lucretia P. Hale. It takes genius to be as stupidly mad as the Peterkins, as they decide to become wise, celebrate the "Fourth," keep a cow, and otherwise strain the resources of the Lady from Philadelphia. Basic book of American humor. 153 illustrations. 219pp. 20794-3 Paperbound $2.00

PERRAULT'S FAIRY TALES, translated by A. E. Johnson and S. R. Littlewood, with 34 full-page illustrations by Gustave Doré. All the original Perrault stories—Cinderella, Sleeping Beauty, Bluebeard, Little Red Riding Hood, Puss in Boots, Tom Thumb, etc.—with their witty verse morals and the magnificent illustrations of Doré. One of the five or six great books of European fairy tales. viii + 117pp. 8⅛ x 11. 22311-6 Paperbound $2.00

OLD HUNGARIAN FAIRY TALES, Baroness Orczy. Favorites translated and adapted by author of the *Scarlet Pimpernel.* Eight fairy tales include "The Suitors of Princess Fire-Fly," "The Twin Hunchbacks," "Mr. Cuttlefish's Love Story," and "The Enchanted Cat." This little volume of magic and adventure will captivate children as it has for generations. 90 drawings by Montagu Barstow. 96pp.
(USO) 22293-4 Paperbound $1.95

THE RED FAIRY BOOK, Andrew Lang. Lang's color fairy books have long been children's favorites. This volume includes Rapunzel, Jack and the Bean-stalk and 35 other stories, familiar and unfamiliar. 4 plates, 93 illustrations x + 367pp.

21673-X Paperbound $2.50

THE BLUE FAIRY BOOK, Andrew Lang. Lang's tales come from all countries and all times. Here are 37 tales from Grimm, the Arabian Nights, Greek Mythology, and other fascinating sources. 8 plates, 130 illustrations. xi + 390pp.

21437-0 Paperbound $2.50

HOUSEHOLD STORIES BY THE BROTHERS GRIMM. Classic English-language edition of the well-known tales — Rumpelstiltskin, Snow White, Hansel and Gretel, The Twelve Brothers, Faithful John, Rapunzel, Tom Thumb (52 stories in all). Translated into simple, straightforward English by Lucy Crane. Ornamented with headpieces, vignettes, elaborate decorative initials and a dozen full-page illustrations by Walter Crane. x + 269pp. 21080-4 Paperbound **$2.00**

THE MERRY ADVENTURES OF ROBIN HOOD, Howard Pyle. The finest modern versions of the traditional ballads and tales about the great English outlaw. Howard Pyle's complete prose version, with every word, every illustration of the first edition. Do not confuse this facsimile of the original (1883) with modern editions that change text or illustrations. 23 plates plus many page decorations. xxii + 296pp.

22043-5 Paperbound $2.50

THE STORY OF KING ARTHUR AND HIS KNIGHTS, Howard Pyle. The finest children's version of the life of King Arthur; brilliantly retold by Pyle, with 48 of his most imaginative illustrations. xviii + 313pp. 6⅛ x 9¼.

21445-1 Paperbound $2.50

THE WONDERFUL WIZARD OF OZ, L. Frank Baum. America's finest children's book in facsimile of first edition with all Denslow illustrations in full color. The edition a child should have. Introduction by Martin Gardner. 23 color plates, scores of drawings. iv + 267pp. 20691-2 Paperbound $2.50

THE MARVELOUS LAND OF OZ, L. Frank Baum. The second Oz book, every bit as imaginative as the Wizard. The hero is a boy named Tip, but the Scarecrow and the Tin Woodman are back, as is the Oz magic. 16 color plates, 120 drawings by John R. Neill. 287pp. 20692-0 Paperbound $2.50

THE MAGICAL MONARCH OF MO, L. Frank Baum. Remarkable adventures in a land even stranger than Oz. The best of Baum's books not in the Oz series. 15 color plates and dozens of drawings by Frank Verbeck. xviii + 237pp.

21892-9 Paperbound $2.25

THE BAD CHILD'S BOOK OF BEASTS, MORE BEASTS FOR WORSE CHILDREN, A MORAL ALPHABET, Hilaire Belloc. Three complete humor classics in one volume. Be kind to the frog, and do not call him names . . . and 28 other whimsical animals. Familiar favorites and some not so well known. Illustrated by Basil Blackwell. 156pp. (USO) 20749-8 Paperbound $1.50

EAST O' THE SUN AND WEST O' THE MOON, George W. Dasent. Considered the best of all translations of these Norwegian folk tales, this collection has been enjoyed by generations of children (and folklorists too). Includes True and Untrue, Why the Sea is Salt, East O' the Sun and West O' the Moon, Why the Bear is Stumpy-Tailed, Boots and the Troll, The Cock and the Hen, Rich Peter the Pedlar, and 52 more. The only edition with all 59 tales. 77 illustrations by Erik Werenskiold and Theodor Kittelsen. xv + 418pp. 22521-6 Paperbound $3.50

GOOPS AND HOW TO BE THEM, Gelett Burgess. Classic of tongue-in-cheek humor, masquerading as etiquette book. 87 verses, twice as many cartoons, show mischievous Goops as they demonstrate to children virtues of table manners, neatness, courtesy, etc. Favorite for generations. viii + 88pp. 6½ x 9¼. 22233-0 Paperbound $1.25

ALICE'S ADVENTURES UNDER GROUND, Lewis Carroll. The first version, quite different from the final *Alice in Wonderland,* printed out by Carroll himself with his own illustrations. Complete facsimile of the "million dollar" manuscript Carroll gave to Alice Liddell in 1864. Introduction by Martin Gardner. viii + 96pp. Title and dedication pages in color. 21482-6 Paperbound $1.25

THE BROWNIES, THEIR BOOK, Palmer Cox. Small as mice, cunning as foxes, exuberant and full of mischief, the Brownies go to the zoo, toy shop, seashore, circus, etc., in 24 verse adventures and 266 illustrations. Long a favorite, since their first appearance in St. Nicholas Magazine. xi + 144pp. 6⅝ x 9¼. 21265-3 Paperbound $1.75

SONGS OF CHILDHOOD, Walter De La Mare. Published (under the pseudonym Walter Ramal) when De La Mare was only 29, this charming collection has long been a favorite children's book. A facsimile of the first edition in paper, the 47 poems capture the simplicity of the nursery rhyme and the ballad, including such lyrics as I Met Eve, Tartary, The Silver Penny. vii + 106pp. (USO) 21972-0 Paperbound $1.25

THE COMPLETE NONSENSE OF EDWARD LEAR, Edward Lear. The finest 19th-century humorist-cartoonist in full: all nonsense limericks, zany alphabets, Owl and Pussycat, songs, nonsense botany, and more than 500 illustrations by Lear himself. Edited by Holbrook Jackson. xxix + 287pp. (USO) 20167-8 Paperbound $2.00

BILLY WHISKERS: THE AUTOBIOGRAPHY OF A GOAT, Frances Trego Montgomery. A favorite of children since the early 20th century, here are the escapades of that rambunctious, irresistible and mischievous goat—Billy Whiskers. Much in the spirit of *Peck's Bad Boy,* this is a book that children never tire of reading or hearing. All the original familiar illustrations by W. H. Fry are included: 6 color plates, 18 black and white drawings. 159pp. 22345-0 Paperbound $2.00

MOTHER GOOSE MELODIES. Faithful republication of the fabulously rare Munroe and Francis "copyright 1833" Boston edition—the most important Mother Goose collection, usually referred to as the "original." Familiar rhymes plus many rare ones, with wonderful old woodcut illustrations. Edited by E. F. Bleiler. 128pp. 4½ x 6⅜. 22577-1 Paperbound $1.00

TWO LITTLE SAVAGES; BEING THE ADVENTURES OF TWO BOYS WHO LIVED AS INDIANS AND WHAT THEY LEARNED, Ernest Thompson Seton. Great classic of nature and boyhood provides a vast range of woodlore in most palatable form, a genuinely entertaining story. Two farm boys build a teepee in woods and live in it for a month, working out Indian solutions to living problems, star lore, birds and animals, plants, etc. 293 illustrations. vii + 286pp.

20985-7 Paperbound $2.50

PETER PIPER'S PRACTICAL PRINCIPLES OF PLAIN & PERFECT PRONUNCIATION. Alliterative jingles and tongue-twisters of surprising charm, that made their first appearance in America about 1830. Republished in full with the spirited woodcut illustrations from this earliest American edition. 32pp. 4½ x 6⅜.

22560-7 Paperbound $1.00

SCIENCE EXPERIMENTS AND AMUSEMENTS FOR CHILDREN, Charles Vivian. 73 easy experiments, requiring only materials found at home or easily available, such as candles, coins, steel wool, etc.; illustrate basic phenomena like vacuum, simple chemical reaction, etc. All safe. Modern, well-planned. Formerly *Science Games for Children*. 102 photos, numerous drawings. 96pp. 6⅛ x 9¼.

21856-2 Paperbound $1.25

AN INTRODUCTION TO CHESS MOVES AND TACTICS SIMPLY EXPLAINED, Leonard Barden. Informal intermediate introduction, quite strong in explaining reasons for moves. Covers basic material, tactics, important openings, traps, positional play in middle game, end game. Attempts to isolate patterns and recurrent configurations. Formerly *Chess*. 58 figures. 102pp. (USO) 21210-6 Paperbound $1.25

LASKER'S MANUAL OF CHESS, Dr. Emanuel Lasker. Lasker was not only one of the five great World Champions, he was also one of the ablest expositors, theorists, and analysts. In many ways, his Manual, permeated with his philosophy of battle, filled with keen insights, is one of the greatest works ever written on chess. Filled with analyzed games by the great players. A single-volume library that will profit almost any chess player, beginner or master. 308 diagrams. xli x 349pp.

20640-8 Paperbound $2.75

THE MASTER BOOK OF MATHEMATICAL RECREATIONS, Fred Schuh. In opinion of many the finest work ever prepared on mathematical puzzles, stunts, recreations; exhaustively thorough explanations of mathematics involved, analysis of effects, citation of puzzles and games. Mathematics involved is elementary. Translated by F. Göbel. 194 figures. xxiv + 430pp. 22134-2 Paperbound $3.50

MATHEMATICS, MAGIC AND MYSTERY, Martin Gardner. Puzzle editor for Scientific American explains mathematics behind various mystifying tricks: card tricks, stage "mind reading," coin and match tricks, counting out games, geometric dissections, etc. Probability sets, theory of numbers clearly explained. Also provides more than 400 tricks, guaranteed to work, that you can do. 135 illustrations. xii + 176pp.

20335-2 Paperbound $1.75

MATHEMATICAL PUZZLES FOR BEGINNERS AND ENTHUSIASTS, Geoffrey Mott-Smith. 189 puzzles from easy to difficult—involving arithmetic, logic, algebra, properties of digits, probability, etc.—for enjoyment and mental stimulus. Explanation of mathematical principles behind the puzzles. 135 illustrations. viii + 248pp.
20198-8 Paperbound $1.75

PAPER FOLDING FOR BEGINNERS, William D. Murray and Francis J. Rigney. Easiest book on the market, clearest instructions on making interesting, beautiful origami. Sail boats, cups, roosters, frogs that move legs, bonbon boxes, standing birds, etc. 40 projects; more than 275 diagrams and photographs. 94pp.
20713-7 Paperbound $1.00

TRICKS AND GAMES ON THE POOL TABLE, Fred Herrmann. 79 tricks and games—some solitaires, some for two or more players, some competitive games—to entertain you between formal games. Mystifying shots and throws, unusual caroms, tricks involving such props as cork, coins, a hat, etc. Formerly *Fun on the Pool Table*. 77 figures. 95pp.
21814-7 Paperbound $1.25

HAND SHADOWS TO BE THROWN UPON THE WALL: A SERIES OF NOVEL AND AMUSING FIGURES FORMED BY THE HAND, Henry Bursill. Delightful picturebook from great-grandfather's day shows how to make 18 different hand shadows: a bird that flies, duck that quacks, dog that wags his tail, camel, goose, deer, boy, turtle, etc. Only book of its sort. vi + 33pp. 6½ x 9¼. 21779-5 Paperbound $1.00

WHITTLING AND WOODCARVING, E. J. Tangerman. 18th printing of best book on market. "If you can cut a potato you can carve" toys and puzzles, chains, chessmen, caricatures, masks, frames, woodcut blocks, surface patterns, much more. Information on tools, woods, techniques. Also goes into serious wood sculpture from Middle Ages to present, East and West. 464 photos, figures. x + 293pp.
20965-2 Paperbound $2.00

HISTORY OF PHILOSOPHY, Julián Marías. Possibly the clearest, most easily followed, best planned, most useful one-volume history of philosophy on the market; neither skimpy nor overfull. Full details on system of every major philosopher and dozens of less important thinkers from pre-Socratics up to Existentialism and later. Strong on many European figures usually omitted. Has gone through dozens of editions in Europe. 1966 edition, translated by Stanley Appelbaum and Clarence Strowbridge. xviii + 505pp. 21739-6 Paperbound $3.50

YOGA: A SCIENTIFIC EVALUATION, Kovoor T. Behanan. Scientific but non-technical study of physiological results of yoga exercises; done under auspices of Yale U. Relations to Indian thought, to psychoanalysis, etc. 16 photos. xxiii + 270pp.
20505-3 Paperbound $2.50

Prices subject to change without notice.
Available at your book dealer or write for free catalogue to Dept. GI, Dover Publications, Inc., 180 Varick St., N. Y., N. Y. 10014. Dover publishes more than 150 books each year on science, elementary and advanced mathematics, biology, music, art, literary history, social sciences and other areas.